Martin Daldrup

M Jambo

To the Horizon and Beyond

Atlantic, Caribbean Sea and Lockdown

"Twenty years from now you will be more disappointed by the things that you didn't do than by the ones you did do. So throw off the bowlines. Sail away from the safe harbour. Catch the trade winds in your sails.

Explore. Dream. Discover."

attributed to Mark Twain

Contents

Prologue: How it all Began

Here I am, back home, sitting on the sofa, trying to put my adventures to paper (or type them on the computer that is). But where to begin? I think it might help if I tell you a bit about the sailor, before I say any more about sailing.

So, who am I? Why do I sail? How did I get into sailing in the first place?

My name is Martin. I'm also known as M Jambo, which is the alias I use for my YouTube channel. I was born in 1964; I am divorced, and have three grown-up children. For most of my professional life, I worked as an engineer before retiring in 2019. If that sounds like a clever plan – well, the opposite is true! At the end of my career, my employer, Caterpillar, reduced staffing levels again, and this time I was out – from one day to the next. That's how publicly listed American companies work.

In my case, however, redundancy turned out to be a blessing in disguise. I had been toying with the idea of taking early retirement for some time because I wanted to focus on sailing, and had started saving accordingly.

Although it had been my dream for ages, I didn't actually start sailing until 2012. Boats had always fascinated me, and I had been lucky enough to spend an afternoon sailing in Chesapeake Bay in the States with a friend one time. I had wanted to do my sport boat licenses, but professional commitments kept getting in the way. In 2012, I managed to give myself the kick I needed and finally got started. The starter package for a license for sport boats, on coastal waters and inland waterways (motor only) seemed a good way to begin then and probably still is now. Later, in 2013, I took the advanced licence, up to the 12 nautical miles offshore, gained the SRC and UBI marine and inland radio communication certificates, and finally, the certificate of proficiency according to the Explosives Act.

In autumn 2012, Anke and I went sailing in Turkey for a week with friends. In case you are wondering, Anke is my partner. We have been together for over ten years. Another blessing! Unfortunately, the wind was no good for sailing except on the last day, but we really enjoyed our week on board the boat. I felt inspired to follow my dream of owning my own boat. Apart from that one sailing afternoon in the States, these were my first 130 NM and they formed the foundation of my sailing life.

The following year, Anke and I spent the spring break in Workum on the IJsselmeer (large lake in the Netherlands). The weather was brilliant, so we decided to charter a sloop for the day. Anke's children, Jana and Mats, were with us, and the four of us set off in the morning. We cruised through the canals of Friesland to the Hegemer Mar and Hindeloopen. We all enjoyed a beautiful day on the water, and it turned out to be a key experience! Sitting together in the evening after I had had time to recap on the day, I suddenly heard myself saying, "It's time to stop dreaming, we are going to buy a boat!" I had made up my mind without even thinking. There was no going back. We started looking for a suitable vessel on all the valid online platforms right away. Fortunately, I had recently sold my half of the house, and so there was a bit of cash to spare.

We wanted to start with a motorboat. It seemed like a good way to begin, especially considering the fact that I still hadn't taken my sailing license for inland waters. As soon as I got that done, I was planning to sell the motorboat and purchase a sailing boat. My first point of call would be the canals of Friesland and the IJsselmeer, where Anke and I had had such a lovely time. We soon determined the object of our desire, a 27-29 foot BAVARIA motor yacht. It even suited our budget. I spent the next few weekends travelling to Leverkusen, Gütersloh, and Timmen-dorfer Strand to look at several different boats. In Timmen-dorfer Strand, I reached a deal with the owner of a 28-foot BA-VARIA, priced at about 68,000 Euros. Some of the paperwork was missing though, and I sent him a short list of the documents we still needed, the next day. I never heard from him again. Something must have been dodgy. Buying a boat isn't as easy as I thought. It is essential to make sure all the papers including the VAT certificate are in good order.

One of the motorboats on offer

The following weekend, we were invited to a friend's birthday party, and told everyone that we wanted to buy a decent boat. Our friends all applauded the idea, but there were a couple of sailors at the party, who advised us not to bother buying a mo-torboat. Instead, they said we should opt for a sailing boat right away, adding that it is impossible to buy and sell boats the way you might buy a car. They also told us that we wouldn't require a sailing license for boats of up to 15 m length in the Netherlands. That clinched the argument for us, and we decided to buy a sailing boat right away. Andy offered to be our technical advisor during the process, to ensure we found a boat equipped with everything a beginner needs: a furling mainsail, diesel heating (essential in the Netherlands), an integrated autopilot acting directly on the steering quadrant, hot and cold running water, and lots more.

Having moved the goal posts, we had to start searching all over again. I set off right away, driving up and down the country to Enkhuizen, Sloten, Hamburg and Neustadt. I actually viewed *Jambo* right at the beginning of my tour - a BAVARIA 34 Holiday, four years old, 10.7 m long and 3.6 m wide, running on ownership charter at the time. She had everything we were looking for, but the price of 73,000 Euros seemed rather high. I looked at other cheaper boats, but soon realised that they lacked the necessary fittings and equipment. Once I included the cost of upgrading everything to the required standard, they turned out to be far more expensive. In the end, I drove back to Enkhuizen on the IJsselmeer, looked at the boat again, and was able to charter it for a weekend – with the charter price included in the purchase price, should we decide to buy the boat in the end.

Anke and I had a fantastic weekend. It was the beginning of July and the weather was on our side. You can't bet on that in the Netherlands at that time of year. Although I was still inexperienced, the harbour manoeuvres went okay – I can't remember anything too disastrous – and I handled the sailing jaunt pretty well. At last, I was able to put some of the theory I had learned into practice. We returned the boat, and I negotiated the terms of sale with the owner the next day. Just a week later, she was ours. It was incredible! What a feeling! Now I couldn't wait to start sailing!

Sadly for me, we were due to go on holiday to Turkey. Anke, Mats, Jana and I set off a few days after *Jambo* arrived, so there was no opportunity to go sailing before then. Suddenly, I found myself sitting in a beautiful all-inclusive Turkish hotel, unable to enjoy myself because I was pining for my boat. On the second day, we went out for a meal and I briefly floated the idea of looking for a last-minute return flight home. *If looks could kill!* I binned that idea immediately, and stayed. But to be honest, I spent two of the most excruciating weeks on holiday I had ever experienced.

Still, time passed, and after our holiday, I booked a one-day single-handed yacht-training course in Lemmer, on the IJsselmeer. My instructor, Kor, and I went out on a BAVARIA 30. Kor was a very experienced seaman, about seventy years old, who had been sailing all his life. It was time well spent. I learnt so much! We practiced all kinds of harbour manoeuvres, boating through locks, spring line docking and lots more - all single-handed. Kor explained each manoeuvre carefully, and demonstrated everything himself, before I repeated the manoeuvres on my own. I sucked up the knowledge like a dry sponge, and at last, I felt ready to skipper my own boat for the first time.

Now things really started to take off. During the following months, I spent almost every weekend aboard *Jambo*. Usually Anke or some friends would join me, but I also took her out on my own every now and then. We sailed across the IJsselmeer, which seemed so big and wide at the time.

I kept *Jambo* in the water over the winter. I really enjoyed the special atmosphere on short winter days, as I sailed out before dawn and watched the sunrise above the water. I would spend all day sailing, and see the sun set in the evening, before we moored in the dark. I think this is when I really learned to sail and got to know *Jambo,* as I put her through her paces.

Was she uncapsizable? She is category A, so she is seaworthy, and should be able to right herself, no matter the angle. I was able to try this out on the back of a stormy low-pressure system, in winds of 8 to 9 Bft, testing the boat's limits – and my own. I probably wouldn't put myself through that kind of ordeal again, but I was so keen and eager at the time and wanted to try out all sorts of things. It turned out to be a good idea, because I gained the confidence I needed to face the strong winds on the journeys ahead.

Jambo in the beginning

I love making movies, so I started filming my experiences as a matter of course. I made a short video of my learning-by-doing tour, to prove to my family that *Jambo* wouldn't capsize in strong winds. It was my way of conveying my faith in my boat to the people I love.

Mats, who was 11 at the time, suggested I put the video on YouTube. *YouTube?* Ok, so I had heard of it, but I had never really looked into it before. In fact, I was rather sceptical to start with, and had no idea how to go about it. Fortunately, Mats was a real expert, and showed me how to set up my own channel. The first thing we had to decide was the name. *Jambo* was not available, sadly. So we had another think and came up with M *Jambo*, with the M standing for Martin – that worked! Our channel was up and running in no time at all. We uploaded the first short video and then forgot all about it, until I had another look a few months later. I was surprised to see that people had not only watched the video but had even subscribed to my channel. Looking back today, after all the films I have shot and uploaded in the past few years, it seems absurd that I started vlogging almost by chance. If you enjoy making films, and people want to watch them. I mean, what more could you want?

It was not long before I began to broaden my sailing horizons, sailing *Jambo* beyond the IJsselmeer. I started planning a sailing tour for a group of male friends, the 'lads'. In May 2014, Heinz, Wilm and I set off for Heligoland. Heinz is Anke's father. He was 78 at the time, but although he was new to sailing, he knew he would be able to pull his weight as required. Wilm had already knocked up an impressive contingent of nautical miles, and had even chartered boats in the Baltic Sea many years ago. So, off we went, out into the North Sea! In Den Oever we had to go through a lock, and then past Den Helder, before we sailed out into open waters. Then we were in the North Sea! What an experience! The swell was quite different to the IJsselmeer. The waves were longer and flatter, with a long, light swell from the west adding to the pattern of the waves.

After we sailed past Juist, it was time to stop for the night. We were heading for Norderney (German island), but just before we reached the marina, the engine failed. There was no wind and *Jambo* started drifting towards the coast in the tidal current. Luckily, another sailing yacht called *Halinka* was heading out of the marina. The crew offered to give us a hand. We threw them our lines and they towed us into the harbour inlet, where we tied up alongside a buoy laying vessel.

We had been very lucky! Anything could have happened. It didn't take long to find the problem - the fuel filters were clogged. I had spares on board, and we managed to change them. Then we sailed on to Heligoland without any further problems. It was a thrilling experience for all of us. The return journey went smoothly and when we got home, I posted my second YouTube video.

That sailing trip was so inspiring that I could barely wait for the next one. In June, Heinz and I spent a long bank holiday sailing to Lowestoft in England and back again. That meant crossing the Channel twice. It was another momentous experience and a huge learning curve. Negotiating the busy shipping lanes, judging my bearings using a pair of binoculars, trying to decide if a cargo ship was going to cross our path in front of us or behind us, all proved to be tricky. I decided to purchase an AIS transponder to transmit my ship's data and receive information from other ships – the principle being 'see and be seen'.

During the summer, Anke and I chartered a boat in Croatia. We booked a flotilla sailing holiday, which was great fun, not least because of the glorious weather and the many 'conobas'.

I was back on my own boat the next year. This time we sailed German islands in the North Sea, firstly to Sylt as I dared to go further again. It was another fantastic cruise with plenty of ups and a few small downs. Somehow, something always seems to go wrong. This time, water got under the forward cabin, where the transducers for speed and depth are installed. We were able find an expert on Amrum Island, who agreed to have a look at the boat. This kind-hearted 'boat whisperer' recaulked the transducers and then everything was fine. The trip was also especially great because Klaus, our ship's cook, joined the crew for the first time.

The lads l. to r: Wilm, Heinz, Klaus and me, Heligoland in May 2015

In summer 2016, I tried out several days of single-handed sailing for the first time. I crossed the North Sea and sailed from the Netherlands to Skagen in the north of Denmark. It was my first chance to test interval sleeping, which I now do all the time when I am on a long solo trip. It's not something I actually enjoy, especially when I am close to the shore. During interval sleeping, you set your alarm clock for the length of time you want to sleep – that can be just fifteen or thirty minutes, depending on whether you are crossing the Channel for example, or on the North Sea with very busy shipping. There are also all sorts of buoys, gas and oil platforms, wind farms, fishing nets and fishing boats you might want to avoid.

Things are very different when you are alone on the ocean. Then I am quite happy to sleep for an interval of up to three hours.

You hardly ever see any other boats, and there are no wind farms or platforms and practically no buoys to circumnavigate. Actually, you'd expect there to be nothing at all, but now and then you do come across something, even in several thousand metres of water, often drifting along by itself. This happened to me once when I was crossing the ocean from Martinique to Heligoland. I couldn't believe my eyes when I had to avoid a solitary buoy that appeared to be stationary.

I always turn the AIS transponder on as an extra precaution to avoid collisions. It connects to an acoustic alarm, which sounds if a ship is approaching. As a backup, the AIS data is also sent via NMEA 2000 to the chart plotter, which has a second alarm. It means I am equipped with two alarms, and they have served me very well so far.

But back to Skagen, from where I sailed on towards the German Baltic coast. Alas, my steering gear failed when I was close to Klintholm. The steering shaft attached to the rudderstock came undone. The screws were jammed, which is why I had thought it was firmly secured when it was not. Unfortunately, I didn't have the right equipment on board and couldn't do the repairs myself. That would never happen to me now. I always pay special attention to the steering gear, and check that connection at regular intervals. There was nothing for it. I had to call for help. I was towed to Rostock by the DGzRS (the German Sea and Rescue Service). I am incredibly grateful to my rescuers to this day. Fortunately, I was able to get *Jambo* repaired quickly and competently, so the cruise with Anke in the Baltic Sea went ahead as planned. The return trip via the Kiel Canal ended up as another enjoyable cruise with the lads.

The weather in the Baltic Sea wasn't great, though, and I started to wonder how far south I might be able sail in two weeks in the following year. As of 2017, I was able to take twelve days of unpaid leave whenever I liked, and the additional costs, (which meant I had a further two weeks of sailing) were fine by me. I worked out a great holiday schedule for 2017 with my boss at the time, Chris, an Australian from Melbourne who is a great guy. It looked like this:

Two weeks' holiday
Two weeks' work
Two weeks' holiday
Two weeks' work
Two weeks' holiday

I started planning the trip. How far would I be able to travel? It took me a while to get my calculations right, but finally I had it all worked out. I could sail to La Coruña in Spain in a fortnight. Then I would be able to spend two weeks exploring the Galician coast with Anke. After that, I would spend another two weeks sailing back to the Netherlands. We would fly back and forth in between the sailing trips, leaving *Jambo* berthed in La Coruña. What a plan! This was another giant step beyond the horizon as far as my sailing experience was concerned. I would encounter the Bay of Biscay and blue water, Spain, and a warmer climate. In the months leading up to the trip, I could hardly wait.

We kept pretty much to plan. I sailed solo to Spain, visiting the British Channel Islands on my way. I sailed the Bay of Biscay single-handed for the first time. How daunted and full of respect the Bay of Biscay made me feel. I am no longer daunted nowadays, but the feeling of respect remains. I remember navigating *Jambo* towards a Spanish port for the first time. *Not bad for an old IJsselmeer sailor,* I thought. At that stage, I still regarded myself as an advanced beginner based in the home waters of the IJsselmeer. I certainly didn't consider myself a long-distance sailor.

Our sailing holiday on the Spanish coast wasn't only magnificent, it was also great fun! Everything was so new and exciting! Sailing home with the lads went equally well, apart from our trip past the Channel Island of Jersey to Cherbourg. I totally underestimated the impact of waves and currents, and got into heavy seas north of Jersey. With winds at Force 7 and a counter current of around 3 knots, the waves piled up 5 m high. Sailing under autopilot, *Jambo* broached twice unexpectedly, putting the upper windows under water. The autopilot I was using at the time was not very reliable, and I ended up steering *Jambo* by hand for several hours. We reached Cherbourg late in the evening, relieved we had gotten off so lightly. The sea had taught us an important lesson. Don't ever underestimate the effect of current against wave. Another experience I wouldn't forget in a hurry.

The next year, 2018, we decided to head north towards Norway and Sweden. The weather was perfect and we spent a magnificent summer sailing. The return journey was almost perfect too, apart from when we ran aground in Limfjord, and ended up stranded for an afternoon. You can find a little anecdote on that story at the end of the book.

In the autumn, Anke and I began making plans for the next year's sailing. As always, one season ends and a new one begins. Where did we want to sail in the coming summer? We definitely wanted to head south. Should we try northern Spain again? Sailing around the Bay of Biscay? But wouldn't it be a lot like our last trip? Sometime during the winter, I had a brainwave. Why not berth *Jambo* somewhere abroad during the winter? That way we would be able to travel further south. We looked at various places and possibilities, and finally decided that the Canary Islands looked like a good option. I could sail there in the summer of 2019 and then back again the following year. It was exactly what I wanted to do, although I would need a new electronic autopilot that was 100% reliable. I did not like the idea of a windvane steering system.

In January 2019, I arranged to meet Tobias Lepper from Lepper Marine at the boat fair in Düsseldorf. He was recommended to me by Bene and Alexia, a sailing couple we first met in Marstrand in Sweden. We spent all morning studying the technology. How I came by the new system is a story in itself, but in the end, I decided not to combine old technology with new, and so we discarded the supplementary package we had just painstakingly put together, and I ended up buying everything new. It is a decision I have never regretted since.

Then in March 2019, I lost my job unexpectedly, and was suddenly free to do as I pleased as of April. The initial shock soon waned as I began to feel that life was giving me a great opportunity. My new freedom meant that there were plenty of new possibilities on the horizon. We were already planning to sail to the Canary Islands. Now, with more time on our hands, the trip would be far more relaxed. And then what? How would I sail home in 2020? Or did I need to come back at all? There were all sorts of options. For quite a while, Anke and I favoured the idea of sailing around the Mediterranean, including southern Spain, and then perhaps making a detour to the Balearic Islands. After that, we could then sail leisurely along the Portuguese coast before I sailed the Bay of Biscay solo, and then headed back to the Netherlands through the English Channel.

However, what really appealed to me was sailing in the other direction. I wanted to cross the Atlantic and explore the Caribbean. Anke and I couldn't make up our minds. For one thing, it would mean being apart for a long time, as Anke could not accompany me because of work. And was *Jambo* really up to an ocean crossing? In the end, I decided to make up my mind when

I reached the Canary Islands. If *Jambo* performed well and I felt up to it, we could then head west to the Caribbean.

I planned to sail across the Atlantic single-handed and see how things went. If everything went according to plan, I would be able to host all my friends when I got to the Caribbean. I hoped to sail back to the Netherlands in May. It was a bold plan, and if I really wanted it to work, I needed to start preparing immediately.

This was another sailing trip that would take me to the horizon and beyond, but this time the distance was a game changer. A brand new adventure was about to begin.

Chapter 1: Failing to Plan Means Planning to Fail!

It is a saying attributed to Benjamin Franklin, I believe, although I first heard it in England. It means that if you don't have a plan, then you are going to fail.

Oh, to be in England – I actually lived there for seven years, in Nottingham, from 2003 to 2010. It is another period of my life that greatly influenced me. Living abroad showed me that there are cultural differences, even if they do not appear on the surface at first. It also taught me to appreciate my homeland more, because some things really are more efficient in Germany. No surprises there. Sometimes you have to do without something before you can really appreciate it. On the other hand, there are plenty of great things in the UK as well.

Now, back to the story!

We have made up our minds - the Atlantic crossing is on the cards! I am not overly excited yet. For one thing, I'm still coming to terms with my new, radically changed circumstances, having only just signed the termination of contract. And now there is a different pile of work waiting for me. The new steering system has to be installed. Of course, I knew that already, but the rest of the boat's equipment needs to be overhauled as well. In her current state, *Jambo* would probably fail an Atlantic challenge. The main problem is power. Having an electric anchor winch would also be a good idea. The batteries should be okay.

There is a long list of things to do and not much time before I plan to leave. I hope to set off on 11 June 2019, after the spring bank holiday. It is the beginning of April now, so that means I only have about two months. Which sounds like plenty of time, but it isn't. Luckily, I am an engineer who can wield a hammer if needed, so I can do a lot of things myself.

I start with installing the navigation system with help from my sailing companion, Wilm. It takes us three days to complete the challenging task and successfully install the new Windex. We spend a whole afternoon drilling holes for the mount on the mast top. We install the radar and plotters. Over Easter, Anke and I do all the wiring. Then, at the end of April, Tobias arrives to inspect our work and do the calibrations.

Old   *New*

New Windsensor   *Working aloft*

We are running out of time, and I have to abandon the idea of an electric anchor winch along with several other could-does.

I had chosen solar panels for the electricity supply, but am still missing a bimini. I had ordered one the previous December 2018, from a sailmaker in Enkhuizen, along with a new sprayhood. Unfortunately, by May 2018 he had still only managed to complete the sprayhood, despite us hounding him with phone calls and telling him to complete our order soon. He had assured us that he would definitely have the bimini finished by this May, at the latest. I have a final discussion about it with him at the end of March, and mention that it needs to be stable enough to carry the solar panels. He then suggests installing an equipment rack for the solar panels. I am delighted. It's a great suggestion – just what we needed. He can start next week, he says.

I should have seen it coming. Of course, he did not start the next week, instead he let us down again. Just before Easter, I finally decided to pull the plug before it was too late. I was running out of time. There is no way I'll be sailing near the Equator without a bimini - exposing ourselves to intense sunlight without any kind of protection. We had already missed not having a bimini the previous summer when we were in Scandinavia! Long ocean crossings without solar panels are too risky, because relying on the engine to charge the batteries isn't enough without a backup. The risk of having to wait even longer and then ending up without a bimini, means that I decide to make one myself.

I have never done this kind of work before, but I think I will be able to manage. I use an old photo of *Jambo*, which clearly depicts the boat from the side. Then I start designing a construction, drawing and redrawing draft after draft, until on the umpteenth attempt, I finally come up with something that might work. My first plausible design. Back on board, I measure up the boat very carefully, and make a bill of material. Then I start sourcing the parts. I manage to find steel construction tubes in the Eifel (Germany) for a reasonable price, and the right fittings near Bremen. The other things I need, small bits and pieces, steel cables and the like, I buy at DIY stores or online. I choose four semi-flexible module solar panels each with 120 Wp and weighing 6.3 kg. I also buy two charge controllers to go with them.

By this time, it is already the beginning of May. *Where has all the time gone?* Luckily, my sailing comrade, Heinz, has plenty of time, and the two of us start building the equipment carrier together. I have to make changes to my original design almost immediately, because some things simply don't work. Then after a couple of days, we have to put down our tools because some parts are missing, and I also need to buy extra material.

It is just five more weeks until our planned departure. Time is running out. The next week, we are able to continue our work at last. We complete our first prototype but, unfortunately, it doesn't do the job.

I have to adapt the design and travel back to the Eifel for some more steel metal tubing. Somehow, we manage to finish the new construction by the end of May, and install the solar panels. A sailmaker makes us a basic bimini and then we are done - it works. We can relax at last.

While I was working on the bimini construction, I suddenly realised that I might have to change my insurance in order to sail

The steel frame is almost finished

Jambo in the Caribbean. In the middle of May, I contact my insurance company and tell them my plans. "That's no problem," they say. "We will send you a quote." I asked them to send it by email, as I am not at home. A week later, I call them again, and hear that everything is proceeding as it should. Then at the beginning of June, I return home to find a letter from the insurance company, informing me that I need to get *Jambo* evaluated as she is more than 10 years old. This is devastating news. If I had known sooner, I would have been able to find a surveyor easily. Now there was just one week left before I was due to depart.

Of course, people asked why I couldn't simply postpone the date. But Anke and I had booked our flights months ago, and I only had just over two weeks to sail to Porto in Portugal. Our return flights are already booked, too. I phone a different insurance company that I had seen at the boat fair the previous year.

All we need now is the bimini

They confirm that I need an official assessment for my boat, if I want to sail the Atlantic. They tell me to send them all the documents I have via email, and offer to contact the reinsurer. I send everything off right away, including all the latest invoices. The next day, the insurance company calls me back to inform me that all I need is a positive attested rig check because *Jambo* is a 2009 model. I am so relieved, and manage to find a rigger who can come at the end of the week. Surely, that will just be a formality, I think.

Wrong. The rig check reveals that strands in the shrouds and anchor plates on the mast are broken. The report recommends changing the rig completely because of the damage. I am dismayed at first, but after a moment of thought, I realise I am not surprised. *Jambo* has been through a lot in the last few years, sailing in strong winds, and covering many nautical miles.

I get a second opinion, which confirms that simply swapping the damaged parts will not be enough. The whole rig needs to be renewed. But who can do it? The rigger who did the check turns me down. He is not available for another four weeks. I spend all day on the phone, following the recommendation of another rigger, who is also not available. I get hold of a company in Stavoren (Netherlands), who can start in a week's time. I drive there by car and sign the contract immediately. I will have to take *Jambo* to Warns and the De Vrijheid yacht harbour after the bank holiday weekend, in order to get the rig installed. This means that our original time schedule will no longer hold. Anke and I re-book our flights. Fortunately, it is not too expensive, and Anke manages to reschedule her time off work. The other good news is that the rig can be renewed without any problems.

We have worked out our final sailing route and schedule. Anke will land in Porto on 5 July. That gives me two and a half weeks' to get there, and means I will be able to make a few nice stops on the way. Then we want to sail to Lisbon together and fly back from there at the end of July.

I plan the rest of the passage quickly too. In August, one leg of the journey will take us from Lisbon to Madeira, and our ship's cook, Klaus, will join me. Then following on from Madeira, I want to sail single-handed to the Canary Islands and explore them, before mooring in Gran Canaria where I hope to leave *Jambo* until the next January.

I'd had a chat with the representative of Trans-Ocean (German sailing association) in Las Palmas, and despite the ARC rally that takes over the marina in Las Palmas in September, things were looking good. "We'll be able to find you a berth somewhere on Gran Canaria," he told me on the phone. He sounded so confident, that I felt reassured, and stopped worrying immediately. Anke and I decide to book all further flights to Las Palmas.

In September, I want to fly home for a couple of weeks, and in October, I am planning to take Anke sailing around Fuerteventura and Lanzarote for two weeks. On week three, Mats is to join us. At New Year, Anke, Jana and I hope to spend eight days on board *Jambo*. If everything goes according plan and I reach the Canary Islands, I should be ready for the Atlantic crossing. That is the goal, but I won't decide until I get to the Canaries.

I have scheduled the Atlantic crossing for the beginning of January 2020, when I will set sail to Guadeloupe. In March and April, I am planning for visitors, starting with Heinz, Wilm and Klaus, followed by Anke, and finally, my daughter Alex and her partner. At the beginning of May 2020, I hope to set off for the Azores, where Anke and I plan to sail round the island group. After that, I want to spend July and August sailing back to Enkhuizen with a lengthy stop on the Channel Islands, including visits to several harbours I have stopped at before, and rather liked. We have finalised our plans and booked all the necessary flights for this year. However, "unverhofft kommt oft", as we say in Germany, which means "expect the unexpected!"

Link to video:

Chapter 2: Emergency Stop in Fécamp, France

On 18 June 2019, at around 12.40 pm, I set off on my great adventure from Marina De Vrijheid in Warns. In Stavoren, I fill up the tank once more, and then sail into the IJsselmeer. With a nice breeze I head for Den Oever, and then on to Den Helder, where I plan to stop for the first time. Everything goes well, and I lock into the North Sea. When I reach Den Helder in the evening, I decide not to dock after all. Instead, I want to sail right through the first night. I have spent so many days in port in Warns and I cannot wait to reach open water.

I want to sail!

How marvellous to be at sea

Setting off at last, with the wind blowing across the North Sea, feels incredible after all the months of intense preparation, the insurance worries and the pressure to get everything sorted. Things could have gone the other way. If I had needed a proper survey, our sailing schedule for the next few months would have been wrecked. And the last week in Warns was very dull waiting for the new rigg.

Here in the North Sea, I feel content, and slowly but surely, the pressures of the past weeks and months start to fall away. Everything is going to be fine from now on. I am certain. As far as I am concerned, I have two and a half weeks to get to Porto, which is plenty of time. It is about 1,100 NM. Although it might sound like a short hectic trip, and would have been a while back, the past few years have taught me how to manage interval sleeping. I am now able to sail through the night single-handed without any difficulty, although I am usually very tired the next day. My average distance travelled in 24 hours is around 130 NM. If I sail through the night, then it means I have done the equivalent of three days' sailing, taking the distance covered in a day to be about 40 NM.

So, I sail through the first night, and head for Blankenberge in Belgium, which is to be my first stop. The night's sailing goes very well, and I pass the entrance to Rotterdam at a decent distance in order to stay clear of all the traffic regulations, and avoid the cargo ships. The next morning I feel so fit, I decide to sail straight on through the next night as well. I set course for the English coast, as the wind conditions there are favourable. I sail past the British cliffs, and then through the Strait of Dover during the night, heading for Eastbourne, under engine. The wind is coming from the west at Force 5 by this time and I cannot start tacking because of the traffic separation scheme (nor do I want to). I want to make good speed towards Portugal and I don't mind some motorised sailing on a long trip.

At noon, Eastbourne is finally starboard and I set course south, with a good westerly aiming to clear the traffic separation scheme first, and then beat the wind toward Cherbourg. From there, I might sail on through the night. The day after tomorrow

I could be sitting in The Crow's Nest restaurant in St. Peter Port, Guernsey, enjoying a well-deserved jetty beer while I look back at the past leg of the trip. Things are going well so far and the prospects look good!

However, suddenly, while I am crossing the traffic separation scheme, *Jambo* points hard to the wind and broaches. Sails are flapping and the speed is down. I start sweating immediately. *What is going on?* The last time this happened, several years ago in the Baltic Sea, the steering gear was to blame. *But I checked everything before we set off, didn't I? Not again, please!* I think aloud as I leap to the wheel and steer hard to port. *Jambo* willingly responds to my steering, and returns to course. I sigh with relief. So, what was the problem? It must be something to do with the autopilot. Could it be the computer, or the wiring, or the autopilot motor? Or, it is something else? I had changed the autopilot motor myself last year when the old one broke.

I am still in the middle of the traffic separation scheme, and steer *Jambo* by hand until I have collected myself and suddenly remember that *Jambo* can sail up to the wind with just some rudder support. I leave the helm for a brief moment to fetch a line to tie up the rudder, and the boat turns into the wind again. Somehow, I manage to fasten the rope and tie the wheel slightly to lee. Now *Jambo* holds course fairly well.

A short while later, I have crossed half the traffic separation area and find myself in the middle between the two seaways. I start looking for the problem, and measure the tension for the autopilot computer with a voltmeter. The computer seems fine, but the Lewmar autopilot motor could be playing up. Fortunately, I know a bit about this because I swapped it myself last year. I know how to get access to the rotary drive. To do so, I have to remove the cladding at the front of the steering shaft. I also need to remove a panel in the quarter cabin to make sure it is accessible from both sides. When I finally get to the motor and check all the currents, it turns out that the motor really is the problem. It is still turning, as I can hear, but the clutch is not engaging anymore so there is no power transfer.

What should I do? This is the end of my plans to sail straight to

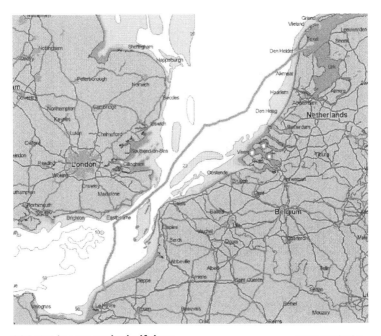

306 NM in two and a half days   *Map: Navionics*

Cherbourg. I should be able to reach Fécamp though, which is another 40 NM away. I could always sail north to Eastbourne. That would be a lot quicker. Intuitively I choose Fécamp because I will be closer to home. This actually turns out to be the right decision a few days later. I sailed there two years ago, and I really liked the town, even though my drone fell into the sea there.

With the rudder in a fixed position, I sail *Jambo* upwind. I don't have to spend the whole time standing at the helm. Here you make use of the play between windward yaw, heel and rudder action. The more the boat heels, the less the effect of the rudder

31

blade, because *Jambo* only has one rudder blade, which is mounted centrally. So on a upwind course, I always have to hold the rudder slightly to leeward to compensate. When *Jambo* bears away slightly, with the rudder set, and heels more, the rudder effect decreases, and the boat automatically luffs. The more acute angle to the apparent wind means the sail pressure reduces, and *Jambo* straightens up a little more, whereby the rudder effect kicks in, and the boat steers to leeward. By taking advantage of this interplay I sail almost all the way down to Fécamp before turning on the engine.

On Thursday, shortly before midnight, I tie up the lines in the marina. Some friendly Belgians help me and ask me where I have come from. They can hardly believe that I left the Netherlands only two and a half days ago. By chance, I was in the same berth two years ago. After two nights' at sea, and all the excitement, I fall asleep straight away and sleep like a log.

In the morning, I phone Tobias as soon as I can. I have already forewarned him, sending a short text message yesterday while I was still sailing. He needs to know the precise motor type, and it is going to take a couple of days with a weekend in between. A break of a couple of days does not suit me at all. I know that Anke will be arriving in Porto soon. I register at the harbour office, and can stay until Monday. I can also extend my stay if necessary. I get permission to use the marina's address for delivery, and although I only speak a few morsels of French and the receptionist's English isn't much better, we somehow manage to sort things out.

I manage to take out the autopilot motor, and send Tobias a photo. To have more options, I phone the Lewmar reps in Le Havre and Dieppe, and find out that there are no spares in all of France, and delivery times for a new motor are five weeks or more.

For the first time on this trip, I am completely at a loss. Five weeks! How can the supplier of a key component have such poor availability of spare parts, and still charge such a high price? The part I need is said to cost 2,500 euros.

Tobias is my last hope, and I phone him, feeling very worried indeed. Luckily, he has managed to find a suitable drive in the meantime, and can send it off at once, so that I will get it on Monday. I am delighted, and agree. I have already stopped thinking about all the costs. The only thing that counts is to get this part as soon as possible so that I can continue sailing. The same afternoon, the new Lewmar autopilot motor is sent per express delivery to Port Fécamp. It should arrive on Monday. I am very lucky to have such brilliant support. It is imperative on such a long trip.

Fécamp beach

I can trace the path of the delivery online and, by the evening, everything seems to be going according to plan. I contact the harbour office on Saturday morning to make sure everyone knows when the delivery is due, and assume everything will be fine. It's lovely weather, and I enjoy my weekend in Fécamp, eat a huge bowl of mussels à la Roquefort on the harbour promenade, and visit the famous Benedictine cloister renowned for its liqueurs.

In the marina, I meet Oliver, and his boat, *Plan B,* for the first time. I am walking along the peer when he says, "Hello," and adds, "I know you but you don't know me!" That is when I realise he knows my YouTube channel. I also meet Carsten, with his sailing yacht, *Stöbi,* and the three of us enjoy a nice afternoon aboard Carsten's boat. That is one of the nice parts of long-distance sailing. You meet plenty of great people all on the same wavelength.

Then it's Monday morning, and according to the delivery notice, my package is at a nearby distribution centre. It is due to arrive today. I spend all morning watching out for the delivery van and driving everyone nuts, asking the marine office if it has arrived. I check the sent details again right after lunch, and see that the packet has now been delivered to someone called Lemetais. I rush to the marine office, but they haven't seen the package. Lemetais must have it. Where is he? The woman at the office says she knows no one by that name. I can't believe this. It now looks as if the driver handed my package to someone whom he assumed must be a marine worker. Now it is lost. It is unbelievable. I am devastated.

Concerned, I phone Tobias again and let him know what has happened. He has found another motor at Lankhorst in Rheine. Should we really have it delivered again? I have no idea what to do, but then I make up my mind. On Tuesday morning, I rent a car; pack up the old motor, which is luckily still under guarantee, and drive the 650 km to Germany and the Lower Rhine area. Anke picks up the engine in Rheine, and we meet at her place.

After a quick coffee, I drive back again, leaving the old motor behind. I reach Fécamp at two o'clock in the morning. I fall into my bunk feeling shattered and ecstatic at the same time.

On Wednesday morning, I manage to install the new motor and get everything up and running again. Puh!

Feeling better now the repairs are done

Of course, I want to head off immediately, but strong winds with squalls are forecast for tomorrow around Cap de la Hague, and with the strong currents there, it is too dangerous for me to sail. With current against wave, a dangerous sea can build up, as I experienced two years ago. I only have to look at the beginning of my own video "Herbstsee" (only in German) to remind myself. I seem to be running out of luck now, and don't want to provoke anything. I'm postponing my departure because of the wind conditions. By the way, this is the first time in my short sailing life that I don't leave because the wind is too strong. I won't leave before Thursday night or even Friday morning, depending on how the weather develops. After then, the wind forecast looks quite good.

On Friday morning, I finally set off with diminishing winds around Force 7. I have lost a whole week, which means that I have just one more week before Anke arrives in Porto. It is roughly 750 NM to Porto. Another stop would only make sense in an emergency. I ask Anke to book a hotel just in case I don't make it in time.

I'm learning that long-distance sailing follows different rules to a holiday cruise, although my well devised plans wouldn't have worked then either, if something this serious had happened. You need reserves of time for difficulties that might occur, such as small repairs, weather conditions and anything unexpected that might come up. I wonder if I have just been very lucky in the past because things always went so well. Probably not, but I at least did not have much bad luck.

I always orientate my plans along recommended travelling periods. It is a good time to sail to Portugal between June and August. Statistically, the conditions are fair, and bad weather is unusual although it can crop up from time to time, as I am finding out now. Keeping your boat in good shape, checking all the important fittings on a regular basis and making necessary repairs is a good idea. That way you lower the risks significantly. Of course, you cannot get rid of them all. It is also important to make sure you bring the right spares. But how are you supposed to what you are going to need?

A few months later, I can exchange the broken rotary drive for a new one, under guarantee. I also buy a spare drive. Somehow, one autopilot motor no longer seems enough for two Atlantic crossings. That means I'm going to start my first Atlantic crossing with two reserve drives. I'm happy to say that the one installed in Fécamp survived both Atlantic crossings, and is still running even as I write these lines.

Link to video

Chapter 3: To Lisbon

But back to the story! I am still on my way to Porto, and the longest leg of the journey so far is waiting for me. As I depart Fécamp at first light, I am very happy to be on the move again. At the same time, I am still feeling down because of everything that happened. At wind Force 7, the sea is pretty rough and choppy, due to the strong current and the swell caused by Force 8 to 9 winds a while back. But *Jambo* copes really well, and the day passes without any problems until I approach Cap de la Hague in the evening.

The wind dropped consistently throughout the day and has now abated almost completely, so that I have to turn on the engine. I start it, but the boat shakes and fails to pick up speed properly. There is also no water emerging from the exhaust. What has happened now? I shake my head. *Is this whole trip doomed from the start?* I wonder. I check the tap of the engine cooling system, but of course, it is on because I used it this morning when I travelled out of the harbour. Something must be blocking the propeller.

I hunt for my wetsuit because I want to dive and have a look at the saildrive. But I can't find it. Luckily, I am not far from the coast, so I have a mobile phone connection and can call Klaus. Perhaps he has my wetsuit at his home. I remember us sailing together on the IJsselmeer last autumn with his sons. At one point, Klaus' mobile fell off the jetty, and his sons wore my wetsuit as they took it in turns to dive for it. They were partially successful. Although they didn't manage to find Klaus' mobile, they did find one Mats had lost in the same place the year before. Of course, it was wrecked, but we were all highly amused by the coincidence (except for Klaus). But Klaus hasn't taken my wetsuit home to wash. Weeks later, I find it hanging in the cupboard. As usual, I forgot to look in the most obvious place.

I try gently moving backwards and forwards. It is the only thing I can think of, and it might work. Sure enough, I soon see bits of plants that must have been freed, floating around the boat, and the motor starts running a bit more smoothly. There is also more water coming out of the exhaust. A tangle of plants must have got caught up in the saildrive. I check the impeller sea-water filter, which is also clogged. I clean it, and then everything is fine. On we go.

As it starts getting dark, the wind increases and Alderney emerges on the horizon ahead. I hoist the sails, and in a gentle breeze, *Jambo* sails between the islands into the dark, with Alderney to starboard and Guernsey on the port side. I am surrounded by silence, and sitting in the bow, I listen to the gentle sound of the waves lapping against the prow as *Jambo* glides through the mirror-like water. In the distance, I see a beacon. This is such a tranquil, unforgettable moment!

I leave the two islands behind, and sadly, the last of the wind disappears with them. I have to throw on the engine again. Luckily, it doesn't play up this time. As it gradually starts getting light, I'm heading for the Atlantic, and the further west I sail during Saturday, the more the wind picks up. In the afternoon, somewhere north of Île d'Ouessant, I can hoist the sails again. During the night, I pass the island, which for me marks the entrance to the Bay of Biscay. I keep well clear, as the current is already contrary and gets stronger closer to shore.

In the morning, here I am sailing the Bay of Biscay – my Biscay, as I like to think of it, or rather our Biscay – I wouldn't be here if it weren't for *Jambo*.

Two years ago, when I crossed Biscay for the first time, *Jambo* and I really found each other. It was a tight sailing schedule to La Coruña and I was feeling unsure how things would go. Was *Jambo* up to it? I kept asking myself. Would the weather hold? I dreaded making mistakes and had no idea what sailing the notorious Bay of Biscay was going to be like.

The second day was perfect for sailing, with a lovely breeze, beautiful weather and deep blue water. La Coruña was just a day's journey away. I stood at the railing, staring out at the endless space around me, a gentle Atlantic swell rocked *Jambo* up and down and I realised I had reached my goal at last. This was where I had longed to be. The Bay of Biscay, a taste of blue water and the ocean before me.

At that moment, all the stress, tension and doubt fell away. The beauty of the ocean overwhelmed me. I could not hold back the tears and just sat there for a long time, letting them flow. Out in the middle of Biscay, I had a profound experience that day. Something that maybe only happens to solo sailors at sea.

I remember thinking, *now for the final nautical miles of our journey to the north of Spain*, and shouting, "Come on, let's go!" Suddenly *Jambo* shuddered and picked up speed. It felt as if she had understood what I was saying and wanted to support me with all her might. Of course, everyone knows a boat is an inanimate object, and that a random gust of wind is the most likely reason for the sudden increase in speed. Nonetheless, there are plenty of sailors out there, who have spent a lot of time crossing the oceans, who would say a boat is more than just an object. Ever since that day, I am one of them.

Now, two years later, here we are again. The weather is glorious as we sail our Biscay. Two beautifully sunny, very relaxing days, and magnificent downwind sailing. I spot lots of dolphins who keep swimming past, luring me out of my cabin with their calls. Two years ago I hadn't realised they were talking to me. I even see a whale spouting water.

The further south we get, the stronger the wind becomes, which is welcome at first, as we make good speed. But on Tuesday, it blows steadily from the northeast at 22 to 30 knots. I have decided to sail to Porto without stopping, and am on course, past Cape Vilan and along the Costa da Morte. The waves are impressive, approximately 4 m high. As they are very long, it is not a problem for *Jambo*. She copes with them very well.

As I head into the next night, things suddenly get rough and we are heavily shaken by the sea, although we are actually still in water depths of 1200 m. It is pitch-black, which is eerily unpleasant, as I can no longer see what is happening outside. I have to stay below deck, letting the autopilot steer, and bracing myself, as the waves pound against the boat. At the same time, I am mesmerised and cannot take my eyes off the various displays. How is the wind developing and how many degrees did that last breaker throw the ship off course? I am in standby mode, with lifejacket and safety harness, ready to steer by hand if necessary. At the same time, I dread the idea of something breaking or failing.

Luckily, after a short while it is over. I set a more southerly course and sail parallel to the shelf edge. The weather calms down somewhat, and the waves hit *Jambo* less violently. I sit up at my chart table until half past one in the morning, before I start to think about sleep. *That was a bit close for comfort,* I think. They don't call it the Costa da Morte for nothing, and no one should underestimate the waters here. Next time, I shall choose a route further west, beyond the traffic separation scheme in conditions like these.

On Wednesday, the wind dies down completely. As often happens, strong winds and slack periods go hand in hand. I sail the final stage of this journey under motor in beautiful weather. Things are quiet all afternoon and there is nothing ahead. Two dolphins approach and swim past, heading north. I go below deck to write up my diary, and get lost in my report of the last leg for the website. When I hear a dolphin calling, the sound pulls me out of my lethargy. *Oh all right, I will go and say hello,* I tell myself. The dolphin swims a boat's length behind *Jambo,* in her wake. Then it surfaces, sees me and turns back north. *That was a short visit,* I think, but as I turn around, I get a real shock when I realise that the path ahead is full of marking buoys with fishing nets.

Immediately, the cruise has my full attention again and I circumnavigate the nets and the buoys. If it had not been for that dolphin, I would have sailed straight into the nets and *Jambo* might have been caught up in the ropes. Was it one of the dolphins who had passed me earlier? Had it come back to warn me? Why did it only stay until I appeared on deck? Throughout the centuries, seafarers have often told tales of dolphins helping them. Had I just experienced the same thing? Maybe it was just a coincidence. Maybe it was a different dolphin. In fact, it probably was. Still, the experience stays with me for a long time.

I am getting closer and closer to Porto. In the evening, I can work out my ETA: about 4 o'clock the next morning. That is not ideal. My Imray cruising guide to the area says the approach to Duoro Marina is extremely demanding. Marinieros meet the yachts and guide them in and back out again. Strong river currents are to be expected, and the estuary is full of unlit small fishing boats at night. Sailors are advised not to enter the marina after dark.

Sunrise is at 6 am and high tide an hour before that, so I have to wait for the tide in the afternoon in order to cruise into the marina in daylight and rising water. It does not look too dramatic on the nautical chart, but Imray's guidebooks have been very reliable so far. Thinking about it, I decide to go in when it is dark after all, an hour before sunrise, in order to be at the marina by dawn. The fact that there is hardly any wind helps. If need be, I can always break off my attempt and anchor in the roadstead until the afternoon. I reduce speed to delay my arrival.

Then it is time: I am approaching the Rio Duoro. The radar is on and I have a torch in my hand. The town and the road on the portside bank are brightly lit, and lights shine on the water. In fact, there are a few smaller boats in the estuary, but they are easy to spot. Without any problems, in almost still water, with good visibility due to the streetlights, I reach the marina and moor at one of the jetties at around 5.30 am. It was one of my easiest night approaches in unknown waters. For once, the guide was off the mark.

783 NM in almost exactly six days and six nights. I am still so wired that, despite being very tired, it takes me some time to fall into a deep sleep. A knock on the boat wakes me up. It is already late morning. A mariniero standing on the jetty tells me that I can't stay here and will have to move the boat later. "No problem," I reply, still sleepy. I need a little time to wake up. My six-day single-handed trip was exhausting.

I spend the day registering at the harbour office, mooring the boat in the right berth and washing clothes, as the last time I could do any washing was in the Netherlands several weeks ago.

This was my longest journey to date. What a ride! I take the opportunity to reflect on how it went.

What went well? The food was great. I had made sure of that and spoilt myself on the trip. I added an automatic coffee machine to the galley equipment before I set off, and couldn't do without it now. Every morning after getting up, I'd sat on deck drinking my coffee in the fresh morning air, staring out at the open sea simply enjoying the moment.

The bread machine I used to bake a fresh loaf of bread every third day is something else that has greatly improved my quality of life. It is a standard machine from Unold, running on 220 v, which are available at all times thanks to an inverter with 1500 W on the whole board circuit.

Interval sleeping also worked well. If I missed sleep during the night, I tried to catch up with it the next day although it is impossible to replace the benefits of an undisturbed night's sleep. The electricity supply from the new solar panels is another excellent improvement. I also did a lot of filming to try to document the trip and catch the atmosphere as best I could, which I believe has worked pretty well.

What didn't go so well? There isn't too much that needs to be mentioned. I knew my battery bank was not that great before I set off. It does not have enough capacity to last through a night without re-charging it with the engine, although the solar panels deliver quite well during the day. However, that wasn't a real problem for this distance.

Washing day

And how do I feel now? Simply brilliant! I really enjoyed the days spent out at sea. I had enough time despite the pressure to make good speed, I also sailed as much as possible, and not just because I wanted to.

Now I can't wait for Anke to arrive and our time together. We are planning a relaxing journey to Lisbon. Just the two of us for once, with a couple of lovely stops, and no night sailing.

On Friday, she finally arrives. We have not seen each other for three and a half weeks now, and are delighted to be together again. We really enjoy the days we spend in Porto, taking a tour of the city and doing a lot of sightseeing. Porto is definitely worth a visit with its ancient city centre and all the attractions.

I also meet up with Oliver from *Plan B* again. That is one of the great things about long-distance sailing: you are likely to meet some of the other sailors on several occasions. On two evenings, the three of us go out to eat in the small fishermen's quarter close to the marina. Chairs and tables are set outside a number of simple restaurants. The fresh fish is cooked on a wood-fired

Oliver, Anke and me (r. to l.)

grill on the street. There are not many other tourists, and locals on the pavement surround us – it all feels very authentic. This is exactly our kind of restaurant.

The food is fantastic and great value for money. We spend some marvellous evenings here and will look back on these few days for a long time to come. It is a shame we cannot stay longer.

During the next two weeks, Anke and I cruise south along the Portuguese coast. Although it is July, it is not too hot because the Atlantic provides a lovely fresh breeze all the time. We visit Figueira da Foz and stay the night. Then we head on to Nazaré where we spend three days. We love area where local tourism and the ethnic origins of Portugal mix in the best way. The food is also great, especially if you like fish – there is plenty of choice and the prices are very reasonable. The area is famous for some of the highest waves in the world. They reach up to 30 m high in the autumn, along the coast, attracting surfers from all over the world. Now, things are quieter. And there are no problems for us sailors. We enjoy the sunny days spending our afternoons on the long clean beaches, diving into the waves. With water temperatures of 20 °C, it feels very refreshing.

Navaré beach

Our next stop is Peniche. We stay just for one night. There are some lovely restaurants and the marina is fine, but we find it difficult to find the harbour office. Luckily, we do find one of the few berths for visitors on an extended jetty. It is a some what choppy mooring as boats sail by, but okay for one night.

We sail 51 NM from Peniche to Cascais. With a nice sailing wind, we tack to a fresh southwesterly until it dies down and shifts against us. Then suddenly it gets foggy, with visibility of about 300 m, although the sun shines through from above. This is probably not an untypical weather situation here and is part of sailing on the Portuguese coast. Of course, we spot some dolphins, as we have done almost every day so far. We are still thrilled every time.

When we reach Marina Cascais, we moor at the registration pontoon first, planning to stay for four days. We have to pay 60 euros per night, which is our highest rate so far. I know that some places in the Mediterranean charge even more, but I think

next time we might anchor in the bay outside of the town, and go ashore in the dinghy.

Nonetheless, we can't wait to see Cascais. Time flies as we explore the town, which we adore. It is such a beautiful place, full of pretty alleyways, lots of parks and squares, great restaurants and historic buildings. We spend a truly unforgettable few days there.

However, once again, we soon have to take our leave, Lisbon is waiting, before Anke and I have to fly back home. I booked a berth at Marina Parque das Nações in advance, also known as the Expo-Marina. It is just outside the city and is very quiet. The berthing fee is also reasonable. We have chosen the monthly rate of 440 euros for the 17-day stay. In some areas, the marina runs dry at low tide, but our berth is in the deeper area. Anyone who knows some of the mudflat harbours on the North Sea coast will recognise a familiar picture.

Lisbon is a fantastic city, and we have two whole days to look around by using the bus. A 24-hour ticket for all public transport costs 6.50 euros per person. We also take the famous tram 28 from one side of the city to the other. There is so much to see and do and two days are not enough.

We meet Eric from the 'Glüxpiraten' in the marina. He interviewed me for one of his podcasts some time back. Of course, he shows us round his *Makani*, a 53-foot Amel. It is a great ship, and we spend a few pleasant hours together.

Then it is time to say goodbye to *Jambo* and fly home. Anke will not be back for a while, but I am only going for 2 weeks. The next leg of my journey to Madeira is due to begin in early August.

A beautiful view across the rooftops of Lisbon

Link to video Fécamp to Porto

Link to video Porto to Lisbon

Chapter 4: From Madeira to La Palma in the Canary Islands

I enjoy the days in Germany and use the time to run some errands. At the end of July, I fly back to Lisbon again to prepare for the long trip to Madeira. Originally, this was supposed to have been my longest leg of the trip, but the non-stop journey from Fécamp to Porto has changed all that. Nonetheless, it will be further away from the coast then anything so far, and marks another personal milestone - the next step beyond the horizon.

I shop extensively, because this time our ship's cook, Klaus, is joining me. I want him to be able to run riot in the galley, so there is tuna, pork filets, rabbit and rump steak for him to play with. This is going to be a culinary adventure as well as a nautical one.

When Klaus arrives, I am delighted to see him. On a Saturday morning, 3 August, we cast off and sail down the Rio Tejo towards the Atlantic Ocean. We pass Lisbon on the starboard side, and briefly admire its beauty, before leaving it behind as we race along at an incredible 9 knots above ground. It is roughly 550 NM to Madeira, and we think the passage will take about four to five days. The wind forecast is looking good, although towards the end of the journey the wind will die down. We plan to arrive in Madeira on the coming Wednesday.

There is a good Force 6 blowing out on the Atlantic. I don't set a direct course. Instead, I choose a slightly more southerly one in order to stay in the wind field. At least that is what the forecast model at Windfinder says. I've bought AIS/DSC transmitters for the life jackets, which we are using for the first time. That means the GPS position is transmitted automatically via AIS and DSC in the event of a man overboard (MOB). The device is activated via a water-soluble tablet, similar to an automatic life jacket. I do a safety briefing with Klaus, and we go through the MOB drill so that he knows what to do in an emergency.

In the evening, Klaus prepares the tuna steaks and serves them in a lemon and cream sauce with fried potatoes and salad. Delicious!

The next day with 3 Beaufort, we decide to take the opportunity to fly the drone and take some photos of *Jambo* in the Atlantic. In the afternoon, we pause for a swim. The water temperature is 22 °C, which is very pleasant indeed, and there is practically no swell. That means it is easy to climb back on board via the bathing platform. Of course, we keep a lookout for sharks but don't see any.

Then Klaus conjures up young Portuguese rabbit in a white wine sauce served with rice and salad. It is a work of art!

The next morning - it's Monday already - we have to start up the engine to keep the boat moving, as the wind is down to Force 2. In the afternoon, the wind picks up a bit, and we decide to practise a single-handed MOB manoeuvre, i.e. simulate an emergency alone on board.

This is the plan: the test person (me!) jumps overboard with the remote control for the electric autopilot around his neck and tries to switch off the autopilot, hoping that the boat will then turn into the wind and automatically reduce speed. Then, while the ship passes, the test person has to grab the line along the stern of the ship and hold on until the ship stops moving, and he can pull himself to the stern. At least, that's the theory. I am going to wear my portable walkie-talkie on my wrist to keep in touch with Klaus in case of an emergency, if we move too far apart.

The first thing we want to do is see how long it takes *Jambo* to lose speed without a helmsman or autopilot. Under full sails, wind at Force 3 and on an upwind course, *Jambo* is currently sailing through the water at about 4 knots. I turn off the autopilot and we wait to see what happens. *Jambo*, however, carries on her way, quite happily, as if she doesn't need anyone to steer. It actually takes about ten minutes before she stops sailing full ahead and turns into the wind. She is still drifting through the water at a speed of 1 knot. That is our first piece of sobering information. If the wind were stronger, she would probably turn to more quickly, but would also drift away faster.

If I do manage to grab the line, I don't want to be dragged along for 10 minutes, so we decide that Klaus should change course as soon as I turn off the electrical autopilot so that the boat stops quickly. Feeling slightly nervous, I move starboard to the shrouds, when suddenly the wind picks up and we start doing 5.5 knots through the water. A little less speed would suit me better, to be honest. After a moment of hesitancy, I pluck up some courage and jump into the Atlantic. I want to reach the lifeline fast and then switch off the autopilot. I manage to grab the lifeline. As I try to press the standby button on the remote control in the foaming water, I lose hold of the line and drift astern. "Abort, abort," I shout into my walkie-talkie. Klaus steers *Jambo* in my direction and manages to pick me up.

I now know that holding on to the lifeline and pressing the button of the controls at the same time doesn't work. In fact at that speed, it is almost impossible to hold on to the line at all. Anyone who has ever done any fender riding will know that it gets difficult to hang on once you are going at about 3 knots. So my manoeuvre has shown us that I have to switch off the autopilot first before grabbing the lifeline.

After a short break, I have another go. This time I don't hesitate as much before I jump off the moving boat into the sea. I manage to switch off the autopilot, but instead I can't grab the line. We don't try again. I am not an athletic swimmer, and am beginning to tire.

It is beginning to dawn on me that the chances of getting back on the boat if I go overboard while sailing solo are slim. If not impossible. To have the slightest chance in an emergency, I need to get hold of the line and hang on. If I miss it, I won't be able to get back to the boat because *Jambo* moves faster than I can swim. I'm glad we tried it out – at least I know what to expect now.

In the evening, I am exhausted after our efforts, so Klaus prepares two magnificent steaks for us with a little side of vegetables. Just what the doctor ordered after such an exciting day.

The next morning, a group of twenty or so dolphins greets us. Their calls wake me up before Klaus notices them. At last, I think, because we have hardly seen any sea life so far, and I had promised Klaus we would see loads. Even the dolphins have been scarce until now. It is an amazing spectacle watching them swim around the boat in formation and then surface occasionally to get some air. We watch them, absolutely fascinated, until they move on.

In the afternoon, we have another go at rehearsing the MOB drill. This time using the engine and a couple of fenders tied together. Once again, we find that it is almost impossible for a man overboard to get back on a boat single-handed, despite the safety lines and remote controls. This is another subduing result. I need to cool down, and jump back into the water to fetch the fenders. Since we set off, it has been growing steadily warmer and it is actually hot this afternoon.

Klaus suddenly spots something in the water, port ahead. I hasten to the bow, and then 200 m away, a whale about 8 or 9 m long leaps out of the water once, and then again – how amazing!

It is almost on a collision course! Standing at the front of the bow, feeling fascinated and worried at the same time, I point my camera, wondering if the whale is about to shoot out of the water right in front of *Jambo*. Thankfully, it skips a jump, leaping out of the water again about 80 m to starboard. Phew! How incredible! We are blown away.

In the evening, there is loin cutlet with peppers, onions, bacon and pasta in a white wine sauce - fantastic!

After dinner, a pod of four dolphins comes to say hello. This time we were ready and waiting with our GoPro underwater camera attached to a boat hook. It is a very inquisitive, playful group. We stop the engine and are able to film the dolphins playing

with the lifeline for minutes on end. What a day! And the perfect ending to this sailing trip.

The next morning we can already see Porto Santo on the starboard side, and Madeira about 25 NM straight ahead. The archipelago is visible this far away because of the high mountains. We spot more dolphins, and this time I get to take some great pictures from the air as they swim alongside *Jambo*.

At lunchtime, we moor at Marina Quinta do Lorde on the east side of Madeira, and our unique trip ends. Our joy at having reached our destination is mixed with a little sadness because

Marina Quinta do Lorde

our fantastic voyage is over. I would have loved to carry on sailing. Apart from spotting the whales and dolphins, my personal highlight is still the first few moments of each day, just after sunrise. I love sitting on deck simply enjoying the never-ending scope of everything as I slowly wake up with a cup of coffee, and the sun glittering in the water shines on me. If it is a cloudless night, you get to see the starry sky so bright and vivid in detail that you will never see on land in populated areas. Here, out at sea, away from the coast, we are far away from any artificial light and can even see the Milky Way.

Klaus flies home in two days' time. I can stay for a couple more days before I travel on to La Palma. But before that, we want to explore the Island of Flowers, as Madeira is also known, and rent a car in the marina.

The road network is a new experience for us. There are numerous tunnels connecting isolated villages separated by cliffs and gorges in the mountains. There are also some very steep serpentines snaking their way up and down the mountainsides. It is all very impressive, and we can't help admiring the Portuguese road and tunnel engineers.

Of course, there is plenty to see. We take a look at Funchal with its marina, the cathedral, the Cristiano Ronaldo statue, the Cristo Rei statue, the botanical gardens, and the tropical gardens, which we enjoy very much. Then we head into the mountains to Curral das Freiras, a beauty spot with a panoramic view across the deep valley. We travel on to the grottos of São Vicente. These are caves found in pipes of lava, which are only ever formed in very special circumstances during a volcanic eruption. All the islands of Madeira have volcanic origins.

Porto Moniz, in the northwest of the island is another lovely tourist spot. We travel back along the steep north coast. We are fascinated by the climate, which is mainly sub-tropical, with several different climate zones due to the high mountains. It is very green in the north, and humid with low hanging cloud. In the east, in contrast, is almost like a desert, without much vegetation. Sadly, it is time to say goodbye to Klaus, who flies home on 10 August.

I stay for another two days, until I start longing to get back on the water again. I can't wait to feel the sea breeze and race *Jambo* through the waves. 5 Beaufort from the northeast are predicted. That should be perfect for the trip to La Palma. It is 250 NM and should take about two days.

The wind blows very steadily at around 20 knots from northeast to east-northeast almost the entire journey. On the first day, the sea is a bit choppy, and occasionally a few breaking waves hit *Jambo* and shake us a bit. With east-northeast winds and a southern course, at times *Jambo* reaches with the waves on the beam. Of course, this is no problem for *Jambo* with wave heights of 2 m.

During the night, the wind shifts slightly, back to northeast and the waves become much more even and only a little steeper. I am actually sailing too fast. We have travelled 138 NM in the last 24 hours and my ETA is before sunrise. I end up having to reduce speed on the second night, as I want to make landfall during daylight, because the seabed rises to the shoreline at a short distance of 3,000 m and the waves are coming right on. On a coast I don't know, I generally like to see if the waves are steep and dangerous as a result. Fortunately, my worries are unfounded. Even though there is quite a decent swell across the harbour entrance, we sail smoothly into the harbour of Santa Cruz de La Palma.

Now I am in the marina of Santa Cruz, which is right next to the small ferry terminal. It is not the most picturesque setting. However, we are well protected from the Atlantic swell by a strong breakwater on the east side. Nonetheless, there is a north wind blowing across the harbour. I make the most of it because today is my big laundry day, and my washing is of course dry in no time at all.

Santa Cruz seems quite nice, but I only look around the small area close to the marina. After two nights sailing solo at sea, and just a few hours of sleep last night, I am far too tired for long walks.

We have reached the Canary Islands at last!

It is 2,100 NM from the Netherlands to here. I have achieved my first major milestone. Looking back, it has been an incredible trip, very varied, with plenty of highlights, and apart from the autopilot motor, luckily no serious downers. We saw a lot of Portugal and Madeira and have had quite a few adventures at sea.

I still have three weeks ahead of me before I am due to fly back to Germany. I intend to tie up in Las Palmas at the end of August, but before that, I want to do a bit of island hopping and enjoy the flair of the Canaries.

Link to video from Lisbon to Madeira

Link to video from Madeira to La Palma

Chapter 5: The Canary Islands of La Palma, El Hierro and Tenerife

The next day starts with no wind at Marina Santa Cruz. I can't believe it! The forecast is very different: wind Force 5 increasing to the south. Of course, I expect the wind to increase due south because the area is renowned for the high wind fields that form between the islands. These are known as wind acceleration zones. In German, we simply call it jet effect.

I am planning to sail to Tazacorte on the west side of the island. The marina there comes highly recommended by just about everyone who knows La Palma. As soon as I set sail, the predicted winds materialise, 4 to 5 Bft. I head straight out into the Atlantic with the full genoa set to starboard, and *Jambo* makes about 5 knots on a southerly course. The further we travel south, the more wind there is. After an hour, *Jambo* is speeding along at over 6 knots in a magnificent force 6 breeze. We are on a run! Then it is even Force 7, and I have to reef the sails downwind. There is a lot of pressure on the sail and it takes all my strength to drag it down about a third.

Off we go, the wind blowing at 32 to 34 knots. At the same time there are waves racing at me from astern, 3 m high, the crests are breaking. *Jambo* surfs the waves at a speed of 8 knots, hitting the troughs with her stern side again and again, as another wave grabs her from behind, lifting her up so she can shoot down again. It's up and down. What a ride!

When we reach the southern point of La Palma, I have to change course. I don't attempt to gybe under sail in the strong wind, but start the engine, furl the genoa, change course, and reset the genoa two-thirds to port. The risk of damaging the sail or capsizing *Jambo* on a gybe is too high. Then we continue on a westerly course on a beam-reach across the waves. It's wild!

All of a sudden, it is over. From one moment to the next the wind dies away and can't seem to make up its mind which way to blow. I'm in the lee of the island. What a picture. The genoa sail is hanging limply in the wind just moments after it had seemed on the verge of bursting under the pressure. I turn on the engine and sail under motor for the next two hours until I reach Puerto de Tazacorte. The wind blows from astern at 6 to 7 knots, while *Jambo* travels at 5 to 6 knots. There is no breeze on board and it is blisteringly hot under the La Palma sun. Nonetheless, I am delighted with my first taste of sailing in the Canaries. Most of the sailing manuals for the area describe it as very demanding and they seem to be right!

Marina Tazacorte

I call the marina ahead of my arrival and organize a berth. The office closes in the afternoon but a friendly mariniero meets me at the fuel ponton, and shows me where to moor. I find my box without any difficulties. I really like the marina, and I have experienced the Canary flair for the first time. It is wonderful. *This is*

63

the place to be! I think, although it is very hot on the leeward side of the island because there is almost no wind.

I'm staying for two nights and can spend a whole day exploring the island. I've decided to hire a car. What can you see in a day on La Palma? Most people would say you need two weeks or more! And they are probably right. But I still have to stick to my schedule and also want to visit some of the other islands. So I choose two destinations which I can easily reach, the San Antonio Volcano, and the observatories on the peak of the Roque de Los Muchachos, which is an extinct volcano. The last erruptions were several hundred years ago.

The harbour office contacts the car hire company for me, and in just half an hour, I have booked a red Fiat Panda for 30 euros. As I get in, I meet the crew of the yacht *Capella,* who hired the same car the day before, and were very pleased with it. Off we go! First to Tazacorte. It is a quiet village, surrounded by banana

The serpentines

plantations. It seems as if every available spot has been cultivated. In some places, the plants are even sheltered from the sun by roofs. I head south, and once again enjoy the unique experience of driving on a beautiful island, although I usually hate driving, thanks to all the traffic jams back home. La Palma does not have as many tunnels or bridges crossing the valleys as Madeira did. Here, the road often winds its way up to the top of the steep slopes in narrow serpentines, and then down the other side. So it is up and down and up and down.

There is a small visitor's centre at the San Antonio Volcano, providing information about the formation of the island and the various volcanic eruptions. San Antonio was last active 300 years ago, and its streams of lava expanded the island. I reach the crater. There is an amazing view inside, and I imagine spewing lava and clouds of ash in the air. I am glad I made the effort to come here.

Volcano San Antonio

I drive back to the marina and stop at a supermarket on the way. I stow everything in the boat, and then set off for the observatories. My satnav informs me they are 53 km away. After one and a half hours, I am already at a height of 2,426 m above sea level on the top of the Roque de Los Muchachos. The little red Panda does a great job. It must have a big engine ☺.

The huge observatory

There is a magnificent view of the telescopes above the clouds. Then I notice the huge concave mirrors used to catch and bundle the light. I walk up to the observation platform. The view across deep ravines and the volcanic mountain range is breath taking. I am stunned. Breathing heavily, I get back to the car. It must be because of the thin air at this high altitude - the ten-minute walk with a small climb leaves me quite out of breath.

Then it's downhill all the way back to Tazacorte in my little Panda. The journey is a bit faster this way round. It has been yet another fantastic day, and I'm looking forward to setting off for El Hierro tomorrow. According to my wind map, the strong wind field in the triangle between the islands of La Palma, La Gomera and El Hierro looks much friendlier than it did yesterday.

I leave at around 8.30 am, which is pretty early for the Canary Islands. As I thought, there is hardly any wind on the leeside of the island, but it is expected to pick up to Force 6 or 7 in the La Palma, La Gomera and El Hierro triangle. I set off under engine on a southern course. The wind should start increasing once *Jambo* is no longer in the lee of the island. I know what to expect now, having sailed out of the wind in the opposite direction just two days ago.

Two and a half hours later, I reach the southern tip of La Palma, where there is a westerly wind to start with. There seem to be large eddies forming near the tip of the headland. Then I see the first breaking waves ahead. This must be the northeast wind already. 10 knots to start with, then 15. Excellent! I set the genoa sail to starboard, first half, and then full. Two minutes later the wind speed reaches 20 knots but we are ok. Another five minutes, and I reef the sails at 27 knots. Then we head towards El Hierro at good speed, sometimes up to 7 or 7.5 knots above ground.

Then I have to reef again, almost to storm size sails because it is blowing 30 to 34 knots. Things stay that way for the next couple of hours. I sail *Jambo* at about 110 to 120 degrees to the apparent wind, and almost across the waves, which fortunately is not a problem with about 2.5 m swell, and a long wave. The waves reach heights of 3 m on occasion and drench the cockpit. Then it is just 7 NM to El Hierro, and once again, the wind disappears from one moment to the next. I have to turn on the engine again. I finally spot a couple of dolphins. I haven't seen any since Madeira, and am delighted.

I radio the harbour office in Puerto de La Estaca on channel 14, as recommended in the cruising guide. There is no answer. Oh well, let's try channel 09 then. Nothing - there is no answer there either. Then I try channel 16, and someone replies, telling me to switch back to channel 14. It turns out to be the crew of the yacht *Capella* I met in Tazacorte, who have been sailing to the same destination ahead of me all day! They tell me that there is no one at the marine office, but that they will help me to moor my boat. Okay! I let them know that I can't put out any fenders and lines until I reach the harbour because of the strong swell, and will need about ten minutes. They suggest I do it before I enter, as the gusts are unpredictable in the harbour and it will be easier outside.

Oh, what is going on here? I wonder. Okay then, I will do it outside. It is not as bad as I thought, because the swell has subsided somewhat. With gusts of up to 25 knots, I enter the marina where three helpers are waiting for me at the jetty. Mooring *Jambo* is no problem. I am quite exhausted though, so I simply tie up at a finger pier. It all works well and I am glad for the help.

I had intended to stay two nights in Puerto de La Estaca, rent a car again, and explore the island, but I change my plans during the night. Gusts of wind of up to 36 knots send half a glass of wine flying through the cockpit in the evening. I take a shower and I hardly needed to dry off because the warm dry wind does the job for me. Beneath deck, the temperature is 31 °C with just 27% relative hydration. I don't really feel very comfortable here, and there is not much going on either, no shops or restaurants nearby. The alternative would be to move on to La Restinga in the south of the island, or on to La Gomera.

The next morning I check the wind forecast. El Hierro is expected to be in a strong wind field of up to Force 8 in the next few days, so presumably I would be no better off in the south. I make my way to the ferry terminal at 9 o' clock to find the harbourmaster, whose office is said to be somewhere in the vicinity. The dock police are responsible. I fill in the forms and ask to pay just for one night. The police officer wants to know why I don't stay longer, and I admit that I'm finding the wind challenging. He nods, and tells me that things are calmer in September and October.

It takes forever to cast off. That is the price for choosing a jetty on the leeside. The wind blows at Force 6 or 7, and only calms to 20 knots every twenty minutes or so. A fellow sailor from Spain gives me a hand, and somehow I finally manage to get going. We are both relieved that the boat manages to cast off without being damaged.

The forecast says the worst winds will be around El Hierro. The further east I go, the less wind there is supposed to be, with a calm forecast for La Gomera. That is how things are in the Canaries. Still in the harbour, I haul in the lines and fenders and then sail out into the Atlantic. There is a Force 7 wind from north-northeast and the waves rush towards me. They are long with an average height of 3 m. I manage to pull the foresail reefing line free enough to tie it up and pull out the genoa slightly. Like an idiot, I miscalculate the necessary length, and the genoa comes out almost halfway. I take a quick look at the wind chart: it is already blowing at 35 knots, with a peak speed of 46 knots so far. *El loco! What am I doing here! I really should have stayed in the marina. Don't push your luck!*

This is too much sail for the wind, but as we head east, it should calm down a bit. Five minutes later, I reef to one third and start feeling better. *Jambo* has to sail as close to the wind as possible to reach La Gomera. Fifty degrees to the apparent wind is just enough to keep pressure on the sail during the course fluctuations caused by the waves, and to stop the sail from flapping. *Jambo* is heading straight east-southeast, but that is okay.

Things go better than expected. Here, beating close to the wind, I finally have the opportunity to test whether the sailing characteristics of *Jambo* have deteriorated since I added the equipment rack for the solar modules. There are an additional 80 kg aft, which I have balanced in the bow with a 50 m, 70 kg anchor chain. *Jambo* still seems to be well balanced, and sails up and down the waves nicely. Even when a wave breaks in an unfavourable way dead ahead and veers to one side, *Jambo* heels another 10 degrees and dips to leeward all the way to the bottom of the railing, but rights herself quickly. Everything still seems the same. *Jambo* is fine, even in these exceptional conditions.

The further east we travel, the less wind there is. It has soon decreased to Force 6 and I can set the mainsail halfway. After

25 NM, we leave the strong wind field behind us. I do not notice at first, because I am catching up on missing sleep from the night before. When I am woken by a radio call, the boat is already sailing very calmly, and the wind is down to no more than 15 knots. Immediately, I put up more sail and set the apparent wind angle first to 40 degrees, and then to 35 degrees. At the same time, the wind shifts and decreases further, Force 4, full sails, then Force 3, and we are on a direct course to Playa de Santiago on La Gomera. Glorious! What a joy and some lovely sailing. *Jambo* is travelling at only about 4 knots speed, but after the last two days with heavy winds, these pleasant conditions are great.

Suddenly, I notice something in the water on the port side ahead. It is light brown. I am sure it is a piece of wood, I think. Then I see it is moving! I turn on my camera straight away when I realise I am seeing a couple of turtles turtling around only 5 m away. What an exciting experience. Dolphins always delight me, as do whales of course, and turtles too. Super!

Soon the good weather is over, and I sail last part of the way to Playa de Santiago under engine power. And I pass two more turtles. I drop the anchor in the bay close to the town. *Jambo* is the only sailing yacht here, although the bay is a recommended anchor spot in my cruising guide. There is a small village on the shore, and there seems to be some infrastructure. In the evening, Lars, from the yacht *Wonderworld,* contacts me on Facebook, and tells me to sail on to Vueltas where the bay is said to be beautiful, very quiet and perfect for swimming.

That night in the bay by Playa de Santiago is quite choppy. Ferries pass close by and the swell rocks *Jambo* accordingly each time.

The next morning, I get the dinghy ready and go ashore to purchase some basics for the next few days. Back on board, I have to tie up the dinghy safely at the stern and then lift the anchor.

I don't bother hoisting the outboard motor for the short cruise to Vueltas.

After two hours of sailing, I arrive at Playa de Argaga, and drop anchor 120 m off the beach at a depth of about 9 m. The sea is calm with just a light breeze across the bay. There are a few other yachts here as well. The cliffs surrounding the beach are impressive. It is beautiful here and I really like it. The small bay is not far from Puerto de Vueltas, and at last, it is time to relax and go for a swim. I want to recover from the past strenuous days at sea.

The Playa de Argaga bay

The water is crystal-clear and not cold at all - really refreshing. It is lovely and warm on the Canary Islands in August, but not too hot. I light up my Cobb grill and cook some chicken wings. In the evening, I watch the beautiful sunset, head to my bunk early and have a great night's sleep. I always turn on two anchor alarms. One goes directly through the AIS system, and the other through the chart plotter, which I recently fitted with a 110 dB

buzzer. It sits behind the cladding but is still pretty loud. I feel safe enough, but still wake up several times during the night, and check to make sure everything is all right.

The next morning I bake some bread with my trusty bread maker. I have brought about 20 kg of bread mixture with me, all plastic wrapped before I set off. It means I do not have to keep my eyes open for a shop in order to have bread on a regular basis. There are many ways to bake your bread, but this works well for me. I enjoy breakfast with freshly milled and boiled coffee in this stunning bay. My morning coffee at sea is as important as the bread. The fully automatic coffee machine was fine during the rougher crossings. It even works when the boat is heeling.

Although things are going so well, I miss Anke lots. I am beginning to realise that I don't like doing everything on my own. It would be fantastic if I could share my experiences with her. So I have learnt plenty again on this trip, not only about further equipment I need to install, but also how I cope with long sea journeys, what does or doesn't suit me.

I spend half a day relaxing and cooling down in the water now and then. Then in the afternoon, I finally make myself take the dinghy to Puerto de Vueltas to see the picturesque village, and enjoy a beer at the harbour restaurant.

The next morning, I don't really want to leave. I would prefer to spend a few more days here, simply enjoying some time off and doing nothing. However, today is already 21 August, and my return flight to Germany is on 4 September. I also want to see a bit more of Tenerife, and need to find a marina on Gran Canaria where *Jambo* can berth for several months. So I hoist the anchor, and cruise under engine towards San Sebastián de La Gomera in light winds.

I have tried several times to contact Marina Las Palmas about finding a berth, but have had no luck so far. Moreover, there have been no replies to my emails. I write to René, the Trans-Ocean base rep in Las Palmas, again today. Fortunately, with EU roaming and mobile data in the Canary Islands, I have had quite good network coverage so far. A few years ago, it was very different, and the roaming charges were extortionate.

A short while later René calls me on the phone. He is a great person, but he doesn't have any good news. This year has been nuts he says, with the berth bookings far worse than expected. Marina Las Palmas cannot take in any more guests. Even some of the permanent berth holders have had to leave the marina and find a space elsewhere. He tells me that the whole of Gran Canaria is difficult at the moment, but I might get lucky in the south.

That had all sounded very different six months ago, but some things are unpredictable I guess. There is nothing I can do. I open my cruising guide and look up a few more marinas to contact later. Now I am heading to the Marina La Gomera. Luckily, I have booked my berth for the night already. Lars, from *Wonderwall,* was kind enough to contact the marina office for me and book me in for two nights.

The entrance to the marina is well buoyed and comprehensively described in the cruising guide. I contact Port Control, and get permission to enter the harbour. I can see the ferry terminal and a couple of ferries at starboard, and the beautiful dark beach on

the port side. I also see the yacht masts straight ahead, interspersed with palm trees. That must be the marina. It looks amazing, I think, and my anticipation grows. At the entrance, a mariniero with a Bavarian accent is there to meet me and guide me in. It turns out he is the Trans-Ocean base rep for La Gomera.

Then I meet Lars, and Kay, who lives here on his catamaran. The three of us spend a lovely afternoon on *Jambo* chatting away and making a dent in my beer supplies. I find other sailors are fascinating people who share similar interests, but are all very different. There is so much to talk about.

The town of San Sebastian is very pretty, with lovely restaurants, a great beach and good shopping facilities. I am pleased I planned a stop here because it is really worthwhile. I buy some rations and enjoy a delightful and reasonably priced meal in one of the small restaurants away from the main thoroughfare.

Seeing as the berth situation on Gran Canaria is so stretched, I start considering alternatives. Although I have sent emails to several marinas on Gran Canaria, I doubt that I will be successful this year. Staying here in La Gomera would also be an option, if only there were direct flights from here to Las Palmas. All my flights leave from Las Palmas to Düsseldorf. It never occurred to me there could be a problem finding a berth on Gran Canaria. If I choose a different island, there needs to be a good flight connection to Gran Canaria.

First, I want to sail to Tenerife and so I say goodbye to Kay and Lars. As I leave the harbour, the wind speed of up to 30 knots feels quite familiar. It is the jet effect between the islands again. As I trim the genoa, a wave hits me and am drenched from head to toe. Luckily, it is a hot sunny day, and the seawater feels wonderfully refreshing.

One and a half hours later, it is suddenly all over, just another five minutes with full sails at Force 3 to 4 before I have to turn on the engine again and furl in the sails. This is crazy - just half a nautical mile away the waves are breaking in the wind field, and here I am motoring along. That is how close the two extremes are.

Looking back, I would say that the sailing conditions in the Canary Islands have been some of the most challenging I have ever seen. Especially close to the coast with steeply sloped shores, you have to be very careful in case of high waves.

Today my destination is the bay at Playa de Masca, which I found in my cruising handbook. It is not long before I see it up ahead. It is easy to recognize with its high cliffs, and the famous Masca Gorge. It is an impressive sight, and I am sure it is going to be as nice as the bay close to Vueltas.

I approach this anchorage at lunchtime. It is not crowded at all. There are only a few motorboats and a few sailing yachts here. I take the opportunity to cool off in the clear water. Shortly afterwards, tranquillity ends when one day-trip boat after another stops here: two large catamarans, a pirate ship and an excursion boat with a water shower. Suddenly there are hundreds of people in the water. Then the boats leave, but soon return with more excursionists. It goes on like this all afternoon. I don't begrudge people their fun, though.

I enjoy the spectacle knowing that this evening there will just be a few boats quietly anchored here. That is exactly what happens. Sadly, the water is not as appealing as it was, as a film of faecal matter has formed on the surface. One of the cruisers must have emptied its wastewater tanks on the way. It demonstrates that I am no longer on one of the smaller Canary Islands, like La Gomera or La Palma, where there are not many tourists. Tenerife is an island with mass tourism. This is one of the downsides of that.

My search for a winter berth on Gran Canaria fails again today. I find the number of a further Trans-Ocean base rep in the south of the island, and give him a call. He informs me that he no longer holds the post, and that finding a berth is generally not easy. He advises me to call the marinas directly, as many of them ignore emails.

The next morning, I depart from Playa de Masca to sail around the south of the island, and then back up north, towards Santa Cruz. I decide to try phoning Marina Los Gigantes, which is only a few nautical miles away, to see if they have a free berth for me. Sadly, no one answers the phone at the marina, so I call the harbour office. The woman explains that they have been having problems with their phone. They have a berth for *Jambo* for the night, which is great news. According to my cruising handbook, it is almost impossible to get a mooring here. I am delighted that I am in luck. I seem to have found the only available berth.

Los Gigantes, Tenerife

The village is pleasant enough, but once again, there are loads of tourists. I take the opportunity to have a look around, and peer into one of the many hotels. It is all very pretty. I used to enjoy staying in hotels on holiday, but since I started sailing, my whole life and preferences have all changed. I buy some supplies but the supermarket at the marina is not well stocked. In the afternoon, I discover a lovely little restaurant and enjoy the fact that I don't have to cook for once. Then I go back to trying to find a berth.

I call the Marina Puerto de Mogan. They offer me a 12 m berth for four weeks. It is not available for longer, and they can't say if anything else will be free after that. It is all very uncertain. The costs are also rather high, so I end up not taking it.

The next day I sail on. For once, it is raining and overcast. This is probably quite unusual weather for the end of August. I think about heading to San Miguel, which is supposed to have a lovely marina according to my cruising guide. Of course, nobody answers the phone. It is a Saturday after all. The marina offices don't always open all hours on weekends, so my guidebook says.

Finally, I get hold of someone in the Marina del Sur Las Galletas, and luckily, the woman speaks English. There are no smaller berths for my size of boat left, but I can have a spot for a 12 m boat if I pay the full price. I gulp, but agree. The woman reminds me to report on channel 09 before entering the harbour. No problem.

I cruise under engine. On the way, I spot two pilot whales, and plenty of the excursion boats I saw two days ago at Playa de Masca, on their way back to the bay.

At 2.30 pm, I approach the marina and radio them. No one answers on channel 09. The marina reception closes at 2 o' clock as I know, but as the woman insisted that I should contact them by radio to register, I had assumed someone would be expecting me, to guide me in. As I don't have a berth number or any other relevant information, I decide not to enter the marina. Today I might do things differently. I always try to fulfil all the requirements, especially in a foreign country, but perhaps I was too pedantic!

I sail on to the nearby bay opposite Las Galletas, and drop the anchor there. The conditions are good, with not too much wind or waves. It is a lovely afternoon, and I go for a swim because the water here is perfectly clean and clear again.

I use the afternoon to send more emails to as many marinas as possible in Fuerteventura (Gran Tarajal and Puerto del Rosario) and Lanzarote (Rubicon, Arrecife and Puerto Calero). The flight connections from Gran Canaria to both islands are good.

The next morning, I sail on around the south tip of the island to the east side. There wasn't much wind on the west side, but now the opposite is true, 6 to 7 Beaufort from the northeast, and 2 to 3 m waves. *Jambo* runs under engine against a southwesterly current, waves and wind, making only 2.5 to 3 knots over ground. Waves flood the cockpit from time to time, and some water pours into the cabin. *Jambo* tosses back and forth, and her bow keeps slamming into the wave troughs with a loud crash. Thank goodness these boats are built to withstand this sort of thing! The diesel tank also gets a good shaking, so there should not be any sediment left in it. I hope that it is all in the filters. Still, I am used to this from many trips in similar conditions in the North Sea. You just have to carry on. The equipment rack is battered as well, and two of the connections break.

I call up a few marinas on the nearby coast on my way, but, nobody responds – it is Sunday this time. Then I get hold of someone at Marina Puerto de Güímar. However, I can't speak a word of Spanish and the woman at the other end of the line can't speak any English. What a pity! I am going to have to make another anchorage stop, which won't be easy in a northeast wind on the east side of the island. The cruising guide recommends Bahía de Abona. On the map, the northern part looks good. I sail in and find a number of mooring buoys close to each other on the sheltered side. They are probably for the smaller boats of the locals. I am sure the bay isn't a great place to anchor, but doubt I'll find anything better now.

I anchor in the middle of the bay. I'm worried that *Jambo* might not be as sheltered as I would like, but with wind Force 5 here in the bay and a swell of 1 m, it should be okay. The anchor is at about 10 m. I have my plough anchor in use with 6 m chain, and

40 m of anchor line connected by shackle. I have to anchor twice more, until I am finally satisfied with the position. Without an electric winch, it's hard work, and my arms ache from pulling up the anchor up by hand, twice now.

Unfortunately, the rocky coast, with white spray and surf splashing, is only about 150 m astern. I 'm not happy with the overall situation and am beginning to realise that this is probably the riskiest anchoring manoeuvre I've done so far.

In the afternoon, I set about fixing my equipment rack. I fix the connections that have come undone, replace any missing grub screws, and tighten the rest. *That was a real endurance test for my equipment today!* I think. The solar panels are fine and coped well with the higher wind speeds. Before I cross the Atlantic, I am going to strengthen the structure by inserting bolts at critical points.

During the night, the wind picks up, and gradually the swell gets stronger and stronger, with some waves actually breaking in the bay. *Jambo* dances up and down, but the anchor holds and doesn't slip. That actually worries me slightly, because it is not necessarily a good sign. It could be caught between a couple of rocks. I hope I will be able to free it tomorrow. I switch on both anchor alarms. Sleep is impossible. Then I do manage to get half an hour's sleep. At 4.15 am, I turn on the engine to load the batteries and drop off.

Then it happens. Both alarms start sounding. I am wide-awake immediately. I look at the iPad that records the boat's movement when anchoring. Right away, I see that Jambo has drifted 30 m from where I dropped anchor, towards the rocky coast. Quickly, I grab the torch and stick my head out of the hatch. The cleat with the anchor line is still locked. I rush on deck and take a quick look in the cockpit to check that we are not too close to the rocks, before dashing to the bow. I pull the anchor line but there is no resistance. A quick glance aft tells me I must take to the helm as quickly as possible. The distance to the rocks is now decreasing very fast and I have to steer *Jambo* into open waters immediately. To keep free of my own anchor line, I move backwards. It would be a disaster for the line to get caught up in my propeller.

With a little more distance to the rocks, I then hurry forward again, and somehow manage to pull up the line while keeping an eye aft. When the end of the rope lands on deck, I see that there is nothing left where the shackle used to be. It seems to have broken, and the thimble of the anchor line looks battered too.

The line, which is lying loose on the deck, still has to be stowed in the anchor locker. Damn, I am not wearing a life jacket. Where the hell is it? Everything happens at lightning speed. I find it and put it on, then return to the fore. Of course, I don't have time to wrap myself up properly. *Jambo* dances up and down in the swell, heeling to either side. With one eye on the approaching coast, I stow the line in the anchor locker. Then I hurry back to the helm, and finally manage to reach the open water. After a few minutes, I am out of the bay and can catch my breath. It is wind Force 6 out here, and the swell is quite high, just like yesterday. I have to put on some more clothes, because it is quite cold.

I start to calm down, and my adrenalin levels seem to drop. Now I begin to realise what has just happened. That could have been the end of *Jambo* - and in the worst case, of me too. I am exhausted. Thank goodness my anchor alarms worked, and that I was mentally ready for something like this to happen. I often play out these 'what-if' scenarios in my head. I had been feeling uneasy about the anchorage beforehand, and so had naturally thought about what I would do if something went wrong.

Still taken aback, I sit on deck drinking my first cup of coffee, and wonder what I might have done differently. Relieved and a bit of frustrated, I sail slowly north towards Santa Cruz.

I hope I can book a berth this time. At nine o´clock sharp, I call the Marina Tenerife to make sure, but no one answers the phone. *Oh well,* I think, *it's Monday morning, let's give them another five minutes.* After numerous tries, someone finally answers the phone at 9.30. But there are no berths available. *Not again!* They suggest I ring the Marina Santa Cruz.

I turn two pages in the cruising guidebook and, *ah yes*, there is a second marina. Perhaps I am still recovering from my experience this morning, or else I'm not quite awake yet (or a bit of both), because I missed it. I spend the next half hour trying to reach someone there by phone. By this stage, I am only 3 NM from the harbour and try radioing them on channel 9. Someone answers immediately and for once, I'm in luck. There is a free berth. The man on the VHF radio tries to give me directions, but I tell him I'll be there in just under an hour and will call him back.

I arrive at Marina Santa Cruz in good spirits, and tie up. There are quite a few sailors on the jetty ready to help a German solo sailor moor his boat. How lovely! Everything is fine now. Despite being pretty exhausted after last night's adventure, I only sleep for a couple of hours. I want to move on again tomorrow and look around town before I go. My flight home is in just over a week, and I still haven't found a place for *Jambo* to stay.

I enjoy strolling through the town. It is a very beautiful place. The marina is near the centre, across a footbridge. I have an excellent late lunch or early dinner. I make a mental note to come back here again with more time to spare. There have been a number of places on this cruise I really liked, and would love to visit again.

Santa Cruz de Tenerife

Finally, the marinas of Fuerteventura and Lanzarote reply. Unlike the marinas on Gran Canaria, each one I contacted sends me an answer, telling me if they have a berth available or not. There seem to be differences on the individual Canary Islands. The Marina Rubicon on Lanzarote appeals to me the most, and there is even an additional 10% discount for Trans-Ocean members, so I take them up on their offer. I want to set off the next day. The direct distance is about 140 NM, but I will have to sail against the wind, which means it could be considerably further, depending on how the wind blows. I am looking forward to Lanzarote so much that I even manage to forget last nights' terrible anchorage for a while.

Two days later, on the evening of 27 August, I reach Lanzarote after 188 NM and 35 hours of sailing upwind! I have reached my target destination and the end of my single-handed journey for the time being.

I am still tired after the crossing. Not just because there was a lot of physical sailing work to do, adjusting the size of the sails according to the strength of the wind, but also, because it is exhausting moving around below deck on tilted surfaces while heeling at 15 to 25 degrees. Having to hold onto something at every move means the muscles in my arms are aching again.

Nevertheless, it was a lovely journey at 4 to 5 Beaufort, and nothing awful happened. Although it nearly did. I encountered two high-speed ferries. Each time, I had to make them aware that they were about to ram me, despite the fact that they were in reach, and my AIS signal will have been visible on their screens. The ferries travel at 30 knots and it is impossible for me to get out of their way.

I radioed the first ferry, one of the Volcán fleet en route from Gran Canaria to Tenerife, two minutes before the possible collision, and asked if they could see me. I received the reply: "Yes, I change course." "Muchas gracias!" I replied. Then the ferry crossed my bow without another word, about half a nautical mile away.

The second time, the *Bonanza Express* came roaring towards me from astern at 33 knots. This time I was better prepared. I radioed them but only got an answer on the second call. I told them formally: "I am the sailing vessel in your direct course line, about three minutes ahead of you." Someone kindly replied, "Yes, we see you and change course over starboard." Once again, I replied, "Muchas gracias." Then, and only then, the ferry changed course.

I had never experienced anything like this before. Had they really seen me? Did the ferries usually head directly towards a vessel until just one nautical mile away before changing course? I don't know, but am highly relieved to have all the instruments I need, so that I know ahead of time what the CPA (Closest Point of Approach) is, how much time is left until then, and what my exact bearings are. I can also see all the dynamic and static data of all the other ships. Thankfully, nothing happened.

After 436 NM around the Canary Islands, and a good 2,500 NM from the Netherlands to here, I have finally reached Lanzarote. The last few months have been very exciting, intense and varied. I have experienced so much, and gained so many impressions that I can hardly process it all. It is good that I have recorded everything in my videos, and managed to keep a diary.

Marina Rubicon is probably one of the most beautiful marinas *Jambo* has ever visited. The yacht harbour is pristine and is next to a lovely holiday resort. There is a swimming pool and the beach is nearby. In addition, there are excellent shopping facilities at the marina and the town is not too far away. I love it here. Plenty of different restaurants line the jetties. I have been doing my own cooking for most of the past two weeks, and missing Klaus in the galley. I am very much looking forward to trying out some of those restaurants.

Marina Rubicon is *Jambo*'s new home harbour for the time being. I have managed to book a berth from now until 5 January

2020. After all the excitement in the Canary Islands, I can finally relax and unwind.

In a couple of days, I will fly home for three weeks. I am looking forward to it very much. Then at the end of September, Anke and I will return here and sail around Lanzarote and Fuerteventura.

Although I really want to do the Atlantic crossing, I still haven't planned the passage I intend to sail in January. My initial plan to reach Enkhuizen in the Netherlands in September 2020 still stands. The big question is how am I going to get there? Sailing to the Canaries with a prevailing wind from astern, and a light southwesterly sea current wasn't too difficult, even though sailing in the Canaries was pretty challenging in itself.

The direct passage home via Spain, France, maybe England, and Belgium is not as easy. I have found out how hard it is to sail northeast on the journey from Tenerife to here, sailing hard to windward and very light on the helm. The other option is to sail across the Atlantic to the Caribbean, and then from there via the

Azores back to the Netherlands. It is generally thought to be the easier route even if it is much longer, and, as far as I can see, not without challenges on the last part of the journey home.

At last, I am in a position to make up my mind. Of course, I want to do it! All the preparations I made in May were designed to make it possible.

I am going to do the Atlantic crossing.

Alea jacta est!

This was no easy decision, and of course, so much depended on how I would cope with the long passages and how *Jambo* fared with all the modifications and new technology I have installed. Now I can truly say that not only has *Jambo* fared well, in fact she has exceeded my expectations. She demonstrated her seaworthiness time and again, especially in the challenging conditions sailing around the Canary Islands. I could not be more pleased. The new equipment I installed in the spring works very well, and gives me the necessary confidence to embark on the Atlantic crossing. The automatic steering in heavy seas and on different courses has proved to be reliable, and is a must. The solar panels provide more power than I had expected, and I am very happy there, too.

Of course, there are still weak points. The consumer batteries aren't very good any more. The nautical shop sells batteries, and I order two new AGM batteries with 175 Ah each from Vetus. The Lewmar rotary drive of the autopilot failed once on the way. That was in the English Channel. To be on the safe side, I take two spares - that should be more than enough. Any defective motor will still be under guarantee, and I will be able to get it replaced en route if necessary.

I spent a lot of time looking at windvane steering, and decided it might not be suitable for *Jambo*. I would have had to install it off-centre due to the bathing platform, which I can't do without because I need it to launch the dinghy. Because of the shallow keel, *Jambo* heels around 15 to 25 degrees on a close-hauled or beam reach course with the sails let out at least half way. Sometimes, she'll heel up to 30 degrees or even a few degrees more, if a wave comes from the side. As a result, a windvane steering system installed off-centre would slope far out of the water on the windward side. I am not sure if it could still work properly. The systems I have been using so far are coordinated with each other perfectly. They have also survived their baptism of fire so to speak. "Never change a winning team!" they say, so I am sticking with it.

I have enjoyed the journey up to this point very much, and have coped well with the lonely, long sea passages. On the other hand, I have discovered that I don't really enjoy exploring new places on my own - I miss Anke and my friends. Shared joy is double joy for me.

I want to do the Atlantic crossing single-handed, but I will make sure that there is room for plenty of visitors when I am in the Caribbean.

Here in the Marina Rubicón, there is time for some peace and quiet. I rest up during the days, enjoying the sun and the good Canary Island food in the nearby restaurants. I do a few minor repairs and maintenance work, and take my two genoas to the sailmaker. A few seams need to be renewed on the first one, but nothing serious. The second genoa has done 2500 NM this year and 1500 NM last year. That is a decent achievement, in my opinion. The UV protection side needs fixing and reinforcing, which costs 260 euros. The nautical shop also sells anchors, and I buy a 15-kg Delta anchor, as it fits nicely onto the holder on the bow. Then I fly home for three weeks.

Link to video La Palma

Link to video El Hierro and La Gomera

Link to video Tenerife to Lanzarote

Chapter 6: The Canary Islands of Fuerteventura and Lanzarote

Today is 1 October. Anke and I fly to Arrecife via Gran Canaria and then take a 45-minute taxi ride to Playa Blanca and the Marina Rubicón. We find *Jambo* exactly as I left her three weeks ago, but she's covered in dust. Marina Rubicón lies on the southern part of the island. As there is an almost continuous northeasterly wind blowing dust across the whole island, all the boats here look as if they have been abandoned for months after just a short while. We will be sailing around Fuerteventura and Lanzarote for the next three weeks, but before we start, we give *Jambo* a good clean up. We can't get rid of all the brown dust, but she looks so much better after we have finished, and we are pleased with the result.

The first leg of our journey takes us to Gran Tarajal in the south of Fuerteventura. It is 48 NM and 8 hours long, on a downwind course in Force 5 to 7. Almost immediately, a group of twenty dolphins comes to say hello and swim alongside us for a while. When we reach Marina Gran Tarajal, we simply tie up in a berth on one of the swimming jetties. It was impossible to make any kind of radio contact before arriving, and the harbour office is only open in the mornings. Here we meet Barbara and Michael, a retired couple, who have been sailing around the Canary Islands in their 17 m steel yacht for quite some time. We spend a lovely evening together.

After completing all the formalities at the harbour office the next morning, we unpack our folding bikes and cycle into town. Gran Tarajal lies on a long black sandy beach. It is the third largest town in Fuerteventura, with just 8,000 inhabitants. There are great shopping facilities and plenty of lovely restaurants.

The next day we hire a car and explore the island. To start with, we drive south and visit Playa de Jandia, the long sandy beach for surfers. The wind conditions here are ideal for kite surfing and everyone is having a great time. From Morro Jable, we choose one of the off-road routes to see more of the island away from the beaten track. It is a very barren landscape, as both Fuerteventura and Lanzarote have very little rainfall. We

see a few goats chewing the sparse blades of grass growing between brown lava rocks, but that is about it. The island is renowned for its goat's cheese, which is a real speciality here. So we hunt for a goat cheese dairy, and find one in Tuineje, which has won several awards for its excellent cheese. Of course, we buy some at a very reasonable price.

Next, we take a look at the main city of the island, Puerto del Rosario, and the new marina there. We are going to sail there tomorrow. We enjoyed staying in Gran Tarajal, which has a nice marina. The sanitation facilities could be better, but that wasn't a problem for us, because we prefer showering on board ship.

Sailing north towards Puerto del Rosario, in the prevailing northeast Force 6 wind proves to be as hard as expected. We sail into the wind under motor, and it takes us six hours for the 24 NM at wind Force 6 to 7. It is a real relief to reach the new marina. The harbour police welcome us and help us tie up.

New swimming jetties have been installed, so there is enough room for guests who used to have to anchor out in the harbour.

The marina is not quite finished yet. There is no electricity and there are no showers.

We sail from Puerto de Rosario to the Isla de Lobos, and put down anchor there. The bay south of the island is well-sheltered, and the anchorage is good. We spend the afternoon swimming and then Anke cooks a lovely meal.

The next leg of our cruise is just 2 NM to Corralejo. As we approach, I try to contact port control and the marina on VHF channels 12, 9 and 16 to register, so that we can enter the harbour. Corralejo is a busy ferry port. So no luck there. We sail in carefully, and find a free berth. We ask our jetty neighbour if anyone else is moored there, and he shrugs. That is as good as a yes in our book.

We head off to the harbour office and ask a security guard for directions. He tells us the office is closed today because it is Sunday. We completely forgot. But he assures us we can stay moored where we are for the night.

We take our folding bikes and cycle to town. Just as we hoped, there are a number of tapas bars and restaurants in the old part of town. We really like them. Then we ride out to the Dunes of Corralejo where there is a beautiful beach. Somehow, we manage to get lost on the way, and it takes us over an hour out in the hot midday sun to get there. We eventually manage to find the beach and a lovely little beach bar where we take a breather, and enjoy a cold cerveza. The dunes are stunning, as is the beach, and we spend the rest of the afternoon there. In the evening, we go back to town for tapas, and then try a few cocktails in one of the harbour bars. It is lovely to relax and unwind.

The next day, I pay the harbour fee at the harbour police office. My Spanish is useless, and the two police officers don't speak any English. I have to fill in a long form, which is all in Spanish of course. If only I'd brought Anke along because her Spanish is quite good. The two police officers are very friendly and willing to help. We use Google translate and manage to fill in the form in the end. It takes about half an hour. Then I pay the fee of 16 euros for one night. Public marinas are great value for money!

We depart from Fuerteventura, heading for Lanzarote. We will spend the next ten days exploring the island. We really enjoyed

Fuerteventura with all the lovely places to visit. And the moorings we found were also fine – things always worked out in the end.

On our trip to Puerto Calero, we have one of the best day's sailing ever in the Canary Islands. With a Force 4 wind, we tack 18 NM close to the northeasterly wind. The weather plays along. During the day it is around 28 °C and at night it cools down to 23 °C. It couldn't be more perfect.

Puerto Calero Marina is very nice, and there are plenty of restaurants. It is run privately, and they speak good English at the reception. However, the mooring fees are twice as high. Everything has its price. Then we drive to Arrecife, the capital of

Lanzarote Island. The marina here is also good, and the city centre is not far away. We enjoy a bit of city life, along with more great food in one of the many restaurants.

Our next destination is the island La Graciosa, which is in the north of Lanzarote. We arrive in the late afternoon, hoping to find a berth. Once again, we weren't able to reach anyone by telephone or VHF radio beforehand. So we sail into the harbour, hoping for the best. We meet a German sailing couple who have moored their yacht on the outer jetty. They tell us that you have to register two days in advance, and that they had to anchor outside for two days before they received a berth.

A security guard on another jetty waves us over, and we sail round to meet him. He and Anke speak Spanish and, as usual, I don't understand a word. They are discussing something, but his shaking head tells me this isn't going to work. And I'm right. Anke tells me they won't give us a berth.

We must look very disappointed, because suddenly he changes his mind and says something again. Anke translates. "We can stay for one night, but we must register at the Capitania at 8 o'clock tomorrow morning."

We are delighted! At 8 o'clock the next morning, we go straight to the harbour office and are even allowed to stay at our berth for another night. That is all though, but is fine by us. The fee is 5.50 euros a night, which is the cheapest we have ever paid.

The town of Caleta del Sebo, which has around 650 residents, is the main town on the island. It has a harbour with a marina, and a ferry port where plenty of tourists arrive every day. It is interesting to note that there are virtually no tarred roads on the island. It feels like stepping back in time.

The next day we rent mountain bikes, the electric version of course, which is a good choice given the gradients and the climate. We cycle to Las Conchas, a famous beach renowned for its beauty. The road is sandy and bumpy, with occasional loose rocks and stones. Even with mountain bikes, you have to be

careful not to get stuck in a rut or hit a stone. Our folding bikes would have been useless. The beach is fantastic, but not safe for swimming - the Atlantic swell breaks on the shore unhindered. We have heard that the Bacardi commercial was filmed here to save money. I don't know if it's true though.

We have lunch in a lovely, hidden away restaurant called Tasquita. It is a great place for fish, and the prices are very reasonable. In the afternoon, we cycle to Pedro Barba and explore the small settlement. It is nothing special.

We really enjoy staying on this island. Somehow, it has managed to preserve its originality. The town is very full during the day, thanks to all the day trippers, but in the evenings, we have the place to ourselves. We love the atmosphere and we definitely plan to come back again some day. I hope nothing changes and time continues to move more slowly here, even if it doesn't stop entirely.

We sail back to Arrecife next, where we pick up Anke's son Mats, and then on to Marina Rubicón.

We decide to hire a car for two days to see the sights. First, we drive to the Parque Nacional de Timanfaya. There we eat half chickens, roasted over heat from the volcano. The last volcanic eruption was in the 19th century, and in some places, the earth is still really hot. It is very impressive. We take a bus tour from the visitor centre across the vast and barren lava landscape.

In the afternoon, it is a short drive to Puerto del Carmen to see the marina where we failed to get a berth. The marina is not designed for many sailing yachts, and really can't accommodate extra guests.

On our second day, we drive through the wine area to the Vega de Yuco vineyard. This is where Yaiza, the local white wine spe-

Mats, Anke and me

ciality, is made. The vines grow in little hollows that are protected from the dry winds by low semi-circular stone walls. Of course, we buy a couple of bottles of wine. Then we go to Mirador del Río, one of the highest villages on the island. It is in the northwest, with a magnificent view over to the isle of La Graciosa. Our next stop is the aloe vera plantation, Lanzaloe, which we really enjoy. Then we move on to Ó rzola. We watch the ferries leave for La Graciosa and order some fantastic paella.

Next, we visit the lava caves of Cueva de los Verdes. Who would have thought that concerts take place down inside the caves? Our final destination is the house of César Manrique in Tahíche. Some of the rooms have been built in old lava bubbles inside the caves, and are connected by small tunnels. The house is surrounded by beautiful gardens. Just imagine living in a place like this!

We spend our last few days on the island enjoying the Marina Rubicón. Then it is time for me to fly back to Germany with Anke and Mats, where I have things to do. My return flight to Arrecife is already booked for December. I need to be back by then to get ready to cross the Atlantic.

Link to video Fuerteventura

Link to video Lanzarote and La Graciosa

Chapter 7: Preparing for the Atlantic Crossing

At the beginning of December, I fly back to Lanzarote on my own, according to plan. I managed to book a real bargain deal, which includes a small rental car. I got it because I am on an anticyclical trip, arriving on Monday and returning on Saturday.

In Marina Rubicón, I bump into Oliver from *Plan B* and Thomas from *Picaroon,* who I first met in Cuxhaven two years ago. We have stayed in contact and, although we don't see each other that often, we always just pick up where we left off the last time we met.

My first task is to clean the boat. *Jambo* is covered in brown dust again. Then I reinforce my equipment rack and drill holes in some of the steel tubes where I want to replace the grub screws with M6 screws. I have to do this at six trouble spots. The equipment rack is now fully finished, and so far, I am quite happy with how it has turned out. Of course, some people might not like the unconventional design or would object to any kind of equipment rack. But that's absolutely fine by me. In the end, we all have different preferences and different ideas about aesthetics and functionality. The new batteries have arrived as well, and I can replace the old ones at last.

I have decided to make a video about preparing for the Atlantic crossing, and I start filming now. I describe my expectations for the journey and the precautions I am taking. I know from my own planning experience how valuable first-hand information can be. Oliver is about to set off on his first single-handed Atlantic crossing. He is planning to leave on 4 December. Of course, I couldn't possibly miss the opportunity to visit him with my camera and see how he is getting on.

Plan B is a Hanse 385, and quite a bit bigger than *Jambo*. Oliver has already stocked up with plenty of provisions and seems excellently prepared in every way. His boat has a windvane steering system at the stern and a trolling generator, but no solar panels. The provisions are neatly stowed in large plastic boxes aft. I could do with some of his sense of order. Things are always

pretty untidy aboard my boat. It's just a different system, I tell myself, to stop feeling guilty.

In the evening, Thomas and I take Oliver to a tapas bar and give him a decent send off. He jokes about this being his last meal before execution. The next day, we help him cast off, take a few pictures and for a long time, we watch as he sails away on course for Antigua. What an inspiring moment! I can't wait until it is my turn.

The days fly by, and soon it is time to return home for Christmas. I love Christmas and always want to be at home for the festivities, if possible. I am away a lot and want to be able to spend this special time surrounded by my loved ones.

I follow Oliver's progress across the Atlantic in *Plan B* excitedly. He posts daily reports on his website and it is possible to track his position. Things go well for a while, but then he starts posting reports about technical difficulties. And then, all of a sudden, disaster strikes. On 13 December, he has to abandon *Plan B* because of a major ingress of water. I am utterly shocked, and start feeling very nervous about my own impending Atlantic crossing.

It sounds like a mix of problems all came together at once. Water got into the vessel via the fastening screws of the windvane control, which had come loose. Oliver thinks a collision could be to blame. Then his autopilot failed. The bilge pump on *Plan B* was in an awkward position, so the water just sloshed past the pump and he spent half the day pumping it away by hand. He couldn't repair or seal the leak. In the end, after a few days, he had to make the difficult decision to give up.

He was in constant contact with Bremen Rescue Service via his satellite phone, who were able to redirect a nearby tall ship, the *Elena of London*, in his direction. Oliver got his life raft ready, quickly grabbed a few personal items, and before leaving *Plan B*, he cut the seawater hoses below the waterline to speed up the sinking process. Then he climbed into the life raft and was rescued by the crew of the tall ship. Dismayed, but in good shape, he had a comfortable journey to Antigua on board the *Elena of London*, because that happened to be her destination.

After Christmas, Anke and her daughter Jana and I all fly to Lanzarote. I have hired another car for the week. For one thing, I want to be able to get around the island and do a bit of sightseeing with the two of them, and I also need to get all my shopping done. The days simply fly by.

Then suddenly Anke falls ill at New Year. She has a dry cough with a slight temperature, and can't really taste anything anymore. She needs to see a doctor. Luckily, there are plenty of them on the Canary Islands. There is even a German doctor in Playa Blanca. She is told she has caught a viral infection and has to spend the next few days in bed. Thankfully, she feels well enough to travel home on departure day. This is the moment, when we have to say our final goodbyes. I drive the two of them to Arrecife and watch them walk into the terminal building, waving until they are out of sight. Now I am all on my own, and that is exactly how I feel. I won't see Anke again until we meet up in the Caribbean in March.

Things are starting to get serious now. I have two days left to buy everything I need, and make one more film before I leave. But first, I visit Petra and Wolfgang on *Mola Mola,* at the marina in Arrecife. I met Wolfgang a few years ago in Dunkirk, when I was sailing home from Northern Spain to the Netherlands. We spend a marvellous morning on *Mola Mola*, a 43 Hallberg-Rassy, and as usual, there is so much to talk about! Then I drive to Lidl and the Mercadona, and work my way down my shopping list. The two supermarkets have everything I need. There is plenty of choice. I fill the first of several shopping carts.

Back at the marina, I stow everything on board and meet Alex, from *Who Nose,* moored at the same jetty. We start chatting away and before I know it, I have been invited for drinks the following evening.

The next day, I go on another shopping tour. I stow everything away on board *Jambo* and start filming a short video about my final preparations for the crossing. It ends up taking up more time than I had expected. By the time I finally manage to load it onto my YouTube channel, it is already evening. Luckily, it is not too late to stop by and see Alex and his wife Dagmar. Alex is a retired marine officer and spends a lot of his time sailing his boat, *Who Nose.* I have forgotten what type of boat, but it is quite big, at least 13 or 14 m long. Alex promises to help me cast off the next day. We agree to meet at lunchtime. I am restless and don't sleep very well on my final night before departure.

Link to video Preparations

Chapter 8: Solo from Lanzarote to Guadeloupe

My diary:

Tuesday, 7 January: Departure

The big day is here at last. It is sunny and not too cold. My adrenalin is at an all-time high, and I haven't been able to get *Plan B* out of my mind for the past few days. Crossing the Atlantic from the Canary Islands to the Caribbean isn't a doddle, and even with the best possible preparation, something unexpected can always happen. Have I forgotten anything? Am I as prepared as I can be? Is there something I still need to do?

In the morning, I complete my final list of things to do - return the hired car; sign out of the marina; pack up the folding bike; hoist and clean the log and echo sounder, which have become encrusted with vegetation over the past few months; fill up the water tank and check that everything is stowed away properly. Is everything in working order? I filled up with diesel a couple of days ago, including the reserve canisters, which means I have 270 litres on board. Then one final weather check. Everything is looking great. There won't be too much wind around the Canaries during the night, but after that, I should have trade winds from the northeast with Force 5 to 6 for a few days. That would be perfect sailing conditions. I mount the cameras and quickly film the first scene before casting off.

We are off!

As soon as I finish filming, I am ready to go – this is it, I think. For the last time, I wonder if I have thought of everything, or if there's anything I still need to do. *Come on, cast off!* I tell myself aloud. Okay, here goes! I pop over to *Who Nose* and knock, but no one answers. On my way back, I unplug the land electricity line and check the wind direction. It is blowing with Force 4 from aft, and *Jambo* is being pushed gently against the finger jetty. It will be all right, I think, and turn on the Navionics App, the AIS and the tracking on my Garmin inReach Mini. Then I start the engine and untie the lee lines. Alex turns up after all, and I am delighted to see him. He gives me a hand with the rest of the ropes. It takes plenty of throttle, but I manage to get out of the berth without any problems. I look at the jetty and see Alex saluting. He wishes me a safe trip. What an honour to be saluted by a retired naval officer as I depart. I think I will remember that moment for the rest of my life. "Thank you very much," I shout.

I leave the boat dock behind and move to the more open part of the marina where I slow down, and bring in the fenders. As I head out of the marina, I radio the harbour office to say goodbye, casually letting them know that I am now on my way to the Caribbean. All I get is a brief greeting in return. Someone setting off on an Atlantic crossing obviously isn't much of a novelty here.

Then I am out on open water and the swell of the Atlantic welcomes me. It all feels a bit odd for some reason. Maybe it is something to do with the fact that I haven't been out on open water for a while. That has happened before. Fuerteventura is straight ahead and I will sail past on the west side. I set both sails and switch off the engine. Sailing on a beam reach, I set a south-southwest course. Then I put a final post on Facebook while I still have a signal.

Everything is going to plan, the sails are set, and *Jambo* glides through the waves at 6 knots in 20 knots of wind. We are a bit slow for my liking. The log and echo sounder were encrusted with vegetation, so the bottom of the boat probably is too. After all, *Jambo* was moored in the marina for several months and I didn't check the underwater hull. It never occurred to me. But it shouldn't be much of a problem. The layer of vegetation will probably be washed away over the next few days. Besides, I'm not trying to break any speed records. All I want is to reach my destination safely.

There isn't much to do now except keep an eye out for other ships. I am starting to relax. The tension and anxiety of the past few days gradually ebbs away. I just sit back and enjoy the sailing, which always has such a therapeutic effect on me. I feel very calm, delighted to be gliding along and listening to the accompanying soundscape.

I am sailing. It feels so good!

I have reached my destination – okay I am not in the Caribbean yet – but I feel as if I have arrived nonetheless. I am on my way, and this is particularly true for sailing: the journey is its own reward. I have been looking forward to this moment for so long, with everything geared towards making it happen. From now on, it is just *Jambo*, the sea, waves, wind and me. Nothing else counts. Everything fades into the background, as I begin to explore my small new world. Well, it is small in one way, but in another way, it seems endless, as I look out across the vast ocean.

I am still a long way from the vast ocean though; in fact, I am still quite close to the shore. My AIS alarm confirms this minutes later, when it goes off. A high-speed ferry has entered my alarm range astern, and I am alerted at once. This is a good test for my two AIS alarms, which go off immediately. I can set the AIS transponder, connected to an alarm buzzer via an app, individually. On my current course and at this speed, I want to be warned half an hour in advance if a vessel comes within 1000 m distance. The second alarm comes from the chart plotter. The plotter processes the AIS information fed from the AIS transponder into the NMEA 2000 network. I can select the radius on the plotter, too, and usually select 2 NM. Both alarms are on now, but there is no danger. The ferry is moving in my direction, but isn't on a collision course.

In the evening, I sail into the sunset. It is time for some food. I have a supply of fresh meat for the next couple of days. Some things will keep for up to ten days. I decide to spoil myself with chicken wings and rice. It is a great meal, which I enjoy very much as I watch the sun go down.

During the night, the wind slackens, and *Jambo* sails quietly past Fuerteventura at a leisurely pace.

Wednesday, 8 January

I wake up to a glorious sunrise. We left Fuerteventura behind during the night. I don't feel too tired after my first night at sea, although I have kept the sleep intervals at thirty minutes so close to shore. I won't be able to extend them until I reach the open ocean.

Although I am not tired, I don't feel that great today. It looks like I have caught a cold. I have a dry cough, a sore throat and a headache. My symptoms are similar to Anke's, who is still recovering from her viral infection at home. Mats was ill, too, and had to rest. We probably caught something when we were sightseeing in the grottos. We were there with lots of people, all crowded together. No one in Europe has heard of COVID at this point, so Anke isn't tested to see if she has the disease. Were we some of the first people to be infected by the virus? Somehow, I doubt it.

I have antibiotics on board, but they are no use for a viral infection. Instead, I stick to my usual cold remedies. Sinupret and GeloMyrtol are my little helpers, and luckily, I have brought plenty. And I take lozenges to soothe my sore throat.

Being unwell is not ideal, but I am not worried. I don't think I will take a turn for the worse, or need to head for a harbour in order to rest until I feel better. The dolphins cheer me up.

I measure the first day's run in the afternoon. It is 112 NM, which is fine, especially considering the light winds during the night. I set the sails wing-on-wing, the mainsail to port, and the genoa to starboard. It is pleasant sailing on a southwesterly course with a Force 5 wind. The wind picks up towards the afternoon, and in the evening, I reef at Force 6 to be safe for the night. *Jambo* and I are now about 50 NM south of Gran Canaria and making good way.

Thursday, 9 January, 2nd day's run 132 NM, total distance 244 NM

This night is slightly rougher than the last. Wind Force 6 to 7 means I have to give up sailing wing-on-wing because with a swell of about 2.5 m, the sails can't hold the wind reliably in that position, and keep flapping. Our course is fine; we are heading almost straight towards Guadeloupe.

In the morning, the wind dies down again, blowing at about 19 knots. Although *Jambo* is not as fast now, it is fantastic sailing. I am still not over my cold though and feel physically unfit. Somehow, I manage to persuade myself to hoist the second genoa on the forestay, when the wind drops to Force 4. This is the classic "trade wind sail" with two genoas on the forestay. It works well on *Jambo*, as the Furlex has two tracks. The two genoas are almost identical, so I don't necessarily have to take the second one down if the points of sail change and *Jambo* is suddenly reaching or running downwind. As I only have one foresail boom with me, only one genoa is poled out, and the wind is kept slightly to this side, with a yaw angle of about 160 to 170 degrees.

It takes nearly an hour. It is far more difficult than if there are two of you, or you have a small crew to help. In fact, it takes three or four times as long. First, I take down the hoisted genoa, which is relatively simple and doesn't take too long. Then I feed the second genoa into the Furlex guide rail, and hoist both genoas with the genoa halyard. On *Jambo*, this comes out at the mast on starboard and runs through a cleat. The first two metres are fine, but I have to keep moving forward from the mast every 30 cm or so to slide the genoa along the rail, because it keeps getting jammed. This means I am constantly tethering and untethering myself, using two safety lines all the time, so that I am always secured by one at least. It takes a long time. Then at some point, it's no longer possible to do this by hand anymore from the mast, and I have to lead the halyard to the starboard winch in the cockpit. There is more distance to cover, and it takes longer again, but is easier to manage now.

Afterwards I am soaked with sweat. Not because of the physical activity or because it is getting warm outside. In fact, it is still actually quite chilly. My cold is getting to me, and I feel run down. To make up for that, *Jambo* is making good speed in wind Force 5. The sea is fairly steady without many waves. *Jambo* rolls gently on this course, heeling about five degrees. It's the perfect time to start cooking. I am doing pork chops and pasta tonight.

Friday, 10 January, 3rd day's run 132 NM, total distance 374 NM

The next night goes very well. There is hardly any shipping about, so I allow myself to sleep for intervals of an hour. However, the wind changes direction several times, and I need to adjust the jib-boom accordingly three times in Force 5 to 7. Watching the sunrise makes me feel better, especially as the sun warms me up. Temperatures drop to 16 or 17 °C during the night.

There are ten and a half hours of daylight, so the days are shorter than the nights. Of course, it is still winter in the northern hemisphere. I keep the temperatures under deck at 23 °C during the day, with the sun supplying additional warmth. During the night, I don't need any extra heating. I only have a small electric heater anyway, because my Webasto diesel heater stopped working at the beginning of December. It won't turn on.

I even contacted the service hotline in Germany, hoping to get hold of a technician who could help. When I did finally manage to get through to someone, after phoning all sorts of different numbers and waiting in loops for twenty minutes or more, the woman at the end of the line told me I had dialed the wrong hotline, and she wasn't responsible. Instead, I was to phone the Spanish one. I told her that I couldn't speak any Spanish, and asked if someone from the German hotline could help organise a technician from a local service centre in Lanzarote instead. "Certainly not," she informed me. "Webasto is a global company, divided into separate country areas." Frustrated, I gave up, and didn't even ask Anke to try using her good language skills again, when she joined me on board after Christmas.

Anyway, it isn't urgent, seeing as we are heading for the Caribbean and it's going to be lovely and warm. Just in case, I have a small electric 1500 W fan heater on board. I will be going back home at some stage. In June, I plan to be in the Azores. and might need it in the evenings in the marinas. In July and August, I should be in the Channel, on my way to the Netherlands, and the temperatures should be fine.

I am still not well. And my cold seems to be getting worse. I have a nasty cough, and my headache and sore throat all seem to be getting worse. I don't think I have a temperature but don't bother to check. It is nothing too dramatic, but I can't do any filming because my voice has practically gone.

The two genoas pull *Jambo* along on an almost direct course in a relatively constant Force 5 wind. With 2.5 m waves, *Jambo* rolls a little more than the day before. Today I cook Chicken Garam Masala, with tomatoes, peppers and mushrooms. There is rice to go with it. I love Indian cooking, and so it all tastes great as far as I am concerned. The food makes me feel a bit better. The cold is a real nuisance.

Saturday, 11 January, 4th day's run 146 NM, total distance 520 NM

Jambo is making better progress than on the first few days. As I had hoped, that must mean that any encrustation on the underwater hull has been washed away by now. During the night, I spend some time doing deck work. I swap the whisker pole from the genoa on port to the genoa on starboard, and back again, in order to make good way, and, above all stay on course. I am starting to realise that it would have been a good idea to get a second pole.

I have been working hard over the past few days and think I can feel every muscle in my body now. This isn't unexpected. I am rarely very fit when I start out on a longer trip. It always takes a couple of days to reach the level of fitness I really need. Thankfully, my cold seems to be getting better at last.

And what a ride! Wind Force 5 and *Jambo* sails along at 6 to 7 knots above ground, almost as if she is on rails. She rolls a little, but the angle of heel remains less than 10 degrees. This is what I imagined things would be like. It is a dream.

Sunday, 12 January, 5th day's run 141 NM, total distance 661 NM

During the night, the wind goes up to Force 6, and around midnight I decide to reef. The reefing line is so tight that it starts to sing. There is still a lot of pressure in the sails.

Today is baking day. I usually get by with one loaf of bread for three days. I always use 500 g of bread baking mix. I have brought several varieties with me. I use a bread maker to bake the bread. It's an Unold appliance that comes highly recommended, and the power consumption isn't too bad. It uses a maximum of 550 W during baking and runs on 220 V. I find it very useful.

The power for it is supplied by my voltage converter with 1500 W, which gets the current from the 12 V on-board power supply. Meanwhile, the engine runs at medium speed. I've put in the forward gear, because diesel engines should always be run under load and not just in neutral. The alternator with 115 A and downstream STERLING charge controller delivers about 70 to 80 A. Power generation has been going quite well so far. The solar panels are delivering more each day, but not as much as usual, as the days are short, the sun is not yet that high in January, even at 24 to 26 degrees north latitude, and the solar panels fall into the shade in the early afternoon, due to our southwesterly course with a trade wind sail.

During the day, the solar panels manage to keep the voltage up. I am annoyed about my brand new AGM batteries. I bought them when the old ones started to fail, but unfortunately, as I found out on the first night, the new ones are worse than the old ones. The voltage drops to 12.6 V shortly after they are fully charged, and it feels like they have less than half the capacity. With lead batteries, you can only actually use about 40% of the nominal capacity anyway, so that would be 140 Ah for the batteries, if they were working properly. That's more than half the daily requirement on board *Jambo,* and should actually get me through the night. At least, that is what I thought. Less than half of that, maybe 50 to 60 Ah, simply isn't enough. So the engine runs for about an hour just before sunset, in the middle of the night, and each morning, to keep the batteries charged. On bread baking days, I turn it on for three hours in the morning.

But the power supply is not a critical issue, because I calculated on using the engine when I planned the trip. So far, we should not have consumed more than 6 litres of diesel per day. I can't say how much exactly, because the fuel needle only starts to move after 50 l have been consumed.

It is still early in the morning, about an hour before sunrise, and I turn on the bread maker, do a little check to see if everything is OK, and lie down on my bunk again for an hour of sleep. There are no ships within range. The wind is down to Force 5 again, but the sea is a bit choppy this morning. Looking forward to freshly baked bread, I drop off to sleep.

At sunrise, I get up as the bread dough is rising. I make my first cup of coffee of the day and go on deck. A pod of dolphins is there to welcome me. I feel the first warm rays of sunshine, and I am entranced by this magical moment. I gaze out across the water and watch the sun glittering on the surface. The dolphins dart around *Jambo* as if they want to play and race with her. Of course, they win every time. They are much faster. I feel blissfully happy. This is wonderful.

Then I go back to bed for half an hour and sleep until the bread machine wakes me up with some loud beeping. The loaf is ready; the lovely smell of freshly baked bread fills the whole salon. It is time for breakfast. I go on deck and set the table in the cockpit. The sun is higher in the sky now and it looks like it is going to be a warm day. I am getting over my cold at last. But my voice is still hoarse and I have a slight headache. I seem to have recovered fairly quickly. No doubt, the fresh sea air helped.

During the night, the wind shifts to east-southeast, so I abandon the trade wind sails and change everything accordingly. Now both genoas overlap to starboard. After that, *Jambo* sails on a beam reach course in Force 3 to 4 breeze.

For the first time, there is another sailing ship close by. *Eternity* is a 14 m sailing yacht from the Netherlands, and we have brief radio contact. There is also a catamaran sailing under an Australian flag, which comes into range from time to time.

There's a weak wind. I am now sailing on a southerly course for the time being, until the wind hopefully picks up enough for me to go on a direct course with trade wind sails. But things are ticking along very nicely at the moment. *Jambo* sweeps along. After 6 days at sea and all the deck work, my muscles ache – but in a good way.

On my journey to the Caribbean, I will pass through several time zones, and have to adjust the time on board accordingly, from time to time. I start today, and change the time from UTC (Coordinated Universal Time) or GMT (Greenwich Mean Time) to UTC-1. In Germany, it is currently 2 hours later than on board. Sunrise is now at 7:24 and sunset at 18:15. The chart plotter displays the times for sunrise and sunset, which are accurate to the minute. This suits my daily routine better. The days are slowly but steadily growing longer as we head south and of course for calendrical reasons.

In the afternoon, I chat with *the Eternity*. The family of four are on their way to Grenada. On board, there are Cris and Klaas, with their grown-up children, Emi and Jörn. The children had wanted to go on this trip with their parents. *Eternity's* homeport is Lelystad, not far from my own home port of Enkhuizen. It really is a small world. Later on, the catamaran, *Triplicity,* comes within radio range. Things are unusually busy for once. They are also on their way to the Caribbean, and on board are the British skipper and the Australian owner's family, with smaller children. At least now, I don't feel quite so alone on this vast ocean. The next day, however, we lose contact again.

In the evening, I cook the chicken breasts. The expiry date is nearly due and I need to use them up. Delicious!

Tuesday, 14 January, 7th day's run 90 NM, total distance 863 NM

A dead calm! At 3 o'clock in the morning, the wind drops completely, leaving the sails flapping idly. I roll in the mainsail completely, and reef the double genoa on starboard so that it stops banging about. Now all I can do is wait. The forecast promises more wind from tomorrow evening. I get the wind forecast via the Garmin inReach Mini, which I have been using for a week now.

I chose it because 350 euros for the device is cheap, compared to an Iridium satellite phone, and it also offers what is called a freelancer contract that you can activate and deactivate, as you like. I only want to use it for the outward journey across the Atlantic and then again for the return journey home. I book the contract with unlimited messages for 75 euros per month.

It offers me an SOS function, and tracking that I can embed on my website. I can also write messages that can be viewed by anyone on the Garmin page next to my track. People can follow me live if they want. I didn't realise this before I set off, but now that I have started the trip, it is an interesting tool. I've been posting brief statements every day on how I am doing.

I also have a text message function with a maximum of 160 characters, so I can stay in touch with Anke. But I am also getting more and more messages from people reading my daily short reports, who write to me via the Garmin website. I always try to answer all the messages. I am glad I chose a fixed rate, otherwise I would be charged per message, and it would be hard to keep an eye on the costs. I also wouldn't be able to keep down costs, because I can't reject incoming messages and would be charged for anything I received. Thanks to the fixed rate, I can use it without worrying. It is great fun keeping in touch with the outside world.

Another available function is weather forecasts. You can get the weather for any point on earth. The price for this is one text message, which I can also repeat as often as I want, thanks to the fixed rate. The normal weather forecast is given for two days in advance, and includes a breakdown of wind direction and strength, probability of precipitation, cloud cover, and air pressure for every six hour period. There is an additional fee of one euro for the marine weather forecast, which is a five-day forecast, including estimated wave heights. I only used it once, just to try it out.

Although I am sailing in the trade wind zone, and the prevailing wind direction is northeast to east-northeast, I really feel safe because I can get additional information about further weather developments via the text messages. Chris from *Quick,* and Chris in Siegen (Germany), are becoming very important weather advisors. This is essential for me, as the spot forecast from Garmin is, in my view, insufficient for such a passage.

Wednesday, 15 January, 8th day's run 130 NM, total distance 993 NM

Apparently, I've found the wind. It has been blowing at Force 5 since midnight. During the night, I manage to hoist the two genoas as trade wind sails, and am on a direct course for Guadeloupe. It takes about forty minutes to get everything set up.

Now we are up and running again, and *Jambo* is making good progress. It is fairly smooth sailing. After all the hard work, I lie down for an interval of sleep. At sunrise, I am back on deck again, so as not to miss this wonderful moment. This morning, a huge pod of dolphins joins me. There must be forty or fifty of them. *Jambo* glides through the water with full sails. Today, the water is tinged with red in the warm morning light. The sun does me good. Lost in thought, I gaze into the distance and savour the moment.

Today is washing-up day. I do this every two days to save water. In the beginning, I did try using seawater in the stainless steel sink, but the knives and forks started to rust. I use about 10 litres a day for all my needs. Since the water tank holds 300 l, I should be fine. The journey won't take more than thirty days. Besides, it is just water for doing the dishes, showering and washing my hands. All my drinking water comes from the supermarket. The bottles are stowed in the aft cabin. I had 150 l at the start of the trip.

On the downside, slowly but surely I am amassing a considerable amount of rubbish. I make it as small as possible, and store it in the locker. I will dispose of it when I get to Guadeloupe. Any leftovers go overboard, but there are hardly any to speak of, just a few scraps of bread on the third day, and any organic waste, like eggshells, vegetable scraps and coffee grounds. I bin everything else. The plastic bottles take up the most space.

Of course, sailors aren't the only ones concerned about protecting the oceans. I think a watermaker might be a good idea. It would give me an almost unlimited supply of fresh water which I could also use for drinking and cooking. With the right filter, it should be safe to consume. I add a watermaker to the list of things I plan to install on board next winter. I need to find out more about the subject. New batteries are already at the top of the list.

Of course, I knew *Jambo* wasn't perfectly equipped before I set out on this Atlantic crossing. I also knew I had the basics I needed to do the trip anyway. This passage is my first chance to try out long-distance cruising. So far, I'm enjoying it immensely.

Thursday, 16 January, 9th day's run 149 NM, total distance 1142 NM

The night is quiet again and there is not much for me to do. *Jambo* makes good way in an east wind of around 18 knots, travelling at almost 8 knots above ground. It is nearly too fast for me, but the sails are holding well and remain taught throughout. Since both genoas are fully set, all the sail pressure rests on the forestay. Nonetheless, I keep things the way they are for the time being.

In the meantime, I have found a good rhythm for myself. My day begins at dawn. I switch on the engine to charge the batteries and then make myself a coffee, which I drink as I watch the sun come up.

When I have checked that everything is in order, I go back to my bunk and lie down again. I have been sleeping in the forward cabin most of the time, because *Jambo* is on a downwind course, relatively upright and quiet. I never imagined things would be this good. It makes life on board very pleasant.

If there were more heel, I would move to the leeward bench in the saloon. I set my alarm for an hour, but often wake up before then. The batteries are full at this stage. The solar panels start producing energy later on, when the sun gets higher.

Then I have breakfast on deck in the warming sun, two to three slices of bread with cheese, salami or honey, or occasionally Nutella. I wash it all down with plenty of good coffee, at least another two to three cups. At the same time, I check the weather and my messages. I work out the best course to take.

Of course, I keep the camera running most of the time to get some nice shots for my videos because, in a few days, I want to start editing the film about this trip. After breakfast, I lie down on my bunk again and try to get some sleep. The morning carries on quietly, unless I have to do any sailing jobs. In between, I send texts and messages and draft my daily short report for the Garmin website. By now, more and more people are following me there, waiting for an update. At lunchtime, I either cook a fresh meal or heat up yesterday's leftovers.

The next day's run measurement of distance travelled is due. Today it is 149 NM, because we are travelling so fast. By now, *Jambo* and I are at about 20 degrees north latitude, Guadeloupe is at about 16 degrees north, and Marina Rubicón at just under 29 degrees north. That means I've come some distance south, following the wind, which tends to be lighter further north.

Then I post my next update, which takes a bit of time, as it has to be split into blocks of 160 characters, and the data speed is nothing to write home about. Sometimes, when loads of messages come in, I am sure it is even slower.

Eventually I get my message sent and do another weather update. I usually choose points at one and two times the day's run ahead, and south and north of that. However, I prefer the daily updates from Chris and Chris via text messages. It is not long before it is evening again, and time to switch the engine on for an hour or so to charge the batteries. Then I usually eat one or two small yoghurts with some fruit.

After sunset, I go back to my bunk and make myself comfortable. I also have my two iPads, my iPhone as an alarm clock, and the remote control for the autopilot. Actually, I don't need two iPads, but I had to buy a new one because my old one got lost. I accidentally bought the wrong one, one that doesn't have its own GPS. So I had to buy a second one with GPS, as by the time I noticed the mistake, the exchange period had already expired. On one of the two iPads, I run the Navionics app with the electronic sea chart, on the other I mirror the chart plotter, and can operate all functions, except the autopilot, and look at the data.

I am still setting my alarm clock to sleep for one-hour intervals. Later I will lengthen that time to three hours, but I don't dare do that yet. There could be sailboats out there without active AIS that I know nothing about. In fact, I only see one sail on the horizon where an AIS signal is missing. Nowadays, it is standard to be on the move with an AIS transponder on such trips.

I set the hourly alarms I need through to the next morning, because if I miss one alarm, the next one will automatically wake me up. It is possible that I do actually miss an alarm now and then. I fall asleep very quickly in the evenings, because I'm always pretty tired by late afternoon. Although I get more than eight hours sleep in total, interrupted sleep at these short intervals is not as restful as a decent night's sleep where I don't have to wake up. I find the three-hour intervals much more pleasant.

After an hour, I am woken up. Immediately I look at the sea chart to see if everything is all right. It is. Then I check the other tablet to see how the wind is blowing. Again, nothing has changed. Next, I check the screen to see if there are any ships in my vicinity. But everything is quiet and there is no ship traffic indicated. Then I open the forecastle hatch and peer out to see if I can spot anything on the horizon. Again, there is nothing out there. Then I take the torch and quickly check the sails. Everything is as it should be. This means I can sleep for another hour. Around midnight, I switch on the engine for an hour. After several more sleep intervals, the morning arrives, and I begin the whole procedure all over again.

I cope quite well with this routine. I am always more tired in the mornings and evenings, and feel at my best at midday. But it takes a couple of days to really get into the rhythm of everything.

Friday, 17 January, 10th day's run 161 NM, total distance 1303 NM

The night is rough. Again and again, gusts of up to 23 knots keep coming. I don't sleep as well this time and get up very late, contrary to my normal rhythm. The swell is about 3 m, and on board it is much rockier than before. There is a strong low-pressure system over Newfoundland, the effects of which reach all the way into the trade wind zone. There is less wind in the north and it is still stronger in the south, which is why I stay on a southwest course, possibly all the way to the 16th parallel, the same latitude as Guadeloupe.

The speed, on the other hand, is really good, at times we sweep across the Atlantic at over 8 knots over ground. The day's run of 161 NM is also an absolute top value, and a new record for *Jambo*. Today is another cooking day. I make egg fried noodles and then spend the afternoon listening to music. I love the fact that I can turn up the volume as loud as I like, because there is no one to disturb.

Saturday, 18 January, 11th day's run 140 NM, total distance 1443 NM

I have now reached the 17th parallel north. The sun is already quite high and it is lovely and warm. From tomorrow on, there is going to be a little less wind, but today I am simply enjoying this beautiful day's sailing with wind Force 5 and a pleasant wave.

Sunday, 19 January, 12th day's run 109 NM, total distance 1552 NM

In the morning, the wind is still reasonably good, but only Force 4 and decreasing. It is now less than 1,500 NM to Guadeloupe. I'm nearly half way! It's incredible how quickly time has gone.

At noon there is almost a calm, with no more than Force 2 to 3 winds, which is not enough to sail before the wind, and the sails hang limp in the wind. Today, I decide to use the day with little wind to check everything on board, especially my steering gear. To do this, I have to clear my aft cabin out to get to the hatch at the stern. Everything is in order there, the screws on the auxiliary rudder arm, which sits on the rudderstock, are tight, and the rudder arm has not moved either. The rudder position sensor is also unchanged in its position.

I decide to pull in the second genoa. Handling two genoas at the same time has been hard work for me so far. Also converting the jib always means going onto the foredeck where, in my view, the danger of going overboard is greatest. Of course, things would be better if I had a second whisker pole. I have added it to my list.

I haul in the genoa, recover and fold it up. The process takes almost two hours. Afterwards, I'm soaking wet and feel exhausted. Inside the boat, I check the keel bolts to see if there are any signs of water ingress. It is something I do every few days, no matter what. *Jambo's* iron keel is bolted onto the hull using eight keel bolts. A few years ago, I also had something called a 'Keel-Connect' done as part of osmosis prevention. This involves planing off the gelcoat around the base of the keel on the hull, and laminating the transition area from the hull to the keel. *Jambo* has a so-called 'Berlin Keel', where the keel is not connected continuously between the upper part and the bulb keel, but with two stays, so that the middle area of the keel can also be laminated. I also had the entire keel filled and sealed to prevent corrosion. This provides additional safety, as the bolts normally are not exposed to the water unless there are cracks in the laminate.

If I did find water were to enter these keel bolts inside the vessel, it would be a sign that keel loss was imminent. It would mean that I would have to prepare to abandon *Jambo* immediately, and get the life raft ready for use at once.

Fortunately, however, everything is in order. Then I do a quick visual check of the engine, clean the seawater filter and check the oil level. I take a quick look at the batteries as well. The bilge is dry, too. Everything looks fine. I also do a quick check of the shrouds. I run my hands along the steel wires as far as I can reach, looking for broken strands. Again, everything seems to be in order.

The wind shifts to north-northeast and blows around 11 knots. *Jambo* is on the beam wind, under full sails, and making about 6 knots of speed. The conditions are perfect for flying the drone today. I get some nice aerial shots of *Jambo* out in the middle of the ocean.

I have a DJI Phantom 4, which has two large leg stands where I can hold it. I launch the drone aft from the cockpit, holding it by its leg stands before take-off. I have to hold it tightly while I'm doing this, because it tries to correct its position by steering against the direction *Jambo* is moving. When I'm ready, I let go, and immediately pull the drone upwards. The battery allows about ten minutes of flight and recording time before it is down to 50%. I have to bring the drone back on board then at the very latest.

To do this, I bring *Jambo* to a halt and fly the drone over to us. Then I go to the mast on the windward side and make sure I am tethered to the boat. I steer the drone towards *Jambo* and catch it in the air. Sometimes it is easy, sometimes it takes forever. This is one time I notice how much swell there is. While the drone automatically maintains its height and position, *Jambo*

goes up and down accordingly. The best landings are when the relative speed of drone to boat is zero, because then you just have to concentrate on the up and down motion. We have managed all right so far. I did lose a drone a few years back when I let it fly from the shore in Fécamp. There was some kind of technical fault, as far as I remember.

Today everything is fine and I get some great shots.

Monday, 20 January, 13th day's run 108 NM, total distance 1660 NM

I sleep for a long time today, in intervals of course. I have now extended the intervals to two hours, because I haven't sighted another ship for days. After yesterday's busy day, it feels good to sleep a little longer at a time. The wind is blowing around 10 knots from the northeast now, and I am making good way on beam reach.

There still tends to be more wind in the south than in the north. I don't want to drop further south at the moment, because otherwise I will be too far downwind, and hardly make any way in the weak wind. I also don't think it's advisable to sail further upwind to pick up more speed, as this would take me too far north, where the wind is weaker. So I keep things as they are for the time being. There is no more wind due for the next few days. So it is slow sailing, but also very beautiful.

These are quiet days, and the weather is nice. Today it is clear to cloudy at a pleasant 25 °C. But in the afternoon, it's almost calm with just 5 to 6 knots of wind. On my course, that is not enough to make good way. I furl in the genoa to a quarter, and let *Jambo* drift slowly downwind, while I spend the day lazing in the sun, listening to music. I occasionally pour a bucket of Atlantic water over my head to cool down. It is wonderful!

Today I set the ship's time to UTC -2 to fit in with my routine. Sunrise is now at 7:04 and sunset at 18:22.

Suddenly I notice something astern. Then I recognise what it is: whales blowing! I am really excited. Slowly they come closer. It's a group of about ten whales. But then I see more spouts of air and water. There's another group, and another one! There are whales everywhere. The first ones are upon us already. They are pilot whales. They approach leisurely, swim alongside *Jambo* for a while, then slowly swim on ahead, leaving us behind.

What an incredible experience! Of course, I keep the camera rolling, taking more and more pictures and stop, as the whales keep coming in larger and smaller groups. Sometimes there are only two animals, sometimes ten or more in a group. Some pass very close to *Jambo*, others at some distance. We are definitely on the same course, but the whales swim a bit faster than *Jambo* is currently travelling.

After three quarters of an hour, I decide to fly my drone. I'm so glad I did. The pictures I get are fantastic. After about an hour and a half, the last whale swims past. I can't even tell how many there were. I try to guess how many animals I saw in ten minutes, and estimate that it must have been more than 150 whales.

What a magnificent day! I have just about reached the halfway point of my trip, and that has to be my absolute highlight so far. I think I have put more nautical miles behind me than are ahead of me, with just under 1,700 NM. Today was a perfect dream, and in fact, the whole journey has been like that for me so far. Before I set off, I was feeling nervous. *Plan B's* fate didn't deter me, but it did make me worry. Now it really feels like a dream to have come this far and have accomplished so many days of sailing already.

Since setting off, I have been in my element, or comfort zone, as you might put it. If I manage to complete this Atlantic crossing, it will be a dream come true. But to experience the journey so far, here and now, feels like a huge privilege in itself, unforgettable and almost surreal. Because this is my first long ocean passage, the experience is probably even more intense than if I were crossing the Atlantic for the umpteenth time. The first time is always special. It is something you will never forget.

Meanwhile, more and more people who are following me on my journey write to me via the Garmin. They often ask me if I don't get bored all by myself on the high seas in the middle of a vast ocean. I always say no, and assure them that I am fascinated by everything I see. On top of that, I am aboard *Jambo*, under sail. My favourite place and my favourite hobby. Sailing is the thing I like doing best, my passion – how could I ever be bored?

I am enjoying this trip, enjoying every minute, even if there are slack days, like today. So far, the trip has been just great for me.

The weather has also been great: blue sky and insanely blue water. I never knew water could be so blue. It's stunning.

<u>Tuesday, 21 January, 14th day's run 95 NM, total distance 1755 NM</u>

I have another unsettled night. At about 2 am I am woken up by the sound of the reefed genoa banging, as the wind has dropped to Force 2. Soon afterwards, a rain front hits us as it moves by, and the wind jumps to Force 5, from one moment to the next. I can see the individual shower cells, also called squalls, wonderfully on the radar.

Then the wind stabilises at Force 4 from the east. I set the full genoa ahead of the wind again, and things go quite well for a while. In the morning the strong wind alarm goes off, hurrying me out of bed - the wind is up to 24 knots. Afterwards, it calms down a bit, and *Jambo* makes good progress, heading west with 19 knots of wind. The weather is dull and grey with dark clouds in the sky, but it is not cold.

I can set the alarm on my chart plotter for different parameters. Apart from warning me about ships approaching, the alarm goes off if the wind speed reaches 22 knots during the night. When this value is exceeded, the alarm sounds so that I can reef the sails immediately. Another alarm tells me when rudder impact is more than 50 degrees. Whenever anything goes off, I am alerted immediately.

In the morning, a swell of about 4 m comes in from the north and rocks *Jambo* hard. There must have been something big going on further north.

After breakfast, the wind speed is down to 7 knots again, and the strong swell means it is impossible to keep any pressure in the sail. To stop the genoa from flapping, I set it at half-size, and make sure it is tight on the boom, so it is just a flat triangle, and can't move much. Once again, the motto is: wait for the wind! As far as the wind is concerned, the only constant now is inconstancy.

At least the sun is slowly asserting itself, which makes me doubly happy. For one thing, like most people, I love good weather, and of course, I need the sun to generate electrical energy with my solar panels.

The four solar panels, with a total of 480 Wp, also deliver more and more energy every day. This is because the days are getting longer all the time. *Jambo* is now at 16 degrees north, much further south than at the beginning, and is sailing on a westerly course, which is another advantage, compared to the south-westerly course in the beginning. Currently, the daily yield is 1.6 to 1.7 kWh, which corresponds to about 130 Ah. That is not bad, but it could be more. The low battery capacity limits the yield in the afternoon, as the batteries are fully charged by then, and the solar charge controllers have to regulate down.

Wednesday, 22 January, 15th day's run 112 NM, total distance 1867 NM

The night is a bit calmer than the previous one, and with the wind at 12 knots, I sleep very well again. Today is my birthday! I am 56 years old. For the first time in my life, I am by myself on my birthday, and sing my own birthday serenade.

My loved ones wrapped presents for me to take on this trip, and today I get to open them: a Lanzarote towel, a photo calendar, a backpack and some other nice things. I am very happy.

A light wind blows from the east during the day. *Jambo* glides towards the west. Slowly, but surely! The weather is great, and it's nice and warm. Feeling very relaxed, I enjoy today, listening to a lot of music.

Thursday, 23 January, 16th day's run 108 NM, total distance 1975 NM

The Atlantic has calmed down enough for me to sail wing-to-wing again, which only works reasonably well if there isn't much wave motion or roll. I keep the mainsail to starboard and the genoa out wide to port. The wind blows at around 11 knots from east to east-northeast.

There is still more wind in the south. I am now even south of the 16th parallel, which is further south than the approach to the island of Guadeloupe. It means that the route is getting longer, and will be more nautical miles than I expected. If the wind forecast is right, I will need to stay on a west-southwest course for a while, possibly even as far as 15 degrees north, as the wind there is actually supposed to blow an average of 3 knots faster.

However, I can only sail wing-to-wing as long as the Atlantic is so calm. If it gets choppier, I will have to dismantle the sails again.

<u>Friday, 24 January, 17th day's run 104 NM, total distance 2079 NM</u>

In the morning at about 5 am, the wind freshens up and blows with Force 5 from the east. It seems to be paying off that I am now further south. I hope it stays like this.

I try my luck at fishing, and after a short while, a fish bites. In the distance, I see it leaping out of the water. Somehow, I manage to press the wrong lever, and let out the line so rapidly that it breaks at the end. I'll have to try again. Fish would make a welcome change to the menu, because I have nearly used up all of my fresh food. I still have a few eggs, but mostly I'm already living off canned food.

How many more days will I be at sea, I ask myself? It's still 1,100 NM to Guadeloupe. If we carry on at this slow pace, and I manage about 100 NM a day, it will take us another ten or eleven days, which would be fine. I'm in no great hurry at the moment. I don't want to give up my laid-back lifestyle on board too soon.

I've got into the rhythm of things, am feeling fit, have everything I want, and absolutely love this beautiful time at sea. I listen to music, spend a lot of time on deck in the warm sun, still pour refreshing Atlantic water over my head from time to time, text lots of messages, keep *Jambo* on course and am delighted to be part of it all. I could not be more content and at peace if I tried.

Saturday, 25 January, 18th day's run 130 NM, total distance 2209 NM

The wind is steady at Force 4 to 5 from the east, and *Jambo* is getting along fine. I'm getting closer and closer to my destination, but although it doesn't look so far on the chart, it's still quite a long way.

I get the rod out again, and another fish bites. This time it doesn't show itself, but pulls very hard on the line. I can hardly reel it in, so I leave it alone for twenty minutes, hoping that it will soon grow tired. Then I slowly reel in the line. It is a slog, and after a short time I am probably more exhausted than the fish. Then suddenly the reel is easy to wind, which does not bode well. All I get is the silvery baitfish hanging on the line; the fish is off the hook. It was probably too big to be hauled on board safely anyway. I guess I need to learn how to fish properly.

Wind Force 4 is slow, but *Jambo* is on a direct course. The current is running with us, pushing an extra knot, keeping the speed over ground at over 4 knots. The current has not been constant, running along a little more or less most of the time, but I have also had days with countercurrents of up to half a knot.

I change the boat's time again, now to UTC -3, which means sunrise is at 6:44 and sunset at 18:09. The direct distance to Guadeloupe is about 770 NM, but it is a bit more for *Jambo* and me, as the wind does not keep us on a direct course. Cautiously, I estimate the day of arrival in Guadeloupe to be 2 or 3 February.

Monday, 27 January, 20th day's run 76 NM, total distance 2388 NM

Today, for the first and only time on any Atlantic crossing, I saw a sailing boat that was not transmitting an AIS signal. It sailed ahead on starboard, about 6 to 8 NM away. After a short time, it disappeared on the horizon. Neither of us made radio contact. The other crew obviously didn't feel like chatting either.

A dead calm! I reef the mainsail completely. I also want to reef the genoa and set it small and tight enough to stop it from banging, and then let myself drift. Nothing happens when I try to furl it in. I keep pulling, and end up with a good bit of line, but the genoa refuses to roll up. *That's odd!* I have to go forward and grab my lifejacket with the lifeline, before I set off. At the front, I notice that the two retaining screws for the guide rail on the Furlex have come loose, and fallen out. So the Furlex turned at the bottom, while the guide rail hung loosely above it. I find the two screws lying side by side on deck. That was lucky!

I have to loosen the backstay so that the forestay is no longer under tension, in order to get the rail down far enough to push it back into the Furlex holder. Before I do that, I wind back the reefing line. I apply Loctite to the screws and screw them back in. After that, everything is back in working order. All the nautical miles, especially with lulls, where the sails bang, cause wear and tear. But apart from that, everything is still fine on board.

Tuesday, 28 January, 21st day's run 81 NM, total distance 2469 NM

The wind is blowing around 11 knots. All along, I've been wanting to try an alternative self-steering system to see how I can make progress without having to stand at the helm if the autopilot fails. I had to try something on a close reach course on the way to Fécamp, which worked well. Now I want to test what I can do on a downwind course if the autopilot fails then.

While I was preparing for this trip, I looked into various autopilot systems and did a lot of research online. In the days when there were no autopilots or sophisticated windvane steering systems, sailors on long voyages developed other ways of coping. On a downwind course, they used bands of rubber. That's what I want to test now. I bought rubber resistance bands of different strengths in a sports shop on Lanzarote. I have band strengths of 15, 25, 35, 45 and 55 kg to cope with different wind speeds, and the corresponding tension forces on the genoa sail.

I set the genoa only, in this case on the port side, and lay the sheet on the wheel. Of course, this won't work without a corresponding device on the wheel. I've got long bolts for this. I attach the bolts to the spokes with hose clips, so that they stick out about 4 cm on either side of the wheel, and fasten a nut to the top of each one, to give the lines some guidance.

Then I lay the sheet over the bolts so that it overlaps about half the wheel. I put a line on the other side, which I connect to the rubber bands, and position another line on the port winch in the cockpit, where I can pre-set the initial tension. In order to be able to tighten the genoa sheet accordingly, I add a reel, which I attach to the boom topping lift, and wrap around the starboard winch in the cockpit.

This way, I now have the system set up and can balance it by changing the pre-tension so that *Jambo* stays on course. In the

light wind, I decide to use the 35 kg rubber band, but I could have chosen one size bigger. It works! In the next half hour, *Jambo* only goes off course once.

So how does it work?

You make use of the different sail pressure at different wind angles and the resulting different forces in the sheet.

I'll try to explain it with the help of a simple diagram. In the first picture, the wind comes from astern, about 150 to 160 degrees, and the rudder keeps *Jambo* on course. The forces are balanced.

The pulling force on the sheet is equal to the pulling force of the pre-tensioned rubber band.

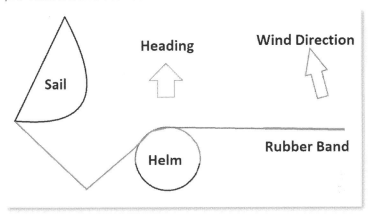

Now, for some reason, perhaps due to a small shift of wind, too much rudder input or a wave, *Jambo* moves too far downwind, and the wind now comes from astern, or slightly from port. The sail pressure decreases, and so does the pulling force in the genoa sheet. Automatically, the pre-tensioned rubber band pulls on the wheel and *Jambo* luffs.

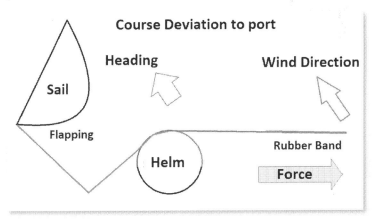

The forces balance each other out again. If *Jambo* starts to luff too much at this stage and is almost at a broad reach, the sail pressure increases strongly, the pulling forces on the sheet increase, and pull the rudder to port again.

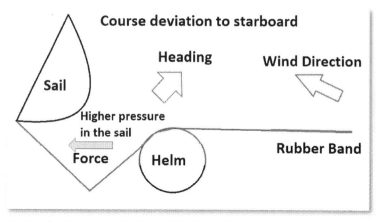

So ideally, it swings back and forth slightly and keeps *Jambo* on course. You have to intervene now and then if the wind changes direction and strengthens too quickly. But it works as an emergency system, so that I don't have to be at the helm all the time. I'm delighted that I was able to get it all set up and can dismantle it again now.

Because of the weak wind, which is likely to continue for the next few days, I actually decide to put the second genoa up again. I'm much better at doing this single-handed now, which will be a help on the way back.

I'm back to sailing in a trade wind position again and hope that I'll be rewarded with higher speeds.

Wednesday, 29 January, 22nd day's run 104 NM, total distance 2573 NM

It rains for a change. I use the bimini to catch water and channel it into a container with a hose. Unfortunately, the water is too dirty to use, because it is full of Lanzarote dust. It is going to take a few more rain showers before the water is clean.

The trip has been trouble-free so far, except for the Furlex, which I was able to fix easily, but now something serious breaks. The ring on the clew of the genoa is almost torn off. Luckily, I notice before it rips off completely. During the night, the wind was very light and I pulled the sheet tight, and the boom rubbed against the tapes that attach the ring to the genoa. It's my own fault, and as usual, mistakes aren't often forgiven at sea. Sometimes they even punish severely. I am beginning to think that phases of light wind often damage the sails more than strong winds, with constant sail pressure do.

I change the genoa. On Lanzarote, I had both sails overhauled, but on this genoa, the area around the clew wasn't re-enforced. On the other one, which I have hoisted now, the same area was repaired. I am sure the final 500 NM will be fine with just one genoa. That's how close I am to my destination!

The wind is blowing at around 11 knots from the southeast, the sun is shining, and it is very warm. If only the wind weren't so unsteady all the time! It keeps changing direction so rapidly that wing-to-wing sailing is impossible. That is why I am sailing a beam reach in a west-southwesterly direction. The course is not ideal, but I way prefer that to sailing downwind at 2 knots on a direct course.

Although my destination is so close, I'm making very slow progress. The last nautical miles require a lot of mental strength. *Jambo* rocks in the waves, and I would like to rock this trip now by getting to Guadeloupe soon. I have had a look at the island in the cruising guide, and it all looks so great, I cannot wait to get there. I am very much looking forward to Guadeloupe.

Thursday, 30 January, 23rd day's run 100 NM, total distance 2673 NM

During the night, there is a good wind. Early in the morning, I can set a direct course, but there is still a lot of sailing work required during the day, in changing conditions.

Friday, 31 January, 24th day's run 105 NM, total distance 2778 NM

It is about 300 NM to go, and roughly three days of sailing in this wind. Today, however, I don't feel good at all. I'm also a bit limp. My muscles ache because the last few days have been hard work. In order to keep up the speed and hold our course during the directional changes of the wind, I put in a lot of work setting the sails and re-fitting the foresail boom.

Today I need a bit of rest, and so I keep the foresail boom to starboard, sailing wing-on-wing when the wind comes from the east to east-northeast. That means I can sail on an almost direct course, or just slightly north. When the wind shifts back to southeast, I get the mainsail on the other side, for a west-south-west beam reach course, and zigzag back and forth.

Today I can't find the strength to refit the boom again. This is surprising after such a long time at sea. But I have heard that phases like this, when you don't feel fit, are common at sea. You have to be sensible and do less. When I'm not fit, I don't feel so safe on the foredeck, and avoid working there.

My food supplies are also slowly running low, as the trip is now taking longer than I had planned. I had only expected to be sailing for twenty-two days. I ate my last yoghurt a couple of days ago, and drank the last of the orange juice today. Of course, I can still prepare some pasta and rice dishes, and have a few canned goods, as well as ham and honey to go with my bread.

I've rationed the canned fruit, to make sure I get some every evening.

I am not going to starve. I still have enough eggs and a few sausages. However, the things I enjoy eating and which have kept the menu a little more varied, are running out. It is definitely time I arrived. My fishing luck has not been great either, although I did try several times. I had one fish bite close to the stern, but not hard, and it jumped off the hook again.

Saturday, 1 February, 25th day's run 92 NM, total distance 2870 NM

With light, changeable winds and a stronger Atlantic swell, it's another busy night, with not many nautical miles to show for it.

But no matter! This is the final spurt! One last time, give it everything you've got! The supplies continue to run out, and the water tank pump drew air for the first time today, which means there's not much fresh water left. Maybe there is enough for two more showers. I really need to get there!

With full wing-on-wing sails, *Jambo* is on a direct course again by midday. The annoying Atlantic swell has subsided to such an extent that the wing-to-wing is possible again. I hope that the wind will stay like this. In the meantime, the situation is starting to get to me.

Sunday, 2 February, 26th day's run 121 NM, total distance,2991 NM

It's a good night, with Force 4 and gusts of Force 5 from the east. Thanks to a bit of easy sailing, I have a quieter night. Today I change the boat's time for the last time. Board time is now UTC-4, which means that I am in the same time zone as Guadeloupe now. Sunrise is at 6:36 and sunset at 18:03.

Now I am very close to my destination. I should be there tomorrow morning. I have chosen the Marina Bas-du-Fort in Pointe-à-Pitre, which looks really good in the cruising guide. I am looking forward to staying there. I am also feeling a lot better now, having overcome the small physical low.

The sun goes down and I sail into the last night. At about midnight, the first lights on the smaller offshore island should come into view. I am looking forward to seeing them.

Monday, 3 February: Arrival

The first beacon comes into view on starboard ahead. This must be the Îles de la Petite Terre lighthouse. I see land for the first time in the first morning light. It is still about 14 NM to the marina. With a light easterly wind, *Jambo* glides quietly towards her destination.

I hoist the French courtesy flag to starboard and the one for Guadeloupe below it. The Q flag goes on the port side, before I sit back and enjoy the last few nautical miles, under sail at a moderate speed, with the best cup of coffee in the world.

Then it is time. I take in the sails and get the fenders and lines ready. Next, I radio the Bas-du-Fort marina to arrange a berth. Luckily, I am able to get hold of someone. They want to know if I have a reservation. "I'm afraid not," I say, "as I've just arrived from the Canary Islands, and wasn't able to phone or email on the way."

There is no free berth in the marina. I was so looking forward to finally having a good shower, doing the laundry, going out to eat in a restaurant, disposing of my rubbish, filling up the water tank and stretching my legs a bit. Now I will have to anchor. I look at the possibilities in the cruising guide. There are a few anchor spots in the lagoon opposite the marina.

I sail into the lagoon and up the Rivière Salée. First of all, I want to go to the petrol station in the marina, which is easy to find. I can get some diesel and water as well, which you can buy here for three euros per 100 litres. Water and diesel - that's one major issue sorted! I also meet the harbour captain, responsible for allocating berths, who tells me to try again tomorrow, although he can't promise anything. I set off to find an anchorage. It's pretty crowded, but I find a suitable spot between the Banc Rose reef and the Îlet à Cochons, and drop the anchor at 9 m depth. Now I need some breakfast, before I get the dinghy ready, drive over to the marina, and see if I can take care of all the clearance formalities. I also want to do some shopping.

It isn't until I sit down with my last piece of ham and bread for breakfast, that I start to grasp what this means: *I've made it! I'm in the Caribbean, with Jambo! My most incredible journey ever! 3,084 NM and twenty-seven days at sea! Wow!* I'm overwhelmed by it all! What an experience!

Link to video

Chapter 9: Guadeloupe

<u>Tuesday, 4 February</u>

At lunchtime, I go across in the dinghy, find the Bas-du-Fort Marina Capitainerie right away, and am able to clear through customs and immigration without any problems. I enter all my data on the computer and print out the document. Then I show it to the woman at the desk along with my passport, pay three euros, she stamps it and that's it. I'm glad everything is so straightforward. I had no idea what to expect, as it's my first time clearing in.

I didn't clear out in Lanzarote, and wasn't even sure if it was doable or not. According to any information I could find, clearance is only possible in Las Palmas on Gran Canaria, and Santa Cruz on Tenerife. According to the marina handbook, the invoice from the marina with the day of departure is sufficient. Here, however, no one wants to see it. The process of clearing in and out, which I experience during the course of my trip, varies considerably, depending on the island state. The process on the French islands is by far the most uncomplicated. It is also the cheapest and fastest I encounter, and I am very grateful to our French friends.

I get a first look at the marina, which is lovely, with palm trees and brightly coloured buildings, but it doesn't seem quite as well-kept as you might expect in Europe. *Hopefully, I'll be able to get a berth there tomorrow.*

I take the opportunity to dispose of the first two rubbish bags — there are eight bags in all. I ask directions to the nearest supermarket, which is not far away, and buy two shopping bags filled with groceries and my first Caribbean beer, a six-pack of Carib. I'm looking forward to drinking a well-deserved anchor beer this afternoon.

I take the dinghy back to *Jambo*. It's a short ride, no more than ten minutes. And there she lies, just as I left her. On board, I fill up the fridge with the things I've bought. The anchor seems to be holding well, as I can see from the track in the app, and *Jambo* is only moving in the usual swing arc. I always run the Navionics app when anchoring to make sure the anchor is set well. By now, I'm starting to feel very tired, so I lie down on my bunk and fall asleep until late afternoon.

When I wake up, it's time for a brief summary, which I record on camera for the video about my Atlantic crossing. I am pleased with the result, and feel great now. Of course, I'm still tired and a bit wobbly after the crossing, but everything has worked out the way I hoped it would. I did hit a physical and mental low towards the end of the journey, but that's part and parcel of a passage like that, and I was able to get over it pretty quickly.

Most of the time I slept well, starting with intervals of an hour's sleep, and then sleeping for two or three hours at a time, seeing as there was no ship traffic at all on many days. I always felt relatively rested in the mornings, but made sure I got some extra sleep throughout the day.

Now, here in the evening, I sit in the sun and treat myself to my first beer in four weeks. Wonderful! I never drink alcohol at sea. It is simply too dangerous for a single-handed sailor. You have to be fully alert all the time. Something can happen at any moment, requiring your full attention or immediate action. Just think of a sail tearing and having to change it immediately. It's far too dangerous to be on deck with any amount of alcohol in your blood. And I don't miss it. It's probably good for me.

The beer tastes great after such a long break. It's a treat I think I have truly earned after sailing more than 3,000 NM and spending almost four weeks at sea. In the evening I cook a quick snack and fall into a deep and restful sleep as soon as the sun goes down. Even though I wake up from time to time during the night to check if everything is all right, I find the experience very tame after all the nights at sea.

The next morning is gorgeous. It is sunny and warm with just a slight breeze. I feel very rested. *What a wonderful morning here at anchor.* After breakfast, I take the dinghy to the marina and ask for a berth at the Capitainerie. I am in luck. I can stay for two nights. The receptionist tells me to come in the afternoon and report on VHF channel 9 so that they can brief me.

I am very happy about this, and head back to *Jambo* in the dinghy. As I pass through the marina entrance, there is a fair amount of wind and some swell in the lagoon. The waves are quite high for my small dinghy. I keep getting soaked as we chug along. Feeling a little worried, I try to spot *Jambo* in the distance. Then I see her. She isn't where she is supposed to be! Instead, she is about 100 m astern from where I left her and only two boat-lengths away from a neighbouring yacht. I can't see anyone on it, but for what good it is worth, there is another yacht a little further off, with a couple watching the spectacle.

At full throttle, I race towards *Jambo* as fast as I can. Completely soaked, I climb on board, quickly tie up the dinghy, start the engine, and manage to sail clear of the boat before *Jambo* collides with it. Then I switch on my navigation instruments. The wind is blowing pretty hard now. I get a reading of 20 knots. I start to pull in the anchor by hand. This is usually not difficult if there's not much wind, because I am strong enough to pull *Jambo* towards the anchor as I haul in the chain. But it is impossible in these conditions. I have to use the engine to help slacken the anchor line before I can pull it up bit by bit.

So I steer *Jambo* about two boat-lengths forward, towards where I think the chain must be. Then I sprint to the bow, pull in the loose length of chain, and then dash to hitch it on the starboard bow cleat before it pulls so hard that I can't hold it any longer. I'm not quick enough, and again and again the chain slips through my fingers, pulling the few metres I have managed to haul in so far back into the sea. Then I have to start again.

I rush back into the cockpit and then forward, over and over again. There's no time to spare, because the anchor is still slipping, and I'm too close to that other boat. Each time, I only gain about two metres distance to the neighbouring boat, and lose one metre each time I'm too slow, and the chain slips out of my hands.

The sailor from the neighbouring boat shouts something. The wind is so loud that I can't hear what he is saying, but I think he is probably offering to help. I could have done with some help a bit sooner, when *Jambo* was drifting towards the other boat without a crew on board. But their dinghy was firmly moored on deck, and they showed no signs of making ready then. By the time they get round to helping me, I'll be long gone. So I signal to him by rotating both index fingers and pointing at my ears, that I can't hear what he is saying, and don't let him stop me.

I go back and forth, between the bow and the wheel continuously. I just keep going, and after a quarter of an hour I have managed to pull in the anchor at last. It is still too early to enter the marina. So I let down the anchor again, further forward and closer to the reef, but on the leeward side. I'm drenched in sweat and feel totally exhausted. I have also hurt my right hand. It's nothing dramatic, just a scratch, which is bleeding a bit. I quickly clean it up and stick a plaster on it.

Now I can catch my breath and calm down. I'm trembling. My pulse and adrenaline are still high. What just happened here? Actually, it is a classic: you've been anchored for a while with hardly any wind, the anchor seems to be holding well and you feel safe. Then the weather breaks and the anchor slips – in my case, it was unfortunate that this happened while I wasn't on board. I'd let out 30 m of anchor chain, which is plenty, and the 8 mm chain is the recommended thickness for my length of boat.

What I did can be quite dangerous, though, and there is a risk of crushing your fingers. In the worst case, you could lose a finger. I add an electric windlass to my list - for convenience and for safety, especially when I am sailing single-handed. I also decide to wear gloves when I'm hauling in the anchor from now on, to protect my fingers.

In the afternoon, and less wind, I lift the anchor again, which is easier after this morning's learning experience. I sail to the marina and radio the harbour captain. He meets me and asks me to follow him. We pass some superyachts and enter the marina. Then we turn into a narrow dock. Every yacht is moored to a stern buoy, anchored with chains that run diagonally below the waterline to the bottom.

I have to be careful to keep clear of the buoys as we approach. *It is really narrow.* Then the harbour captain points to a box, which is on starboard for me. Luckily, the wind is coming from directly ahead, which helps me turn in.

The harbour captain waves me past, and indicates that he is going to push me in with his dinghy. It works. I'm in, and as I hand my line to someone on the jetty in front of me, the harbour captain ties *Jambo* up at the stern, and shouts for me to take the line. "Merci!" I call, and then he leaves. No doubt I would have managed to dock on my own somehow, but of course, this was a lot easier.

I'm delighted with my berth. There is a single-handed sailor from France next door. He was the person who helped me with the lines on the jetty. We have a quick chat. He sailed across the Atlantic single-handed just a few weeks ago. His wife is flying in from France in the next few days, and they want to spend some time here together. Sadly, she still has to work, while he has already retired. "That's a bit like us," I say. Anke is coming to Sint Maarten in March. I miss her immensely.

After paying the mooring fees, I start looking for a restaurant. Fortunately, the first one I see looks great and they are actually serving food. Restaurants usually close here in the late afternoon. I really enjoy eating out after all this time. In the evening, I crawl into my bunk, and sleep soundly through the night for the first time in a long time.

I start the next day by doing the laundry. I bought the coins for the washing machine and dryer when I paid the mooring fee yesterday. I start the first wash with towels and bed linen, and have breakfast while I wait. By the time I've finished breakfast, the laundry is done and I put it into the dryer. Then I wash colours. As the clothes are temperature-sensitive, I can't put them in the dryer, and will hang them out to dry on board. After an hour, the

washing machine and dryer are finished, and I go back to *Jambo* with two full bags of laundry, and hang up my clothes. While everything is drying, I stroll through the marina, taking everything in. I also walk a bit further afield. In many cases, the houses and streets look a bit run down, but that seems to be normal here. There is a row of restaurants in the marina, and I plan to go for lunch a bit earlier today.

I really like the marina with all its Caribbean flair. I would love to stay a few days longer, and ask again at the Capitainerie. But nothing can be done. In the afternoon, I stow my dry laundry away, change the sheets, tidy up the boat and buy provisions for the next couple of days. Next door, the single-handed skipper is delighted when his wife arrives. I'm happy for him and think: *Anke will be here in just a few weeks.*

The next day we get ready to depart. My French neighbour is also leaving. He has already called the Capitainerie and booked a mariniero for 10 am. I'm happy to go along with this. It's very windy today, and even here in the marina it's already blowing with Force 5 to 6. I keep glancing at the wind indicator and the windex, and hope that I'll manage to cast off in the narrow docks. I needn't have worried. Everything here is routine. First, the mariniero unceremoniously grabs the neighbouring boat by the stern and pulls it out of its berth into a wider area, where the yacht can turn. Then it's my turn. I let go of the stern line. I'm only steering gently, with no throttle. It works fine. I am grateful for the great service.

I have chosen the Des Saints archipelago as my next destination. I want to go to Anse du Bourg, because there are mooring buoys there where you can moor for a fee. The wind blows from the east at Force 6. I sail on a close-haul and really enjoy it. After a nice 27 NM leg, I reach the bay ahead of the archipelago in the evening. It is well-protected from the trade winds in the front part.

Somehow I actually already expected this: there are no free mooring buoys, and the free anchorage area behind the buoys is also very crowded. I find a gap at the beginning of the anchorage, and hope it will do. I let out 30 m of chain, which looks okay from my point of view. A woman on a neighbouring yacht disagrees: I can't believe she is standing at the bow of her boat shouting at the top of her voice, trying to chase me away. I find her behaviour uncalled-for, and ask her to radio me. Shortly afterwards, the skipper very politely and almost apologetically answers my call in the finest English, and explains that they have let out 50 m of chain, and my anchor is too close to theirs. There really is a danger of getting in each other's way. I wouldn't argue with that, and am happy to give in, now that they have remembered their manners.

I have to lift the anchor in medium conditions. To avoid any further conflicts, I position myself at the end of the anchor area with plenty of distance to all the other boats. The bay opens to the Atlantic in the northeast here, and the east wind is stronger. I don't really like the spot, but I anchor at 10 m depth and let out the whole 50 m chain, as the gusts of wind reach 24 knots. For safety's sake, I lower the 20 kg plate anchor to port and, although I attach the line to the bow cleat at the end, I just leave the line loose on deck. In the unlikely event that the first anchor does slip, the second one should provide some extra grip. At least that's the theory. Fortunately, the wind gradually dies down. But I don't think it is safe to leave *Jambo* alone so soon after arriving, so I don't go over to the island today. Instead, I enjoy a relaxing afternoon on board.

The next day is also very windy, but there's a brief calm forecast for 4 pm. I want to use that time to have a look around the small town. The wind dies down quite punctually in the afternoon, and I see a dinghy being lowered into the water from the neighbouring boat. Apparently, we have the same plan. It takes me ten minutes to drive to the town in acceptable conditions. After the experience at Pointe-à-Pitre, I don't feel particularly comfortable leaving *Jambo* on her own. I hope everything will be all right. At least the second anchor reassures me a bit. On reflection, I have decided the second anchor's only real purpose was to reassure me. I have no idea if the plate anchor would have provided any additional hold on the sandy seabed, it is not really likely.

I moor the dinghy to a jetty for fishing boats, and lock the outboard motor with a 7 m wire rope and padlock. I pass the rope through an eyelet in the dinghy, so that both are bound to the jetty via the wire rope. This will be my standard procedure when I go ashore for the rest of my Caribbean trip - even at night at anchor. Better safe than sorry.

The town looks lovely. It is neat and tidy. Everywhere the houses are painted bright Caribbean colours: blue, red, orange, yellow. Yes, this is what I imagined it would be like. I have a drink in one of the small restaurants and keep an eye on my dinghy. Unfortunately, the kitchen is not open yet. Towards evening, I head back. The wind has picked up again, and I am glad to see *Jambo* still safely anchored at the spot where I left her.

The forecast for the next week is for winds of Force 6 to 7 from the northeast. I am not happy, seeing as we aren't well-sheltered, and there isn't much to do here. So, the next day I decide to sail to the leeward side of Guadeloupe in the hope that things might be calmer there. Now I have to lift the anchors under difficult conditions, wind Force 6 and a light swell. Although I'm quite good at this by now, it takes me forty-five minutes to pull up both anchors. I jam my finger, but only lightly. Thank goodness I am wearing gloves! There is always a risk of getting my fingers caught in the anchor line on the cleat and injuring myself badly. Due to that experience I put the electric windlass at the top of my list.

I contact the Marina de Rivière Sens via e-mail, but receive no reply, so I choose the small bay of Anse à la Barque as my next stop, which is a few nautical miles north from the marina. It's rough sailing through the archipelago to the main island of Guadeloupe at first, but on the leeward side of the island things improve greatly. The bay is very nice, and there are already several sailing yachts moored there. I drop the anchor to 7 m and let out 30 m of chain. It is wind Force 1, which is a stark contrast to the last bay, where it was Force 6. I like it here. It's raining, but the rain feels good and cools me down a bit. It is very hot today.

I stay for one night, and then I'm off again. It is beautiful here, but there is nothing to do. Îlets Pigeon and Malendure are about 5 NM further north, and there is a little more infrastructure. When I raise the anchor, it is rainy again, but not cold.

After a short sail, I arrive and like what I see. I anchor in just under 10 m water depth about 300 m offshore, and let out 30 m of chain. I go swimming, and it is already afternoon when I go over to the beach in the dinghy and moor at an excursion jetty. I get caught in a heavy shower. I like it here, there's a lovely beach with stalls and restaurants, even if there are lots of tourists, and it is quite crowded. I am lucky, because I manage get a table in one of the restaurants. I really appreciate not having to cook again today.

The next morning, I take the dinghy and head to the southern part of town. There is an access channel to a lagoon where the locals moor their small motor boats. I leave the dinghy here and have a look around. It doesn't take long to find a supermarket where I can buy groceries for the next few days, before I return to *Jambo*.

At lunchtime, I go back to town, and have lunch and a beer for 15 euros in one of the typical restaurants. I really like the fact that they are so rustic and authentic.

Luckily, I am back on board when the wind picks up strongly in the afternoon. At the anchorage, the wind is up to over 32 knots from the east, even though we are on the leeward side of the island. The neighbouring yacht's anchor slips, and the crew have to lift it and then anchor again. Suddenly, my anchor alarm goes off. I check the Navionics app, and see that *Jambo* is slowly moving west. Now I have no choice, and have to pull up my anchor too. A young couple on a catamaran watches me with pity.

I look for a new spot, let out my entire 50 m chain in 10 m water depth, and drop the plate anchor again. The wind is now blowing steadily at 32 knots. I won't be going ashore in the dinghy today. It's too risky. I see the two people on the catamaran, which is about 60 to 70 m ahead on the port side, get their dinghy ready and go ashore. I think: *They must have a guardian angel and a really reliable anchor.*

About an hour later, I am sitting on deck, leafing through my cruising area guide to find out more about my next destinations. I look up randomly and notice that the catamaran is quite close, no more than 30 m away. I put my book down at once, and check *Jambo's* position on the electronic sea chart. Everything is fine, but the catamaran is moving slowly but surely astern, towards the open sea, and possibly speeding up. I try to spot the crew somewhere on the shore. But all I can see is their empty dinghy lying on the beach. Slowly, the catamaran drifts past to port.

What should I do? Launch the dinghy and sail over? That would be putting *Jambo* in danger if her anchor were to slip without me on board. I also don't feel entirely comfortable going out in the dinghy in offshore winds. If the outboard motor were to break down, it would be impossible for me to row back safely, and I would be putting myself in danger. And what might the owners think if they come back and find me on board their boat, far from their original anchorage? It could lead to some tricky questions. Would they believe me if I said I was trying to rescue their boat, not trying to steal it?

I decide to send out a sécurité VHF radio message to warn the other ships about the drifting catamaran. Promptly, the Maritime Rescue Coordination Centre in Martinique answers. I explain the situation. But, there is nothing they can do, as there are no ships in the vicinity. They ask me to keep an eye on the catamaran.

The catamaran has already passed *Jambo,* and is in slightly deeper water, 15 m according to the chart. It is drifting towards a spot marked with some diving buoys. There is a wreck there, and divers often sail over to go diving from their boats. Fortunately, there is no one there at the moment.

The catamaran passes between the buoys, and then comes to a sudden halt. The anchor must have got caught in the wreck. *How lucky they are!* An hour later, I see the couple approaching their anchorage, looking for the catamaran. They stop at a neighbouring boat and ask the crew, who first point to the catamaran, which is now about 200 m further out to sea, and then to me. At full throttle, the two of them race their dinghy over to their boat. Very quickly, they raise anchor, which goes amazingly well, and sail a nautical mile further south and anchor there, as far away as possible from the scene.

In the evening, the wind dies down and a dinghy stops beside *Jambo.* It's the couple from the other neighbouring boat. Two lovely Americans who have come to the Caribbean to sail for a few months and are on their way south. They overheard my radio call, and told the two catamaran sailors that I had contacted the rescue centre. We chat for a bit before they go back to their boat.

What an exciting afternoon! Although, I have to admit that I don't like the fact that my anchor slipped again, for the second time running. It gives me food for thought. The bottom of the anchorage was sandy both times. But there is also some vegetation, as I could see when I pulled up the anchor. I bought this Delta anchor in Lanzarote. Maybe it's not so good? I also think that a stronger chain, which would also be heavier, might be a good idea. So I add the following items to my list: 10 mm chain and Rocna anchor.

The next morning, I decide to sail to the next bay. It is a short distance to Anse Deshaies, a really beautiful bay. But it is very crowded and the wind is blowing again at Force 5 to 6. I try to find a good place to anchor. I let down the anchor and then decide I am too close to the rocks, so I have to pull it up again. The second time, I'm too near a smaller boat, and as I drop anchor, we get so close that the yachts almost touch each other.

So I raise the anchor again and let *Jambo* drop back a ship's length. People are watching sceptically, but *Jambo* is three boat-lengths away. Nobody says anything, so it must be okay. The anchor is at 7 m depth with 40 m of chain let out. Of course, I'm exhausted after having to anchor by hand three times. Nothing seems to be going right today. I wait to see if the anchor is going to hold before I venture ashore. I put two exclamation marks after the electric windlass on my list, so that I don't forget about it after I've put *Jambo* in storage for the winter. It's odd, but when I am at home, my sailing experiences fade away, and then there is always a chance that I'll forget something important that needs doing.

The next morning, the wind is still blowing at Force 5 to 6, and I lower the second anchor again before going ashore in the dinghy. At the jetty, I ask how to pronounce 'Deshaies' to get the name right in the video. It's pronounced 'Dee', I'm told.

I walk through the tranquil town, and here, too, I get those authentic Caribbean vibes. Pretty streets, small shops, a beach with palm trees where a few locals are barbecuing food. There are also plenty of restaurants. At lunchtime, however, it is very crowded. Luckily, I find a spot near the water, and can keep an eye on *Jambo* in the distance at the anchorage, tugging away at the anchor chain while I enjoy my meal. I'm a little restless, and head back as soon as I've finished. My experience two days ago means I'm more nervous about going ashore now.

The next day I want to sail on again, and choose Port-Louis as my next stop. There is a marina marked in the cruising guide, and on the nautical chart, and I plan to stay there. The guidebook also warns of a shallow entrance, but on the chart it doesn't look so bad, and the harbour basin is marked in white, with a water depth of 2.7 metres.

I set off at dawn and use the time under engine to bake a loaf of bread. Today the wind is blowing strongly from the east at wind Force 6. The swell coming from the northeast is about 2 to 3 m high. So I'm in for a rough ride and a slightly tougher day of sailing. I sail as close to the wind as possible, and so far north, that I get a glimpse of Antigua and Montserrat to the west, and Guadeloupe to the south. They are all quite close together. After tacking, I'm on a good course of about 140 degrees, with the bearing for Port-Louis at 150 degrees. This is fine, and I can easily adjust my course later on.

Then I'm in the lee of Guadeloupe where the wind drops a little, and the swell goes down a lot. Port-Louis is to port, and I sail along the long white beach towards the marina. I can already see the masts of a few sailing yachts, which seem to be a similar height to *Jambo's*. *So, my hunch was right. The cruising guide is wrong again! If those yachts could get into the marina, then so can Jambo - with her shallow keel and a draught of 1.55 m.*

I approach the harbour entrance and everything looks fine. The water depth is down to 2 m. I continue at a slow speed. Then the depth gauge measures 1.6 m. I've never tested to see how accurate it is; there is probably some level of uncertainty. The next moment I'm grounded, and the depth gauge reads 1.2 m. I wonder how the others got in? The tidal range is only 15 cm, so it doesn't make much difference, and can't be the problem.

But for now, I have other things to worry about. I entered the marina very slowly and should be able to get out if I move backwards, I think. I put the engine into reverse, but nothing happens. I increase the power until we are on full throttle, but *Jambo* doesn't budge. *Damn it! I'm such an idiot, getting stuck here in the harbour entrance, despite all the warnings in the cruising guide!*

I keep a lookout for other boats, but there's not much going on here, practically nothing in fact. Then I see a few people walking on the small quay wall, but they don't take any notice of me. What do I do now? Launch the dinghy and get help?

Heeling is the magic word. The wind is still blowing from the east, from starboard for me. It is only Force 4 here, but maybe if I can get *Jambo* to heel enough, we can set her free. I hoist the mainsail first, and *Jambo* tilts slightly to port, with the engine running on full throttle astern. But, *Jambo* doesn't move. So I hoist the genoa as well. Now *Jambo* heels a lot more, and starts to turn leeward. The problem is, that's not what I want. The harbour entrance is wide enough, thank goodness, but I'm not happy yet, and *Jambo* fails to move further out to sea.

She is standing upright across the entrance with the wind coming from astern. I apply full throttle astern, because I don't want us to drift onto the stones of the rampart. It will definitely be shallower close to the edge of the harbour entrance. Fortunately, *Jambo* keeps on turning until the wind comes from port, so that the sails turn and she heels more strongly. I back the genoa, and at full power ahead, *Jambo* starts to move very slowly at first - then all of a sudden, she is free. Thank God!

Mortified, and soaking wet from all the exertion, I head out into the open water, haul in the sails, drop the anchor off Port-Louis to a depth of 6 metres, and let out 30 metres of chain. Feeling very cross with myself, I manage to calm down. Then I fetch my snorkel mask and inspect the underwater hull. As far as I can see, there is no damage, except for the coat of antifouling at the bottom of the rudder blade, which looks a bit scraped. Everything really is okay.

Jambo is the only yacht anchoring. In the bay of Anse Deshaies, there wasn't much room, and I was close to all the other boats. Here I experience the other extreme. It's just me and a kilometre-long beach. I don't really like this either, as I'm a bit worried about uninvited guests who might take advantage of the lonely setting. I watch any passing boats very carefully. By evening, there are a few boats out, mostly local fishermen, and I see my worries were unfounded. Guadeloupe is a safe island.

Today I use up the last of my provisions. There's not much left. I find a vegetarian lentil stew. I have no idea who bought it or when, but it is still edible, and tastes delicious. Feeling very tired, I watch the sunset and then crawl into my bunk. I am looking forward to exploring the town tomorrow.

It is a quiet night and I sleep really well. At noon, I take the dinghy over to the marina, as it is easier to moor it there. I noticed breaking waves on the beach this morning, and decide it doesn't look safe to land there. Arriving at the marina, I tie the dinghy to one of the floating pontoons. Of course, I still haven't got over running aground yesterday, and take a look at the yachts in the marina. There are a few catamarans, and one larger boat. Of course, most of them have shallower draughts, but there are also a few keel yachts here, about the same size as *Jambo*. Presumably, they all have shorter keels and shallower draughts.

Having inspected the boats, I make my way to the centre of town, and spot the first restaurant at once. It looks really nice, but I need to find a supermarket before I can stop for something to eat. Ten minutes later, I've reached the church in the middle of town, and ask my way. Some of the houses here are quite dilapidated-looking. The town has obviously seen better days. I find the supermarket, and then I head back to the beach, where there are plenty of restaurants. Here, too, they are quite full, but I manage to get a table, and enjoy not having to cook again. After lunch, I go to the supermarket and stock up on food for the next few days. I spend the afternoon swimming and reading the cruising guide to learn more about my next stop: Antigua.

The past twelve days here in Guadeloupe have been fantastic. This is my first time in the Caribbean, and I have been able to get a good impression of the place. Even without being able to speak much French, I have managed to get by. Tomorrow I sail on to Antigua and I'm really looking forward to it.

Link to video

Chapter 10: Antigua and Barbuda

Saturday, 15 February

I've weighed anchor, the sails are set, and I am on my way to Antigua. *Jambo* is making good progress, and with winds of 5 to 6 Beaufort, I have reefed the sails considerably. There's a moderate swell of about 2 meters from east-northeast.

Then Antigua appears on the horizon, and shortly afterwards I see a large sailing yacht behind me. I have to stay on course, because the other yacht is in the overtaking sector. *Sailing Poland*, a Volvo Ocean 65, comes close, but then drops off to port at the last moment. It is very impressive to watch her sail by so close. Everyone waves.

Now it is about 1.5 NM to the entrance of English Harbour. First, we enter Freeman's Bay. It's lovely, but full. My cruising guide tells me there are anchoring possibilities and some mooring buoys at the back of English Harbour. So I leave Freeman's Bay to starboard for the time being, sail on into English Harbour, and pass Nelson's Dockyard, where some superyachts are moored. When I reach the rear part of the harbour, I am not impressed, especially as the yachts here are quite close together.

So I turn around and sail back to Freeman's Bay. I spot a gap in the anchorage area, and am about to drop anchor, when the skipper of a small sailboat calls to say I can't stop there. While I am still debating with him, someone in a smart-looking dinghy comes by, and suggests another spot. He informs me that the small yacht is probably hanging on just one anchor line, and has been swinging in wide circles. I'm happy to accept the suggestion, and sail to the recommended spot, where I drop anchor at 3 m depth and let out 12 m of chain.

Done - I am now in Antigua, in the famous Freeman's Bay. This is a real highlight for me! I savour the moment but soon decide to get the dinghy ready and go ashore to clear in. It doesn't take me long to find out where to go. All the offices are in one building at different counters. First, I have to go to Customs, where I am told that I must enter all my details on the PC. There are three PCs; one of them is free. Here I first create an account, and then click through the various questions. It takes a while, but I manage okay.

Then I return to Customs, where the woman wants to see all my documents. She asks me where I have come from. "From Guadeloupe," I tell her, and show her my customs clearance document from Pointe-à-Pitre. Then she wants to see my other clearance document. "Oh dear! I completely forgot about clearing out," I admit. She is not amused, and gives me a good telling off, which I endure with a rueful look on my face, apologising as best I can.

Thankfully, I do not have to sail back to Guadeloupe and clear out properly. I guess I am not the first person this has happened to, because all I have to do is write a letter to the Customs Office in Guadeloupe, explaining when I left and why I had not cleared out. The officer hands me a blank sheet of paper and a pen, and tells me to start immediately. So I write the letter and include an apology for my mistake.

When I give the woman my letter, she examines it carefully before adding it to my other documents, still scolding me all the while. I apologise again, promising to mend my ways, and am curtly sent off to Immigration, which is at the next counter. Another woman checks my documents, photocopies my passport and my ship papers, stamps my docket, and sends me back to Customs. There, everything is checked again before I am sent to the Port Authority, which is at the counter next to Immigration. Here, I am asked how long I will be staying, and then the permit is issued. At the next counter, I pay the cashier about 140 Eastern Caribbean dollars. That is the local currency and the equivalent of just under 40 USD. I am then sent back to Customs, where the woman checks everything one last time, and stamps another document. At last, she hands everything back to me and hopes I will have a pleasant stay.

I have managed to pay the mooring fee for Freeman's Bay and the sailing permit in one go, am cleared in, and have completed all the necessary formalities. I can stay in the vicinity of Antigua and Barbuda for almost four weeks. After that, I am allowed to extend my stay or will have to leave. The whole procedure took less than half an hour. Although the process was quite complicated, it was very well organized. And it was all my fault anyway. I don't think I will ever forget to clear out again in my entire life!

I plan to stay here for a few days and then explore Antigua and Barbuda, the two main islands of this twin-island nation.

The next morning, I have a chat with the people from the neighbouring yacht who so kindly helped me yesterday. They are an American family cruising the Caribbean on their catamaran. A couple of their friends are on another sailing yacht, also with kids, all between the ages of six and fourteen. The kids spend all day playing together on the two boats, swimming and sailing the dinghies. It feels a bit like paradise. I don't ask about school, although I do wonder. They invite me round for the next evening, which is very kind, and give me a few more tips, like where to find the dinghy jetty, rubbish bins and the supermarket.

I head off in the dinghy to dispose of the first few bags of rubbish. I have accumulated quite a bit since leaving Pointe-à-Pitre. I wander through Nelson's Dockyard. The historical marina is named after Lord Admiral Horatio Nelson, who was stationed here several hundred years ago. Today, it is a small open-air museum. Many of the historic buildings have been preserved, and there are even some cannons on display in a well-kept park. I also find a sailmaker, A & F Sails. Without further ado, I go in to ask about getting my genoa sail repaired. The clew ring, which nearly tore off on the last miles of the Atlantic crossing, needs to be sewn back on again. I'll bring the sail over tomorrow.

I feel wonderful, and really enjoy walking across to the Falmouth Marina. Everything looks lovely, with plenty of Caribbean flair. I also pass a few restaurants. The prices seem rather high to me, and almost everything is listed in USD, not in Eastern Caribbean dollars (EC).

At midday, I treat myself to a delicious lunch of chicken wings and steak, in one of the restaurants in Nelson's Dockyard, right beside the pier. I haven't eaten this well in a long time. I treat myself to a couple of Carib beers to wash it all down, and end up paying 70 USD, which I have to pay in USD. The prices here are far higher than in Guadeloupe.

 At the pier, I meet Kwami, from the diving school. He does all kinds of underwater work, but as far as I know, *Jambo* doesn't need anything done. I

take his card just in case, and go back to the boat, where I let the day wind down very pleasantly.

The next day begins with beautiful sunshine and more useful tips from my neighbours. I learn that I can buy SIM cards with data volume at the Crab Hole Supermarket. So I take the dinghy over again at lunchtime. I have another nice meal, in a different restaurant this time, and then buy a card with 10 GB data volume in the store at the pier. Shawn, at the counter, kindly reconfigures my mobile phone for me, so that the SIM card works.

In the afternoon, I film a small live update, which I cut and render on the laptop straight away. When I am finished, I upload it, ready to be published the next day. In the evening, I go to visit my American neighbours. Another couple joins the two families I have already met. Cate and Deaken come from near Boston, and their boat is called the *Yankee*. We have a lovely evening. They make this single-handed sailor feel very welcome.

Bottom right: Freeman's Bay
In the background: Nelson's Dockyard

The next morning, I upload my video and then jump into the dinghy to drop off my sail. It will be ready in a couple of days. This time, I find a French restaurant for lunch, and enjoy it very much. In the afternoon, I edit the next video.

During the night, the wind picks up, and I decide to drop the second anchor for safety. Things calm down again, but the wind shifts several times, and I end up with my two anchors tied up in knots, and not holding very well. *Jambo* starts to drift in the morning, and I wake up to friendly shouts nearby. We are too close to a French yacht that dropped anchor here late yesterday. As far as I'm concerned, the boat was a little too close to *Jambo* to begin with, but I don't say anything. They are keeping clear of the stern with a boat hook.

But it is not a problem. I start the engine, and drag my anchor in the direction that is free, which should give me a bit of time. Then I untangle the anchor lines and drop the plate anchor and line again. The main anchor is so heavy with the bundled chain ball that I can't get it on deck. I actually have to free the knotted chain wrapped around the anchor under the water.

Obviously, I am no great anchorman, I think, just as a yacht drops anchor at a good spot with plenty of room. I decide to move *Jambo* across. It is almost where I originally planned to anchor, and happens to be next to the *Yankee*. I drop the anchor to 5 m depth, let out 30 m of chain and make sure the anchor is well set. I stow the plate anchor away. Now I can stop worrying for the rest of my stay. Cate and Deaken are great neighbours who keep an eye on *Jambo* when I am out.

I say hello to everyone in the neighbouring boats, and make sure they are happy for me to anchor here. They all are.

Atlantic rowers keep entering English Harbour. They usually set off from the Canary Islands, and cross the Atlantic in a rowing boat with one to four rowers on board. These are, of course, high-tech rowing boats with keels, small berths and electric autopilots. Nevertheless: what an achievement to cross the Atlantic using just muscle power! I am truly in awe!

In the afternoon, I go shopping again, and meet Guido, who is from the Black Forest, on the pier, and whose yacht, *Imperia* is moored here. We have a beer together. And so the days go by. There is always something to do, and plenty of lovely people to meet. Like the German sailing family from Hilden. Nina, Ron and their three-year-old daughter Lea, are sailing their yacht *Cheers,* round the Caribbean. They drop anchor not far from *Jambo*. Of course, I pop over to say hello, and they invite me in for a beer. We have a lovely afternoon and arrange to have dinner together on one of the next evenings.

I am beginning to feel restless, because I have been in Freeman's Bay for six days now. But I am also having a lovely time, enjoying the relaxed rhythm of life here, with my small social network, good infrastructure, and plenty to do. On Thursday evenings it's Reggae Night at Shirley Heights, and of course, I join in. Here too, I meet all kinds of people. It is great fun.

The next day I pick up my sail. It costs 180 USD, which is more than I had expected. Last time, I paid 50 euros to have it mended in Germany. Of course, I'd expected a certain Caribbean surcharge, but not this much. Once again, I have to pay in USD, as the local currency, EC, is not accepted here either. The work has been done very well though, and I'm glad it is sorted.

Someone tells me that the divers here provide great underwater services, and I'm reminded of Kwami, who gave me his card at the very beginning. Since then, I have noticed that a lot growth accumulated on *Jambo's* hull during the crossing, including small barnacles. I want this removed. Without further ado, I drive over, and for 4 USD per foot, that is 136 USD for *Jambo*, they agree to do it.

The next day, two divers arrive in a dinghy, and clean the underwater hull, using a metal spatula for the rough stuff and the shells, and a plastic spatula and coarse cloth for the final polish. After three quarters of an hour, they are done, and *Jambo* looks wonderful. I am thrilled. They also clean up the saildrive, and notice that the front large anode is badly corroded and needs to be replaced. They don't think it will survive the return-trip. They could do it, but I decide to talk to Kwami first, regarding the price.

Unfortunately, I am missing some anodes. I was sure that I still had a spare set on board but I'm wrong. I installed the last on last winter. This is annoying. I talk to Kwami, and he suggests I look in the Budget Marine shop. He offers to do the work for nothing, since I've won him a few clients. In fact, I did recommend him to some of the sailors on neighbouring boats.

I decide to walk to the Budget Marine shop, which takes about twenty minutes. It's not a big store, but they have all sorts of anodes. It would be a huge coincidence if they happened to have the right one for my saildrive, but in fact, they have two - and I buy one of them. Very satisfied, I take it back to the diving centre, and Kwami promises to send over his two divers' the next day. They arrive in the afternoon and get the job done. I am very grateful.

The next day, I want to take the bus to St. John's to see the town, but it is a Saturday, and the bus does not arrive. Buses obviously don't run as often on weekends. So I postpone my trip until Monday. I'm planning to leave on Tuesday. On Monday, the buses are up and running again, and I take the opportunity to see the island's capital. It is not as great as I expected. Everything seems a bit run down. In the harbour are two large cruise ships, and the streets are full of American tourists. I am lucky to be able to grab some lunch at Hemingway's Caribbean Cafe.

On Tuesday, I am ready to leave, when my electric toilet stops flushing properly. I have to postpone my departure. I guess the seawater pump must be to blame, so I remove it and have a look. However, the pump seems to be in perfect working order, so I install it again, but it only works briefly before stopping again. After an hour's work, that means I am back to square one, but I'm soaked in sweat now, because it's 30 °C below deck. I check the control relay, but that's not the problem either.

Then I disconnect the hose, and lo and behold, the pump starts working. *Of course!* It is a pressure-controlled pump that shuts down when the pressure on the output side is reached, just like my fresh water pump here on board. Therefore, the fault must be somewhere in the toilet itself. So I have to dismantle it completely. It's a lot of work, but not a problem, since I know how everything is mounted, because I put in the toilet myself a few years ago. I notice an extra valve you only need when you use water from the fresh water tank to flush the toilet. In my case, it is redundant so I bypass it. I put everything back in and the toilet flushes this time, but no water is pumped out.

So I remove the toilet again, only to discover that it is clogged with bits of a brown, rocky substance. Removing and re-installing the toilet has loosened deposits in the hoses on the pump-out side. Now comes the gross part of the job. I remove the hoses and pipe sections, which I have to clean and free from muck. It is nearly evening before I am finally finished, and I feel well and truly whacked. Sailing is fixing things in the most beautiful locations, as they say. Fortunately, it doesn't happen that often.

Wednesday, 26 February

It's Wednesday, and I've been here for ten days now - much longer than originally planned. But things keep coming up. Today, the weather is not so good, and I toy with the idea of staying another day, but quickly decide against it. If I don't leave now, I will be stuck here even longer, as another good reason to stay is sure to crop up in the next few days.

Slowly, I'm beginning to understand why sailors feel they'll never get away, because something always keeps coming up. The longer you stay, the harder it is to weigh anchor or cast off the lines.

I make a final trip to Nelson's Dockyard in the dinghy, to say goodbye to Shawn at the Crab Hole Supermarket, and to Kwami, and all my other friends in the bay. After that, I lift the anchor and take on some more water and diesel at the petrol station, before finally heading out of Freeman's Bay into open water in the early afternoon.

The day is cloudy and rainy; the wind blows with Force 5 from east-northeast. I have chosen Green Island to the east, as my next destination, where I would like to drop anchor. It is a good course and I get there in the early evening. There is only one sailing yacht here, the Norwegian *Hello World*. I sail on into the bay to check the water depths. Unfortunately, my chart is not as accurate as I would like, and the front of the keel briefly touches the ground.

I head back over to the Norwegian yacht to see what the people there think. There is a very nice Norwegian couple on board, enjoying some time off on their boat. They warn me that it gets flat to the north, as I have just found out. I drop the anchor close to their stern, and allow *Jambo* to drift out with the wind as the anchor digs in. Everything holds firm with 30 meters of chain. The weather improves, and I spend a lovely evening relaxing.

The next day the weather is beautiful again. But rainy days are all part of the Caribbean experience. The climate is warm and humid, which is why the vegetation is so lovely and green.

I take the dinghy over to the beach. Green Island is actually un-inhabited, but is leased by a charter company that brings guests over daily on two catamarans. However, other visitors are al-lowed to land on the island and swim on the beach. It is still early, and so I am all alone on this magnificent white beach. The water is brilliantly turquoise and clear. It is like a dream come true! This is exactly what I imagined the Caribbean beaches would be like. I love this.

Afterwards, I explore the area some more, sailing to Nonsuch Bay in the north, and on from there to Brown's Bay, where Har-mony Hall is supposed to be. My cruising guide says it is a lovely restaurant. I find Brown's Bay, and see a sign to Harmony Hall,

but I'm not in luck because the restaurant is closed for renovation. *Too bad!* I go back to *Jambo,* and go snorkeling on the nearby reef, which is interesting, but not very colourful.

In the afternoon, an American couple comes by. They are moored in Nonsuch Bay, and just want to say hello, because they have got a BAVARIA, too. We enjoy a pleasant chat before they go on their way. In the meantime, a French yacht has also arrived. I drive over and greet the young family. They have a permanent berth in Guadeloupe, and fly over during their holidays to sail here. That is a nice concept I haven't considered before.

I feel happy and content, enjoying my time here, and although I am a solo sailor, I don't really feel lonely.

The next day, I want to go further into the northern part of Antigua, and have set my sights on Long Island. East of Antigua there are many offshore reefs, and only a few safe passages. In some places, sailors have left warning notes on the electronic chart, saying when the chart is not accurate. I decide to sail the long way around the northeast side of the island, and then head from north to south, as this looks doable on the chart. I sail on a northerly course along the east coast, with a good sailing wind. Then suddenly, I see a catamaran zigzagging through the reefs to port.

I study the chart again, and see that the boat is sailing through the Bird Islet Channel, which I had considered too risky and therefore did not take. If the map is right, it looks doable after all. There is no user note on chart accuracy here, but if the cat can do it, then so can I. I haul in the sails. I also remember the forward-looking sonar scan, which I haven't used at all so far. I turn it on and select a range of 25 m ahead, and sure enough, it shows me the bottom structure, with depths in that range. I wish I knew how accurate the information is at this point.

I head on a westerly course into the reefs and the Bird Islet Channel. I'm only cruising at 4 knots under engine. Sure, the cat has made it too, and has passed me by now. But of course, there is no way of knowing what draft it might have. I can see reefs in the water ahead, everywhere. You can spot them because the waves break very gently above them, and the colour of the water is a little greener than the rest of the sea. My pulse rate and adrenaline levels shoot up. I am very tense, and keep shifting my gaze from the sea chart to the water and forward scan, and back again. Now I have to swerve past something for the first time, and sure enough, the forward scan shows an obstruction, like a wall beneath the water - so there is a reef there. This is what the chart says as well, and I change course to the south. The forward scan shows clear water ahead, but shortly afterwards, I have to change course to southwest, because of the next reef, and then again to the west.

I make good time, but my heart is racing. Then Long Island appears up ahead. I am doing okay. My tension eases slightly. I see the first small green buoy to starboard. All I have to do now is pass between Long Island and Maiden Island, and get the bay on the west side of the island. But suddenly the scanner shows only 2 m water depth ahead, which means just two handbreadths under my keel. I can't go that way. I must be too close to Long Island. I change direction towards Maiden Island, and make way safely without grounding.

Relief! Jumby Bay is very shallow, and I stay away from the shore before dropping anchor at 2.7 m depth. As I slowly calm down after all the excitement, I take the opportunity to leave a quick note in the Navionics nautical chart, saying that the Bird Islet Channel is navigable, and the chart is correct, with a nice greeting from yacht *Jambo*.

So here I am in Jumby Bay. *Jambo* is the only yacht moored here. I've got a fantastic view of the bay with beautiful turquoise green water. On the shore, a resort blends in beautifully with the palm trees. There are plenty of sun loungers on the beach, but most of them are empty. It's noon, and it is probably too warm for most people at this time of day. It seems odd that there are so few yachts here. Perhaps it is just too shallow.

The cruising guide says there is a restaurant on the beach that accepts guests from anchored yachts who follow the dress code. It is supposed to be a bit up-market, but sounds nice. I put on my best swimming trunks and a fresh polo shirt, and take the dinghy over to the shore to have a look at the restaurant, and reserve a table for the evening if possible.

When I reach the jetty where I hope to moor the dinghy, a security guard comes rushing up and asks me what I am doing. When I tell him, he informs me in a friendly but determined manner that this is private property, and I am not allowed to enter the facility. I tell him I want to have a look at the restaurant, whereupon he says that this is also not possible. To placate me, he says he will ask at the restaurant if I can eat there in the evening, and asks me to wait while he disappears in the direction of the buildings. He returns ten minutes later, and tells me that there are no available tables at the restaurant this evening.

What a shame. I say goodbye, and the security guard kindly wishes me well. I spend the afternoon on board, swimming and lazing around. Towards evening, a British yacht drops its anchor some distance away. When it is dark, I hear music coming from the beach. There seems to be a party going on. I would not have enjoyed that really, I think. I could have dressed up a bit, because I have long trousers and a shirt with me, but I'm not sure if I would have felt comfortable among all the well-to-do guests. I'm actually happier being here on *Jambo* tonight.

The next morning I am greeted by a beautiful sunrise over the island. After breakfast, I raise the anchor and head north through the reefs, out into open water, where everything is fine and not too narrow. I sail to Barbuda with a nice east wind. My destination is Cocoa Bay, in the southeast of the island. As I approach the shore, I turn on my forward scan again, and am relieved to see the water depths are fine. In the bay itself, it is very crowded, and I find a spot at the end of the anchorage area. Unfortunately, I end up anchoring a bit too close to another BAVARIA for my liking, and have to lift and drop the anchor again. After that, I am satisfied, and call across to the neighbouring boat. There are no objections.

Here I am, moored in the next beautiful bay. The sand on the beach is brilliantly white. I know Hurricane Irma wreaked havoc here a few years ago and destroyed most of the infrastructure and buildings. I can still see some dilapidated buildings in the background, but there are a few newer buildings directly on the beach, and there seem to be some tourists there as well.

Hoping to find a restaurant, I get my dinghy ready. I would quite like to eat out again, because I have been cooking for a few days now, and my supplies are starting to run out. I should have bought more food when I had the chance, but I had been expecting more opportunities to dine in a restaurant.

At the beach, I tie up my dinghy, head to a beach bar, and ask if they will be serving food later. No, I am told, and the nearest restaurant is in Codrington, eight miles away. That means cooking for myself again tonight. I spend the afternoon swimming and lazing around.

The next day, I sail around the southwestern headland to Low Bay, on the west side of the island. The forward scan serves me well again. By now I am feeling more relaxed about the reef approaches, having gained some experience. I drop anchor opposite the ruins of a hotel. Here it is much emptier than in Cocoa Bay. I see a paradisiacal, mile-long white sandy beach, stretching out to the north. It is deserted. Here, too, the water is turquoise green. It feels like being in a dream.

I read in a note on the nautical chart that the spit of land that used to separate the inner lagoon from the open sea is gone,

and you can now take a dinghy from Low Bay to Codrington. Codrington is the only town on Barbuda. I imagine strolling along the harbour promenade to a lovely restaurant.

The trip there takes about twenty minutes against the east wind. Arriving at the harbour, I notice that everything here is very basic, and there is no sign of a harbour promenade. There is only a run-down small fishing port. I tie up the dinghy next to another one at a crumbling concrete pier. Then I set off towards the town centre. I pass partially dilapidated and badly damaged houses. Everything looks deserted.

I check Google Maps for restaurants. There are not many. Wanda's Food Palace sounds best to me, and appears to be open. A pleasant casual atmosphere! That sounds good! I walk through almost empty streets. Now and then, I see a car, but there are hardly any pedestrians. When I reach the spot where the restaurant is supposed to be, I can't find it at first. According to the picture in Google Maps, there should be a purple building somewhere here.

Then I find it. But it doesn't look like a restaurant at all. It doesn't even have a sign outside. There is a small stand in front of the building where a few locals are gathered round, chatting. I walk up and see pots on the stand. Then it dawns on me - this must be where the food is sold, and the woman behind the stall must

be Wanda. I ask if I can have something to eat. "Yes, fish or chicken?" I go for chicken, and would also like something to drink. I can get a drink inside, the woman tells me.

So I step inside the house, into an almost empty dark room. There are a few locals sitting on some chairs, and a woman standing behind the bar. They all eye me from top to bottom. I hadn't seen any other light-skinned people on the way either, and must look a bit out of place here, in my red polo shirt with a rucksack on my back. "What do you want?" the woman behind the counter asks sharply. "A beer, please," I reply, and all the guests laugh and nod. What else would anyone want here? Is that what they are all thinking?

I pay 3 USD for the beer. Wanda hands me my food in a disposable box with plastic cutlery, outside. That costs 10 USD. I find a place to sit at a table in the front garden between three other guests, who don't mind me joining them. I am glad that I have found something to eat at last, even if the food is not quite hot anymore. Never mind, at least the beer is cold.

After eating, I make my way back, and as I walk away from the restaurant, everyone watches me leave. I think they must be wondering where I have sprung from. But I enjoyed the experience. On the way back to *Jambo*, I make a detour to the long white beach. There is nobody there. I sit down and enjoy the sound of the waves and the view out into the open water.

The next day I sail back to Antigua and Dickenson Bay. As far as I can tell, according to the map, there seems to be some good infrastructure there. The approach through a few reefs goes well. There are several resorts along the beach, and I amble along until I find a restaurant, where I get a great steak served with some nice cold Corona beer. For a few days now, I have been hearing worrying news from Germany, about a virus with the same name, which is said to be circulating.

In the morning, I sail on to Jolly Harbour, where I find a good place to anchor. I ask my neighbours on an Austrian boat where the Customs and Immigration office is, because I want to clear out and sail to Nevis the next day. I go ashore in the dinghy, taking a few rubbish bags with me. There is a special jetty where yachts can moor briefly, in order to complete the formalities. Customs, Immigration and the Port Authority are all located in one small building. It is very crowded on the porch in front of all the entrance doors. Some people are having a discussion. I ask where I have to go to first. Customs, I am told.

But there seems to be a problem. One crew is engaged in a discussion with the woman at the Customs desk. They leave the office but more people show up, then the woman is on the phone. At some point, I manage to squeeze into the office, where someone tells me to use the PC. I have no idea what I am supposed to do. In between the woman dealing with a complicated case and all the other people waiting, it takes me a while before I can ask what I need to do next.

I find out that I don't have to enter anything on the PC to clear out. The woman writes a note and sends me over to Port Authority next, where the clerk in charge is having lunch. However, I don't have to wait long before she is finished. After a few questions, and some written comments on the note I handed her, I am sent back to Customs, where it is still a bit chaotic and very crowded. A short time later, I manage to get into the office, and there are still discussions going on with the same crew. The woman tells them to write a letter and sends them out.

Then she takes a deep breath, and starts to explain what has been holding her up. She tells me all about the charter company that has not included its guests on the crew list. She has had to call her boss several times to discuss the proper procedure. I nod sympathetically. The solution, she says, is for them to write a letter explaining the issue. I know this already, and can't help smiling to myself.

After that, she sends me to Immigration. Here, I am not allowed into the office. The official comes out, disappears briefly with all my documents, and then hands everything back to me, and tells me to go back to Customs. That's my last stop. I get the last stamps, and after one and a half hours, I've done it. I think things are quite well-organised here, overall. I decide to make a short video in English on the spot, and explain the usual five steps for clearing out here: first Customs, then Port Authority, then Customs again, then Immigration and then Customs again. Behind me, I hear laughter. I didn't realise that people waiting were listening to what I was saying.

I soon find out where the supermarket is, and how to dispose of my rubbish. I go to the end of the marina where I can moor the dinghy. A few restaurants are open and I manage to find something to eat. Who knows when the next opportunity will arise? Then I make my way to the supermarket. When I get there, I can't believe the variety of goods in stock. It seems that they have everything, almost like in a German supermarket. I can't resist and buy a few things that I have not had for a long time.

The next day, I lift the anchor early, because it is over 40 NM to Nevis with a moderate wind from astern. Yesterday, I picked Charlestown on Nevis, to clear in on the island state of St. Kitts and Nevis. I also want to pay a short visit to St. Kitts, the neighbouring island. The nautical chart shows mooring buoys marked in the bay in front of the town, where yachts arriving are expected to moor, first at the yellow ones before clearing in, and then at the white ones after clearing in. This sounds logical. Anchoring is prohibited in the bay. There is a note in the cruising guide describing the town as very picturesque with friendly people. It all sounds very inviting.

I arrive there at around 4 pm, but there are no mooring buoys. A few boats are at anchor, so I decide to drop anchor not far from a Swedish sailing yacht, although my guide says this is not allowed. There is no one on board the other boat. After a short time, however, a family of four arrives in a dinghy. I wave. The man lets his family climb on board before he sails over to me. He excitedly tells me that they have just tried to clear in, but that it was impossible. They've been told to register online, but with no mobile data here, they now need to find an internet café. I do not have any mobile data either, because it is a different network here. "The officers were very rude," the man says. Their passports were taken away and they didn't get them back for 45 minutes. He says he has been in the Caribbean for two years now, but has never experienced anything like this. He tells me they have given up, and are going to find a nice bay for the night. He advises me not to try clearing in here.

Quite honestly, after hearing this story, I have no desire to expose myself to possible arbitrariness of the authorities. My previous experiences with clearing in and out haven't been too bad, so far. Of course, there were some difficulties in Antigua, but that was my own fault. I decide to follow the hint, and find an anchorage. I pick Ballast Bay, which is on the west side of St. Kitts, and offers good protection from the east wind. Maybe I will clear in at Basseterre on Saint Kitts, tomorrow.

After a short trip, I reach the bay and find a good anchorage. Of course, I set the Q flag, since I am not yet cleared in. This is the usual practice. Although there is a small beach club with music playing on the shore and the pleasant smell of food keeps wafting over, I stay on board, according to regulations.

In the night, the water is a bit choppy, and I check to make sure everything is all right at quarter to four am. I also check the sea chart, and notice a comment I hadn't seen before. It says that it is forbidden to anchor here with a Q flag, and that the coastguard checks regularly. If you are caught, it costs 250 USD, and they search your boat.

I immediately raise the anchor, turn off my AIS and motor out of the bay. I don't want to clear in in Basseterre now either. Around sunrise, I am already at the northern tip of St. Kitts with St. Eustatius ahead. My destination today is Sint Maarten, where I am expecting my first visitors to arrive in just a few days' time: Heinz, Wilm and Klaus, the male crew with whom I have done so many cruises.

In the early afternoon, after a great day of sailing with wind Force 5 from the east, the island is straight ahead. It is divided into two parts. The northwest belongs to France, and is called St. Martin. The southeast is independent, and is called Sint Maarten, and belongs to the Kingdom of the Netherlands. The local currency is the Antillean guilder, but mostly you pay in USD, as I am about to find out.

Ahead there are lots of boats cruising off the coast. Apparently, there is a regatta taking place. As I find out later, it is the Heineken Regatta, which lasts a week. A large racing trimaran passes in front of me. It is an incredible sight. Then there is a gap big enough for me to sail across to the bridge that marks the entrance to Simpson Bay. You are allowed to anchor in the bay and then complete all the formalities. Although the bay is crowded, I still manage to get a berth at the edge of the channel. Most of the boats are waiting for the bridge to open, but some are also moored here.

I make my dinghy ready, and ask the crew of a neighbouring boat where to clear in. "The building is right next to the bridge and is blue," they say. I sail across. I can moor the dinghy at a relatively high wall, and manage to scramble up to the top. Sure enough, there is the building. All the departments are in one room, and I first inquire at the cash desk about the procedure. "Goede middag," I say and receive a frown in return. The clerk only speaks English.

I first have to fill out a form, and then go to Customs and Immigration, which is all processed at the same counter. I am cleared in quickly, and can pay the bridge fee at the same time.

Then I hurry back to *Jambo*, because the bridge is about to open. Then off it goes. A large crowd of yachts is waiting to pass through. They start to move - and of course there is some pushing and jostling. I am in the front end of the queue, and manage to get through fairly quickly to Simpson Bay. I have checked out the anchorage north of the bridge. On the map, it looks quite good. I am still in heavy traffic, and decide to head out of the buoyed channel. The chart shows a water depth of 2 to 5 m.

Then another dinghy crosses my path. While I am paying attention to the dinghy and the other shipping traffic, *Jambo* shudders all of a sudden, and a quick glance at the depth gauge tells me that I am running aground. I immediately release the throttle and put the boat in reverse. Fortunately, I can free myself again immediately, and head straight back into the channel. I have already learned that the charts here can be inaccurate, but I hadn't expected quite such a deviation in such a frequented area of Simpson Bay. I stay in the fairway for a while, and then decide to sail back into the anchorage area where other yachts are anchored. *There wouldn't be any yachts there if it wasn't deep enough,* I reason.

Fortunately, everything works, and there is enough room in the middle. At about 3 m depth, I drop the anchor. It is a bit noisy here, because the anchorage is next to the airport, and the flight path is directly overhead. However, there are only a few of planes in the mornings and evenings, so there is not too much disturbance. Now I have a few days left to relax. Next Monday the lads are flying in in.

Link to video

Chapter 11: Sint Maarten, St. Martin and St. Barts

<u>Thursday, 5 March</u>

In the afternoon, I decide to go out in the dinghy and explore the area. The Simpson Bay Marina is here, where I have booked a berth for Monday and Tuesday. We have chosen Sint Maarten as a starting point for all our visitor trips, because the flight connections from Germany are good, and the surrounding islands very interesting. I also book a berth for all our planned visitors' arrival and departure dates, so we don't have to ferry all the luggage back and forth in the dinghy, which would be hard work. I book enough days to receive a small discount. Nonetheless, 68 USD per day is pretty expensive, I find.

Then I discover the famous beach bar, Lagoonies. As luck would have it, it is happy hour and soon I'm having a great conversation with some other sailors over a few Presidentes - the most popular beer here. Mostly it is about the regatta, and where we have just come from and where we are all heading. It's a great afternoon with nice people in a lovely atmosphere.

The next day I go to the Budget Marine shop. It's a huge store, and they seem to stock just about anything anyone could ever want. If they don't have it, they can usually order it for you. It's paradise for any sailor who wants to buy more gear. It is also interesting financially, as prices are similar to Europe. I only buy a few guest country flags for Anguilla, Sint Maarten, (I have only set the Dutch guest country flag once so far), and St. Barts. On the way back, I bump into Ron, Nina and Lea, from *Cheers*, who have just arrived in Simpson Bay as well. It is a great reunion and we arrange to have a barbecue on *Cheers* the next day. They also tell me where to refill my Campingaz gas bottles, and I am grateful for the tip.

Next, I need a SIM card for mobile data, and ask around until I end up in an electronics shop. Unfortunately, they don't have any cards, but one of the employees is kind enough to show me a store about ten minutes away. He tells me that only a few people here speak Dutch, and that although Sint Maarten is under the Dutch crown, they have their own parliament, and the administration is independent of the Netherlands. In the store, I buy a SIM card with data volume, and reward my guide with a cold Presidente for all his help. Back on board, however, I don't manage to get any mobile data - probably due to the settings. I could do with someone like Shawn from the Crab Hole Supermarket in Antigua, who always helped me there. At least I can use the card to make cheap phone calls.

On Sunday, I go to Lagoonies at lunchtime for a bite to eat, and meet Guido, from *Imperia,* again. Here, too, I'm delighted to see him. We chat all afternoon. *Imperia* is anchored well outside the bridge. Meanwhile, he has booked a place on a freighter for his yacht. It is being transferred to Majorca in April. We stay for happy hour, and afterwards I meet a lot of other sailors at the bar. We have a lot of fun and one round follows another.

In the morning, I wake up with a buzzing head and can't remember how I got home. Thankfully, nothing hurts except my head, and the dinghy is properly lashed to the stern. *I must have had one too many*. But it was a very nice evening.

Then I notice an unusual, quiet crackling sound in the hull. In seconds, my hangover is gone, and I am wide awake. What could that be? The noise is definitely coming from the hull, from somewhere in the middle. I check below the floorboards, but there is no water intrusion. It sounds like a rope has caught on the keel, and is banging the hull in several places because of the current. I put on my diving mask and dive down to have a look.

I can't see anything unusual on the hull, or anything caught anywhere. I also can't feel anything out of the ordinary at the transition from the keel to the hull.

I take the dinghy to the marina, since there is free Wi-Fi there, and research the phenomenon on the Internet. I can only find something about pistol shrimps, but no meaningful explanation. I go back and swim down to inspect the hull again. But I don't find any crabs or other animals on the hull. I never did find out what caused that noise! But when I moved to the marina the next day, the sound disappeared and never came back. It remains a mystery to this day.

I am now berthed in the marina, and am expecting my first visitors to arrive today. Heinz, Wilm and Klaus took off from Paris earlier on, and are on their way here. I need to get sorted. The aft cabin has to be cleared, and things cleverly stowed away so that there is enough space for two people to sleep in the aft cabin, and one in the saloon. It's quite cramped on board with four people. When we went sailing together before, it was easier because it was a trip close to home. Now, on a long voyage, I have much more stuff with me, so we've reached the limits space-wise.

My friends arrive late in the afternoon, and it is so wonderful to see them. The lads settle in, and we celebrate the reunion with a jetty beer. In the evening, we eat at the nearby Jumbo restaurant, where the new arrivals get their first taste of the Caribbean. The spare ribs here are probably the best in the world. They are cooked in a slow oven at just the right temperature for hours on end, so all you have to do is suck the meat off the bone. It is a dream.

The next day my new crew members need to rest up. The time difference and jet lag are getting to them. In the meantime, I go to Customs and Immigration, and officially add the three of them to my crew list and check out for the next day, because we want to go to St. Martin - the French part of the island. Actually, I find out that I don't have to clear out from here for St. Martin itself. For once, the advice in the cruising guide and on the Internet don't agree. But it makes no difference, because we want to continue to Anguilla later on, and have to clear out any way.

We spend the afternoon enjoying happy hour. Afterwards, we find a nice beach restaurant and have an early dinner there, before my new crew members crawl into their bunks.

The next morning, we get underway and cast off. We pass through the bridge at 9 am. Then we head west under engine. Along the way, we pass Maho Beach, famous for being so close to the airfield where landing planes fly in just above people's heads. From a distance, it looks very dangerous, but of course, there is plenty of room. After a few hours, we reach Marigot Bay, where I manage to clear in at a marine store without any difficulty. Then we continue north, because we have chosen Îlet de Pinel as our next stop.

The approach does not look easy on the chart, because the water is shallow in places, and the swell of the Atlantic goes right up to the entrance. Someone has also already left a message on the electronic sea chart, warning about breaking waves. Today the swell is about 1.5 m, and we can already see the breaking waves from a distance. Right in the middle, where it is deepest, things seem a bit better, and we are only pushed forward occasionally by a somewhat steeper wave. Still, I am relieved when we finally drop anchor in the shelter of the island. We can already see beach bars and restaurants under the palm trees along the beach, and look forward to going ashore.

We spend almost all of the next day there, enjoying a few Coronas and cocktails. We have a fantastic time, with Caribbean feeling at its best. The next day we head on to Anse Marcel. This is another bay, badly damaged in one of the recent hurricanes. However, there are several buildings under construction, and they should be rebuilt by next season, unless a new hurricane destroys everything again. There is a restaurant and a marina. We drop anchor. As we can't all fit in the dinghy at once, I have to make two trips to get us all ashore. The beach restaurant is open for lunch only. It is a little bit more upscale, but really nice. We have a great day.

The next day we are planning to go to Anguilla. However, we learn that Sint Maarten has issued a ban on entry for people who have been in Germany within the last twenty-one days. This is due to the Corona pandemic. No one was expecting this! The world has been fine here so far. We never dreamed the virus would catch up with us. In retrospect, it seems so naive, but none of us guessed the extent of the pandemic at that time.

This means that Anke's visit will probably be cancelled, and she might not be able to get her planned flight to Sint Maarten next week. We discuss what to do. We can't go back to Sint Maarten, because Heinz, Wilm and Klaus are no longer allowed to enter the country. Having cleared out, they have officially left the country, and their passports have been stamped accordingly. So it means they can't take their return flight from Sint Maarten to Germany now either.

We also decide not to stop in Anguilla. It is too risky. We might end up stranded there. In the end, we decide to sail to St. Barts. This far from home, we realise we feel safer on the French islands, which are a part of Europe. We will work out what to do next when we get there.

Feeling slightly dismayed, we sail to St. Barts, or Saint Barthélemy, as the island is officially called, though most people call it St. Barts. We arrive in the early afternoon, and anchor in the capital, Gustavia. I take the dinghy to the harbour office where I hope to clear us in. They only allow two people in at a time now. "Because of Corona," the port commander explains.

Back on board, I phone Anke, who is already looking for alternatives, and has found a flight to Fort-de-France on Martinique, which she can take tomorrow. We both agree that she should catch the flight, and then fly on to St. Barts from Fort-de-France. We can meet her there, and then decide what to do next. If necessary, the men will have to stay in the Caribbean for another two weeks, and then fly back from Sint Maarten as soon as possible. That means there will be five of us on *Jambo*, including Anke. It's likely we are all thinking the same thing. This is going to be a tight squeeze.

In the evening, we take the dinghy to Gustavia to get something to eat. At the quay wall, there is a small area between the luxury yachts, reserved for dinghies. I moor ours between all the others. Ladies in high-heels, holding champagne glasses, stare down at us from the neighbouring megayacht. They watch us rather poor-looking sailors crawl ashore on our knees, and scramble up the wall. We couldn't care less.

St. Barts, and Gustavia, especially, are famous for attracting the rich and beautiful. We stroll through the town, which we all agree is lovely. But the restaurants are all too expensive. Eventually, we end up in a beer garden, and buy something to eat at a food truck. There is no sign of the pandemic here, and there are no restrictions. However, St. Barts has already reported its first four confirmed Corona infections, and sadly, also a first death.

Anke is already on the plane to Martinique, and has booked a holiday apartment, because she has to spend a night there, before catching her flight to St. Barts the following day. The night is not very quiet at the anchorage. In the early morning hours, I can't sleep anymore, and do some research on the Internet about the current situation. Reports about the Corona pandemic are coming in thick and fast now, and here in the Caribbean more and more islands are locking down.

Around 5 o'clock, I wake Klaus up to discuss the situation with him, and then Heinz and Wilm join us. After a short crisis meeting, we decide to cancel the trip immediately and tell Anke not to fly on to St. Barts. Klaus tries to call the airline to rebook the flight from Sint Maarten. But, after two hours he still has no success. We decide to transfer to Martinique. The lads book flights

from St. Barts to Fort-de-France for the same day. Fortunately, there are seats available on a midday plane. I am going to sail *Jambo* to Martinique single-handed. By now, it is too risky for the four of us to sail there together. The trip takes two days, and with things changing so rapidly now, it is impossible to know whether we will be allowed to enter Martinique in two days' time.

I drive to the harbour office at 8 o'clock to clear us out, while the lads pack their things. Back on board, we weigh anchor and I moor *Jambo* at the ferry terminal briefly, in order to let my friends disembark with their luggage. There is also a cab stand nearby. Hastily, we say goodbye, and I cast off. That was it: our shortest lads' trip ever. Just a moment ago, we were sitting in the coolest beach bars imaginable, and suddenly we find ourselves in the middle of a global crisis that has caught up with us faster than anyone could have anticipated.

I sail *Jambo* south, while the three of them fly to Martinique, where Anke has also arrived safely in the meantime. She has managed to book a room for Heinz, Wilm and Klaus, so that they can stay there until they manage to book a flight back to Europe. They all meet up in the evening. Luckily, my three friends are able to get a flight to Paris the next day, and then have to make their own way back to Germany. The German borders are already closed, but there are still some exceptions for family reunions.

Most of the countries in Europe have now closed their borders, which could affect my own return to Europe if the situation does not improve quickly. There is a big question mark hanging over my return plans.

While I am near the coast, I talk to my daughter on the phone, because she and her boyfriend are hoping to visit me on Sint

Maarten in April. It is impossible to say if that will be possible at this point.

I continue under engine, because there is no wind. I have got just about enough diesel to last me until Martinique, but I need to go more slowly than usual to keep the consumption per nautical mile down.

Chapter 12: Lockdown off Martinique

Tuesday, 17 March

Two days later, I arrive in Fort-de-France before sunrise. I have chosen the boat refuelling station CAP DCML as my destination,  because it is possible to clear in there, and I desperately need diesel and fresh water as well. In the early morning hours, I call Anke and she tells me that on Martinique everything will shut down at 12 o'clock. She already went shopping yesterday with Marie, her landlady at the holiday apartment, and is hoping to go back to the supermarket again today before it closes.

Martinique is going to close! It is a huge shock! The petrol station should be open at 8 o'clock. That will be okay. Shortly before 8 o'clock, two British sailors arrive in a dinghy. They have just come from the customs office at the ferry terminal where you normally clear in, but everything is closed there, they say. Although the office should have opened at 7 o'clock, there's no sign of life. My uneasy feeling intensifies, and I actually start to feeling queasy.

I swap telephone numbers with the two men before they head off again. We promise to let each other know if we hear anything. In the meantime, it's half past eight, and there is still nothing happening at the petrol station. I call the two British men, but everything is still closed where they are too. They say clearing is supposed to be possible in Sainte-Anne at the Boubou Bokits snack bar, and are heading there next.

I am getting more and more nervous. I desperately need to buy some fuel, because my tank is already on reserve, and I can only travel a few more nautical miles without filling up. I decide to see if I can find anyone who can help. Behind the petrol station, I see boats in dry docks. It is a shipyard, and I can see people working on a motor yacht in a large hall. I ask someone why the petrol station is still not open. He tells me that that is odd, and calls the proprietor. After a short phone call where I understand nothing because they speak in French, he tells me that the owner is on his way and will be there very soon.

That reassures me a little. I phone Anke. Marie will drive her over as soon as they have been to the supermarket. Then the man from the petrol station arrives. He runs in and locks the door behind him so that I don't get a chance to speak to him. After a while, he comes out and locks the door again. I speak to him in English, but he doesn't understand me, just shakes his head and disappears again.

Now I am starting to panic. I am cleared out, and in the worst case, I won't be allowed back in again and will end up stranded at sea between the islands. At about 9 o'clock, the British people come back again and tell me that everything is still closed where they are.

Finally, Anke calls me. She is standing with Marie in front of the barrier to the compound, and they can't get in. I run over and at last, we see each other again for the first time in two and a half months. There's no time for more than a fleeting kiss and a short greeting, because we have more pressing issues. It all happens too quickly, like in some tacky movie.

It is too far to carry everything from the barrier to the boat. I ask one of the workers if we drive the car through. Kindly, he comes with me, and opens an element of the fence so that Marie can drive through carefully. As soon as we reach *Jambo*, we load everything on board as quickly as we can, so that Marie can get home. At 12 o'clock everything is going to shut, even public transport will come to a halt then. I ask if the petrol stations are still open, because I urgently need diesel. She thinks we should be able to find one, and offers to drive me. So I grab five reserve canisters and we drive to the next petrol station. I have just entered the country illegally without border controls, and am actually trespassing on French soil. I couldn't care less right now.

As we drive, Marie informs us that for the next fourteen days, public life will be reduced to a minimum everywhere on the island when everything closes at 12 o'clock. She says people will have to stock up on food. Many grocery stores are sold out already. At the petrol station, I manage to squeeze 130 litres of diesel into the five 20-litre cans. We drive back to *Jambo*, open the fence, close the fence, and stow our goods onboard *Jambo*. I press Marie's hand, thanking her, and giving her 100 euros for driving us. Anke has her phone number, and if anything happens, we can call her. Necessity welds us together. We are really grateful. I go back to the fence with Marie, and close it behind her after she drives through.

Then Anke and I cast off and head out to sea and an uncertain future. *What is going to happen to us?* If everything is locked down here, we will probably not be able to clear in. Other islands are already closed, or will follow suit in the next few days. Sailing to a new destination, only to find out that we are not allowed to enter, feels very risky to us.

We decide to sail to Sainte-Anne and take things from there. But we won't arrive before Boubou Bokits closes for the night, and the next day it will also be closed, because it only opens on certain days. We sail against the strong east wind along the south coast of Martinique. The tacking angles are lousy, but I don't want to use the engine, because who knows when or where I

will get the chance to refuel again. In the evening, we arrive in the bay of Sainte-Anne and drop anchor between all kinds of yachts. There must be nearly a hundred boats moored here. I lower the Q flag, because I don't want to attract attention. After some pasta with tomato sauce, we drop into bed exhausted. What a day!

We wake up to a beautiful sunrise. I call the British guys to find out how they got on. They did manage to clear in eventually, but the store is closed now. We talk for a while, and they mention that the boat refuelling station in Le Marin, just a few miles into the bay, is open. I quickly say goodbye, we lift the anchor and head for the petrol station as fast as we can. A few other crews must have heard that the petrol station is open, too, because several yachts are sailing in the same direction. I give full throttle, and ten minutes later, we reach the floating jetty where the petrol pumps are. Several boats are already circling ahead of us. We ask who is last in line, and join the queue.

After half an hour, it is our turn, right next to a boat sailing under the Swiss flag. We can get water here as well, and they also sell Campingaz bottles. Things are starting to look up. Anke chats with the Swiss crew, who mention that they hope to clear in right here at the Capitainerie at Le Marin. I prick up my ears, and ask if they are serious. They think it should still be possible here, and give me rough directions. I hurry to get everything finished quickly. The tanks are soon full with diesel and water, and I buy two additional bottles of Campingaz.

We cast off immediately to look for a good anchorage, and drop the anchor as soon as we find a place. I launch the dinghy and

head over to the marina, where the Capitainerie is supposed to be, as fast as I can. I find the dinghy pontoon and moor there. "So where is the harbour office?" I ask someone, who points me in the right direction. Then I ask someone else who is going the same way to give me a lift. He is going to the Capitainerie, too. When he knocks on the door, it only opens a crack. The man asks if he can remain moored at a buoy in the marina, because he has lost his anchor and is waiting for a replacement. He is told he cannot do that, and that there are no berths available in the marina either. Sounding quite desperate, he demands to know what he should do without an anchor. Eventually, the officers relent, and allow him to stay at the mooring buoy for a few days longer.

Then it is my turn. A man with a mask looks at me and asks what I want. "Customs clearance," I reply. He nods and opens the door wide enough to let me in. Inside, I have to keep my distance. All the officers are wearing masks. I have to disinfect my hands before I can make my request at the counter. Then I am shown to a computer that is sprayed with disinfectant. I enter all my details, and the form is printed out at the counter. While I pay 5 euros, I explain that it was impossible for me to clear in the previous day in Fort-de-France, because everything was closed. The woman at the counter apologises, saying: "These are crazy times." She is right. I am extremely relieved to be cleared in properly at last, and go back to *Jambo* feeling much better.

Back on board, Anke and I start to calm down at last and take a deep breath. We have managed to avoid the worst. We've got some food and drinking water, and the tanks are full. For the next days, we will be able to get by. Now we have to wait and see how long the petrol station will stay open. We need to keep an eye on that, and if it has to close, we will make sure we fill up again beforehand.

The next day, I decide to go shopping, because I've found a Carrefour that isn't too far away. I take the dinghy to the boat dock at another marina, and then walk to the supermarket. When I get there, there is a long queue of people waiting outside. This is because they are only letting in a limited number of people at a time. After an hour, it's my turn, and I pack as much as I can carry into my shopping cart. The shelves are empty, and there is

almost no pasta or rice left. Somehow, I manage to get every-thing I want to buy. Things could be a lot worse.

For the next few days, not much happens. We are in close con-tact with home. Heinz, Wilm and Klaus had a real adventure, getting back from Paris, but have arrived home safely now. We are very relieved to hear that. Fortunately, we can use our phones in Martinique with our normal contracts, because the usual EU roaming charges apply, and we have a fixed rate for phone calls and texts. We just have to top up our data package occasionally. In our situation, it is a great help to be able to stay in touch with the outside world, and keep up to date with what is going on.

We meet Jenny and Stefan, from the *Solviento*, who are anchor-ing outside Sainte-Anne. They suggest we should join them. They say the water is much clearer where they are, it is not far to Sainte-Anne, which has another supermarket, and they get to see turtles every day. I am not so enthusiastic at first, because it is much further from there to the petrol station, and to the Leader Price supermarket, which is even closer than Carrefour, and better stocked.

In the end, however, we decide to relocate the next day. Before we go, I call at the marine electronics store, and am able to buy three batteries to boost my weak battery bank. It hardly lasts through the night because of the fridge. Since the temperature below deck is never less than 30 °C, even at night, the refrigerator keeps starting all the time, and consumes a lot of power.

I go to Leader Price first. It is practical, because you can take your shopping cart to the jetty and simply load everything straight into the dinghy. But here too, I have to queue forever,

before I am allowed into the supermarket. I stand in the heat for two hours. At least they have a very good selection of goods and the shelves are full.

The staff here are all wearing protective masks, and they disinfect the conveyor belts at the checkouts after each customer. When we tell our families in Germany about this, they are astounded by these measures, because at this point, there are no masks or disinfection procedures, and no admission restrictions in the supermarkets in Germany.

Chris is another person we met here. Usually he takes people out on cruises from Le Marin on his catamaran. He tells us the secret of the well-filled shelves, even though everyone has been hoarding purchases for a week now. Le Marin is a large charter base, so the supermarkets around the marina normally cater for a huge demand. With charter guest numbers now down due to the pandemic, but supplies still rolling in, there is always enough. We have been lucky to find this place, I think. It's a small ray of sunshine in all the gloom.

The next day we try to lift the anchor but, unfortunately, I can't pull it up, not even using the engine to help. It won't budge. Heike and Jürgen, from the *Valentine,* also had problems lifting their anchor here a few days ago. They had to dive down and free it, because it was caught in an old, heavy anchor chain. I guess that means we need a diver as well. We phone around, and Jenny puts us in touch with Franck, a French skipper on an X-65, also moored off Sainte-Anne. He is a full-time skipper and takes care of the big luxury yacht for a German owner.

Franck is also a freelance diver. He comes round in his dinghy the next day. He dives down briefly, and when he comes back up, I ask if he there is anything he can do. He tells us he has freed our anchor already. He simply pulled it out of an old chain. Well, that was quick! We are able to lift the anchor without any problems, and can sail to Sainte-Anne and *Solviento.* This is the start of eight weeks of lockdown anchored in the most beautiful bay off Sainte-Anne.

As I write this, I am sitting in wintery Germany in another lock-down. When I look outside from time to time and see the cloudy weather, I like to think back to the lockdown we spent off Martinique. In retrospect, it was probably the most beautiful lock-down in the world for us.

Of course, there are plenty of restrictions and not much to do. On land, we are only allowed to move with a self-issued confirmation of exit. All the restaurants are closed at first. They start to offer take-away food after a while. Supermarkets are open, as is a small fish market, where local fishermen can sell their catch. We are not allowed to meet up with other yachts, as there is a contact ban there as well.

The municipality of Sainte-Anne installs a fresh water connection for the yachts at the jetty, so that the crews of the yachts can tap water. This is a brilliant idea. The municipality of Sainte-Anne also takes care of our rubbish. It is just great. We are very grateful to France, Martinique and the municipality of Sainte-Anne for everything. All the measures are implemented very strictly, but also very fairly. A helicopter circles over the bay once or twice a day. A patrol boat also regularly passes between the anchored yachts to check that people are not meeting up, and no more than one dinghy is tied to the stern of each boat.

In the evenings at 8 o'clock, most of the boats sound their foghorns to remember and thank the people on the front line who are caring for us in these times. Every morning, a small boat arrives, going from yacht to yacht to sell fresh bread, fruit and vegetables. We buy a baguette every morning, and sometimes a little more. On Saturdays, there is a delivery service run by a restaurant, and we take advantage of that offer once or twice as well.

We adjust our lives to the circumstances. After breakfast, we have a swim, and then we go into town to do our shopping. In

the afternoons, we sometimes meet up with fellow sailors for a sundowner, out in the dinghies, or very occasionally on board, when it is dark, and impossible to see if there is more than one dinghy tied up to a boat. Alternatively, you pick up your guests, and then take them back to their boat again.

On Tuesdays, we do the laundry. Several dinghies head off to a water park. This is also closed, but the small area on the beach under the trees is well-protected, and it is a good place to meet secretly. At first, it is just Jenny, Stefan, and us.

From there, it is only a short walk to the launderette. It is located in a building below a restaurant, where it is possible to order a take-away, which of course we do. While the laundry is in the machine, we eat out under the trees at the water park. We almost get caught there once, and have to flee from two gendarmes out on patrol. Fortunately, someone warns us. When a voice shouts, "Gendarmes!" we pack up our food and run to the launderette, before the two gendarmes get to the beach. Several people are allowed in the launderette at the same time, but they are not allowed to eat together out under the trees. The rules are not always very logical, even here.

The next time there are seven of us. A gendarmerie helicopter circles over the bay and flies close by. We sit frozen at the table. Then it flies far out into the bay. So no one saw us. That was lucky! Then, the helicopter turns and flies right at us. We leap in all directions in panic. Some of us hide behind a wooden shack, others under the table. I find cover behind a tree. For a while the helicopter hovers over the water opposite where we are hiding, remaining there for a moment before it flies off. We stop meeting there after that. Even today, I still flinch when I hear a helicopter approaching. It's funny how an event like that can come back to haunt you.

In the meantime, Anke's return flight has been cancelled by KLM, and she is in regular contact with the airline to try to book an alternative flight. They keep fobbing her off, and she has had to inform her employer that she can't return from her holiday as planned. It turns out not to be a problem, however, because her company has announced short-time working for all employees, as business has slumped due to the crisis. Anke is also entitled to paid time off because she has worked overtime.

The situation in Europe is still very tense. Portugal has closed its borders. It only allows Portuguese yachts and pleasure boats in distress to enter the country. In the Azores, you can anchor outside Horta, but you are not allowed in. However, you can order provisions, water and diesel, and have them brought to a jetty in canisters. France and Spain have also severely restricted any travel. Slowly but surely, the world is grinding to a halt.

On board many yachts in the Caribbean, people are feeling increasingly anxious and uncertain about where to go when the hurricane season begins. Between June and October, it's not a good idea to keep your boat anywhere between latitude 10 and 30 degrees north, and we are in Martinique, at 14.5 degrees north. Almost everyone, including us, has joined various WhatsApp groups where there is a lively exchange of information. Some people need extra crew members to support them on the return trip, who now can't fly in due to travel restrictions.

Anyone wanting to sail back to Germany can register on a privately organized website. I do this. The data is forwarded to the German Federal Police, who send me a confirmation e-mail. The Piracy-Prevention Center Directorate is responsible for overseas recreational shipping. I send a few more details, and inform them that I do not need any assistance at present, and that I intend to arrive in Germany in July. At that stage, I will need information on current quarantine regulations, and where to clear in and moor my boat.

Meanwhile, the situation is escalating, and people are starting to panic. Using social networks, some sailors manage to attract the attention of the media with shocking headlines. The media leaps on the story, dramatizing it slightly, so that it becomes worthwhile news. The German Broadcasting Company ZDF is interested, and asks me to participate in a feature. I do an interview, and send them a few recordings. In fact, the feature is broadcast on 29 April in ZDF's 'Nachtjournal' news programme. Our situation is not that dramatic, though. I was always planning to sail back single-handed, regardless of the current situation.

Anke increases the pressure on the airline, and manages to set a deadline. The airline agrees to fly her home by the end of April. This actually has an effect, and Anke gets a return flight for 16 April. It's a pity that she has to fly back so soon. But she can't refuse the flight, as she would lose any right to a return flight if she didn't take it. She will fly via Paris to Amsterdam, from where she can take the train to Germany.

Thursday, 16 April

We are very sad on the day Anke leaves. Despite everything, we've had a great time, even if we could not carry out our original sailing plans. Jenny and Stefan give us a hand, and ferry

Anke across the bay in their dinghy, while I take her luggage. The cab arrives on time, and we say goodbye in tears. Our wonderful time together is over and I am left behind on *Jambo*, all alone.

Now I have to start preparing for my return journey home. I want to leave on 10 May. First, I do an inventory of all my supplies, and make a list of things I still need to buy. *Jambo* is in good shape. It might seem a bit unusual that there is nothing to repair, but she really is fine. In the meantime, I've bought a portable petrol generator to charge the batteries in the mornings. I want to use it on the passage home, and have to buy a few reserve canisters to make sure I take enough petrol with me.

One by one, the first yachts leave the bay on their way back to Europe. Other yachts are loaded onto cargo ships in Le Marin bay. Tina and Bernd, from the *Festina Lente,* have a cargo appointment, and sail their yacht towards the Azores with another couple. Jenny and Stefan are looking for crew members, as are Nina and Ron, who are stuck in Antigua in the meantime. Guido's *Imperia* is already on a freighter bound for Europe.

Trans-Ocean launches the Rolling Home Initiative, offering support to yachts during their passage to Europe. As a member of Trans-Ocean, I sign up of course, but will only receive limited information. My Garmin inReach Mini can't receive complete emails. At least I will be able to send daily position reports and short messages via the text messaging function.

A group of us decide to sail in a loose group, all setting off together around 10 May. But in the end, it doesn't work out, because some of the boats don't make it to Martinique, and stay longer in the south of the Caribbean, while others leave a week earlier from Guadeloupe; one yacht unexpectedly gets a place on a freighter, and the last one ends up staying in the Caribbean.

Sunday, 3 May

I get my first wind forecast on windfinder. For the coming weekend, it predicts wind Force 5 from the east in the Lesser Antilles. This suits me very well, because I will be sailing north initially. I am curious to see how things develop further north. According to the Pilot Charts, (wind and current charts based on many years of weather observations), it is statistically a good time to travel, and you are more likely to have to deal with lulls than too much wind.

Today is 'Tatort' day again. I bought a Wi-Fi package here. It's not very strong, but is enough to keep me up to date with German news broadcasts, and allows me to watch the German Tatort crime series. Thanks to the media libraries.

This week, the countdown starts. Since Anke left, I can't wait to leave. I hadn't wanted to leave earlier because of the weather. I had also been hoping there might still be a chance to sail in the Azores.

I aim to plan my exact passage en route, and will decide if and where to dock on the way. But I have supplies for a non-stop trip to Germany. It should be enough for at least 60 days. I have stowed most of it on board already, and only need a final trip to the Leader Price supermarket shortly before I leave, to buy some fresh things. I have 110 litres of petrol for the portable Honda generator. Charging the batteries at anchor has worked very well so far, although my shore power charger with 45 A is not very powerful. It just takes a little longer. It will be interesting to see how it works at sea. I have the engine and also 260 litres of diesel for power supply backup, if it fails.

Then I have to clean the underwater hull. After all the weeks at anchor, it is encrusted with growth again. Jürgen, from the *Valentine,* lends me a bracket to attach to the hull, similar to brackets used by a glazier. This is a great help. With a scrubber that has an edge on one side, I can reach the middle of the boat if I stretch my arm, and give the entire hull a good clean. It takes me four snorkeling sessions of 45 minutes each, and I am exhausted after each one. After four days I finish the job, and where I started, a first light film of algae has already formed again. The antifouling is probably not as effective as it was when I started, but in these conditions, the hulls of most of the yachts anchored here for several weeks look similar. I also pull up the

log and forward scan, and clean them too, so that everything is working properly.

<u>Saturday, 9 May</u>

Jürgen from the *Valentine* lends me his dinghy. It is much bigger than mine is, and can hold much more, so I only have to go to Leader Price once. Here I buy all the fresh food I will be taking with me, including yogurt, meat, cheese, sausage, fruit and vegetables.

In the afternoon, I say goodbye to everyone I know who is still here. I am leaving tomorrow and am starting to feel very excited.

Link to video

Chapter 13: Non-Stop from Martinique to Heligoland

My diary:

Sunday, 10 May

It's departure day, and I just have a few final chores to do. I top up the water tank with water from my canisters, until it is completely full. Then I go back to the jetty in Sainte-Anne one final time to fill them up as well. Apart from the 300 litres in the inboard tank, I have 3 x 20 litres in canisters, and 95 litres in 5-litre water bottles, which we bought as drinking water, and kept for this purpose. That means I am starting with 455 litres of fresh water, which should be enough for more than 6 weeks, assuming an average consumption of about 10 litres per day. Also, I will be able to collect some water from the bimini. I am sure I will have more than enough for a non-stop trip. I still haven't decided if I'll include a stop somewhere on the way, though.

I check the weather: the forecast for the coming days is fine, with an east wind. I want to head north first, and then set course for east-northeast or northeast, on the same latitude as Bermuda. There is a large high-pressure area, stretching from the Azores to Bermuda, which is a little less prominent in Bermuda.

I shoot a video and complete the last checks. Then it is nearly 2 o'clock in the afternoon. I have no idea where all the time went so quickly.

I am ready to hoist the anchor, but it's really difficult to raise. Something must be entangled in it. Stefan, from *the Solviento,* comes over in his dinghy and takes the wheel, so that I don't have to keep running back and forth. I finally manage to pull up the anchor, along with a thick old hawser that was wrapped around it.

Stefan throws the rope into his dinghy, I go to the wheel, and steer *Jambo* between the anchored boats. I have my foghorn with me, and blast a signal. On the *Solviento*, Jenny waves, and honks back. We call out to each other, and then their yacht is already astern. That's it. "Au revoir, Sainte-Anne!" It is a very poignant moment for me. I am on my way now, and I can't wait to see how this trip will unfold.

I set sail, and make good way south. The wind is Force 5 to 6 from the east, because I need to go around the headland before I can head north. With a good swell, *Jambo* climbs the waves and glides down the other side. It is fantastic fun. I realise that this is what I have been missing during all the past weeks at anchor: sailing!

After almost two hours, I tack as planned, and head north-northeast. I hope I have done enough, and won't need to tack again. I am on a close-hauled course, not far from Martinique. This close to the coast, the Atlantic swell hits the shallower area off the island, and the sea stays choppy until the evening, when I have several hundred metres of water beneath my keel, and the waves grow longer.

What a fantastic start, I think, as the sun over Martinique disappears behind a few clouds on the horizon. We carry on at great speed with around 20 knots of wind. The first night lies ahead of me. I cook a bite to eat, and start the generator to charge the batteries, before I make myself comfortable on the port bench for a first round of interval sleeping. There's not much shipping traffic, but since I'm sailing fairly close to shore, I choose to sleep in intervals of 30 minutes.

When the alarm clock goes off, I do all the usual checks (electronic chart: course, speed; plotter: wind, ship traffic; check the AIS transponder to see if the lights are all green; take a quick look out, shine the torch onto the sail, check the battery voltage, check the running lights). I can do all of this so quickly now that I don't bother to wake up properly, and go straight back to sleep as soon as I have finished. Of course, this is only possible if nothing unexpected happens, and I have no sailing jobs to do.

In the middle of the night, I switch on the generator again and recharge the batteries. To do this, I jack it up on one side with wooden blocks, so that it stands a little straighter when heeling and the oil distributes evenly throughout the engine. Although I have increased the battery capacity with the extra batteries, it is still not enough.

During the night, the wind rises to 23 knots and I reef the mainsail twice, to half the sail size. I can leave the genoa as it is, because I furled it out a little more than half.

Monday, 11 May

In the morning, I feel pretty groggy. It's not just the short intervals of sleep that are getting to me. The first days at sea are always difficult, because I have to get back into the rhythm of things again.

Every single muscle hurts, and I can hardly move. It is also quite exhausting to have to hold on tight every time I move while we are heeling about 25 degrees. I am way to unfit, due to the lack of movement over the last few weeks at anchor, during the lockdown. I have to be especially careful because the risk of injury on board increases if you are too slow.

So today, I am trying to take it easy, and recover as much as possible. I need to get back into the swing of things and get fit as soon as possible. Sailing on a beam reach, it would great to put in the foresail pole. But I can't, because it's too risky at the moment. I will do it when I feel better in a few days' time.

The sea is quite choppy, with higher waves washing over the deck from time to time. But *Jambo* makes good way, and in the early afternoon the first 24 hours are over. The first day's run is 156 NM, which is really good. It's a new personal best for *Jambo*. No doubt, the Antilles Current helped a bit, but our speed through the water is extremely fast. Several times, we nearly reach the hull speed limit of 7.5 knots. All that hard work cleaning the underwater hull before I left has paid off.

Soon I am heading into the second night. I have already passed Guadeloupe on the port side, and everything is going well. The wind is blowing at Force 5 from east-southeast. *Jambo* is on a beam reach and on a target course of 000 degrees. The sea is calm, with 4000 m of water under the keel. This is plain sailing.

Tuesday, 12 May

The night goes well, with no special incidents and no sailing work needing doing. As expected, I am weak and tired in the morning. I feel a bit better than I did yesterday, but the muscles in my arms, legs and shoulders really ache.

Today is my first baking day, and at sunrise, I put the baking mix and some water into the bread machine and turn it on. Three hours later the bread is ready. Freshly baked, warm bread for breakfast is one of the little pleasures I'm really looking forward to on this trip.

I keep the target course practically the same, at 000 to 010 degrees. The wind is still coming from the east at Force 5, but will probably ease later on.

I am very pleased with the second day's run of 138 NM. That makes a total of 294 NM so far. It is a beautiful afternoon. The wind is already down to 4 Bft. from the southeast, and I luff the boat to keep the speed up. The sun is shining, it's about 27 °C and I enjoy the last warm days. The further north I get, the cooler it will be. Everything would be perfect, if only my muscles didn't hurt so much.

After another beautiful day sailing, I get ready for the third night. It is incredible how quickly time passes at sea. With wind Force 5 and a fair sea with gentle, long-drawn waves about 1 to 2 m high, *Jambo* stably but determinedly holds the course through the Atlantic, and lulls me to sleep as she dances in the waves.

Wednesday, 13 May, 3rd day's run 131 NM, total distance 425 NM, position approx. 20 °N 60.5 °W

Calm! After wind speeds of 15 to 20 knots, the wind has died down almost completely this morning. The sails are completely furled in, the engine is running and the batteries get charged by the alternator. Fortunately, there is only a short lull in the wind, and by afternoon, it is blowing again with Force 4 from east-southeast. Another lull is predicted for the late afternoon and evening. The swell is moderate at 1 to 2 m, and it is sunny and warm. Everything is fine!

Then the wind drops as expected, to no more than 9 knots from the east. Nonetheless, *Jambo* does okay. Every day I thank my lucky stars for deciding to clean the overgrown underwater hull before I left.

<u>Thursday, 14 May, 4th day's run 119 NM, - total distance 544 NM, position approx. 22 °N 60 °W</u>

With wind Force 4, I have another good night. I detect a small squall on the radar, and the wind goes up to 5 Bft for a short time as we pass through it. I am starting to perk up a bit, and in the morning, my muscles are not so sore anymore. I enjoy the beautiful sunrise. The forecast for today is 8 knots of wind from the east until the evening. So it looks like it is going to be another easy-going day.

The wind decreases further in the afternoon, to between 5 and 7 knots from the east, which is just enough to keep the boat moving with a swell about 1 m high. In smooth water, the limit is 4 knots of wind. The current course of 60 degrees to the apparent wind, means a northerly course over ground. This is the optimum angle for light winds, and *Jambo* reaches her highest speeds - about 4 knots through the water at present.

The day evolves as I had hoped – relaxed, sunny, and warm. Now and then, I make sure to pour a bucket of Atlantic water over my head.

In the evening, there is more wind again. For quite a while, it blows very constantly at about 12 knots. The forecast for the

night is the same. So I spend a long time trimming the sails for maximum speed. A bit more depth for the genoa, and the mainsail as well, the sheet lead of the genoa a handbreadth further forward, the traveller a touch to windward. *Jambo* speeds along at over 6 knots. I am delighted. Suddenly, the winds go up to 17 knots, and I have to reef. All that work for nothing. That's a sailor's life for you. You never really know what the wind will do next.

Friday, 15 May, 5th day's run 120 NM, total distance 664 NM, position approx. 24 °N 60 °W

The night is quiet, and I sleep a lot (in irregular intervals up to 3 hours). Anke texts me to say a large low-pressure system seems to be forming between Florida and the Bahamas, which may move east and cross my course line. Hans-Uwe Reckefuss, from INTEMAR, who runs the Rolling Home initiative, and does their weather forecasts, together with Trans-Ocean, reported it. The selective weather forecasts from the Garmin don't provide this kind of information. I will bear it in mind, continue on course for now, and decide what action to take from day to day.

Every day, I send a short message with my position and direction headed, to Astrid Ewe, who is my contact person at Trans-Ocean. In case of emergency, or if my daily texts stop arriving, she will launch a rescue operation.

The weather is still good, but it is already getting cooler. During the night, the temperature in the saloon is down to 27 °C. Fortunately, I am getting fitter every day, and my muscles have almost stopped hurting. I have also got into the rhythm of things. My daily routine is very similar to my Atlantic crossing to the Caribbean, a few months ago. Shortly before sunrise, I get up and start the generator to charge the batteries. Then I drink my first cup of coffee on deck. I turn the generator off again after about an hour, and lie back down in my bunk to sleep for another hour. Then it is time for breakfast, and afterwards I have another nap. At lunchtime, I'm at my best as usual and feel very rested.

In the early afternoon, it is time for my hot meal of the day. I usually cook every second or third day, and reheat the food on the following days. I alternate between rice and pasta dishes. For this first week, I also have fresh meat and some potatoes. After I have eaten, I sleep for an hour. Then in the afternoon, I do various tasks, including navigation, until the evening.

After sunset, I run the generator for about one and a half hours to charge the batteries. Then it is bedtime again, and I set my alarm clock to go off in three hours' time. When I wake up, I turn on the generator again for another one and a half hours. I make sure I stay awake while it is running, because it is too risky to go to sleep while there is a real danger of exhaust fumes entering the cabin without me noticing.

It is a serious risk. I always run the generator upwind. This means on a windward course I put it at the stern, and when we are running downwind I have it amidships, to keep the danger as low as possible. Even then, something might happen if there is turbulence, for example. I also keep both side windows open in the saloon when the generator is running at the stern. Exhaust fumes below deck can cause carbon monoxide poisoning. First, you get dizzy, then you lose consciousness, and if it lasts too long, you don't wake up.

So I don't risk it and just stay awake. But my measures seem to be sufficient, and everything is fine. I add a carbon monoxide alarm to my list.

Saturday, 16 May, 6th day's run 121 NM, total distance 785 NM, position approx. 26 °N 59.5 °W

Although the wind blows from the east at no more than 12 to 20 knots, it is a rough night because the swell is at odds to the motion of the sea. *Jambo* keeps slamming into the trough of a wave. I don't sleep at all, but manage to catch up on sleep the next day when conditions improve.

Yesterday there must have been a backlogue of messages, because Anke sent me an extensive weather update about the low-pressure system, consisting of many messages. Now they start coming in one by one. I am on a fixed rate, but it seems as if the rate has gone down, because I only receive a handful of messages per hour. The next morning, things improve.

In the meantime, there is a lull, and I have to sail under engine for a couple of hours, until the wind picks up to Force 3 in the afternoon. That is enough to hoist the sails again, because the sea is much calmer than it was a few hours ago. *Jambo* sails close to the wind on a course roughly north-northwest, which is good, because there is supposed to be more wind to the west.

Sunday, 17 May, 7th day's run 101 NM, total distance 886 NM, position approx. 27.5 °N 60 °W, 3 Bft northeast, course north northwest

Another pleasantly calm day with light winds. It looks like it is going to be a while before there are any stronger winds.

Monday, 18 May, 8th day's run 117 NM, total distance 1003 NM, position approx. 29.5 °N 60 °W, 3 Bft east-southeast, course northeast

The wind continues to blow lightly, bringing some lovely sunny weather, but it is a bit cooler again. In the meantime, I have

235

reached 29.5°N latitude, which means I have come 15 degrees of latitude north. The temperatures below deck reflect this. In the morning, it is only 25 °C. I am in a weak wind zone, approaching the area where the pronounced high-pressure zone between the Azores and Bermuda starts.

The lower swell and waves make for great sailing on a close reach in this glorious weather. The conditions are ideal, so I take the opportunity to fly my drone, and take a few lovely shots of *Jambo*, with the North Atlantic looking stunningly beautiful.

Unfortunately, things are about to change. The low-pressure system has picked up so much energy off the coast of Florida that a tropical storm has formed. The low, christened as Arthur, is currently moving east between the Bahamas and Bermuda, and may well affect my trip, although it is impossible be sure. I am staying on my northeast course for now, and am expecting a southerly wind to set in tomorrow evening.

Tuesday, 19 May, 9th day's run 111 NM, total distance 1114 NM, position approx. 30 °N 58 °W, 3 Bft southwest, course east

The wind shifts first to south-southeast and then to southwest. At Force 3, the swell is small. Tropical Storm Arthur is approaching from the west, and all the weather experts advise people to stay south of 30 °N and let the storm pass. I get this information thanks to Anke. Chris from the *Quick* and Chris living in Siegen also keep me up-to-date with regular, reliable weather information via text messages.

It is 22 °C, much cooler than it has been, and even during the day the temperature below deck is 25 °C or less. It is time to unpack some warmer clothes.

Wednesday, 20 May, 10th day's run 100 NM, total distance 1214 NM, position approx. 30.5 °N 57 °W, 3 Bft southwest, course east

I spend the morning cleaning up the aft cabin and rearranging my provisions, as *Jambo* sails along nicely on an even keel. Before I left, I stowed things in the order I thought I might want to use them. It didn't really work. I ended up needing stuff right at the back, and getting everything mixed up. So now it is all again - until the next time I need something that is in the wrong place.

I am still being told to wait for Tropical Storm Arthur. As recommended, I don't stay too far north, because things are supposed to be wild there. Here in the south, there still isn't much wind - it is Force 3 from the southwest, and we cruise at a leisurely pace. The barometric pressure is quite high at 1028 hPa.

In the afternoon, I take the opportunity to clean out the fridge, wipe it dry and re-fill it. Then I transfer fuel from a 22 litre reserve canister into an 11 litre canister, in order to fill up the generator. I use a huge funnel, which works well, so that nothing gets spilled. I've used up the first 20 litres of petrol now, which means I still have ninety litres left. That is not too bad. If the consumption stays the same, I will have enough petrol for forty-five days. I think that is on the safe side.

I cook a tasty meal: spaghetti with a bacon and onion cream sauce. Almost all my fresh food is finished now, but the bacon will keep in the fridge for up to three weeks.

Wind Force 5 from the southwest. That means we will be heading east for the next night! According to the reports, Arthur seems to be getting weaker. We have been fine so far.

Thursday, 21 May, 11th day's run 128 NM, total distance 1342 NM, position approx. 30.5 °N 55 °W

During the night, I see flashes of lightning in the distance. They are visible in every direction, but I cannot make out a real thunderstorm cell. Although I don't hear any thunder or see any forked lightning, I am worried of course. I only ever experienced one thunderstorm at sea, a few years ago on the Baltic Sea, but fortunately, it wasn't directly overhead. A lightning strike on board would wreak havoc with the electrical system and all the electronics on board.

The wind is getting gustier. You can literally feel the low approaching. During the night, for safety reasons, I remove the foresail boom, which I had added on the broad reach course. Just in time! Shortly afterwards the wind goes up to 30 knots and turns to west-northwest.

Arthur has caught up with me.

At noon, the wind is blowing again at Force 4 to 5 from the southwest and it is raining. Then in the early afternoon, there is a sudden near calm with a Force 2 wind from the northeast. I am in the eye of the low-pressure area. I take down the sails and motor sail on a northeasterly course. It is still raining, and after just two hours, I have collected ten litres of water on the bimini. I never expected to get so much water in such a short time.

I secure what I can to be prepared for the upcoming strong wind. I take the Honda generator below deck and put it in the bathroom. I secure the boom on both sides with a preventer. I also check the anchor fastenings and the dinghy – they are okay. I check all the latches on the windows to make sure they are locked, which they are. That's all I can do. Hopefully, everything else should be okay.

In the late afternoon, the wind increases very suddenly, and from one moment to the next it is blowing at 15 knots, though it is still coming from the northeast. I hoist the sails, first the mainsail and then the genoa. Although I am still running against the wind under engine, the mainsail is okay. As soon as the mainsail is up, I furl out the genoa, but make the mistake of not changing course by 20 degrees beforehand, so that it can fill out past the mast.

It was bound to happen: the genoa starts filling out towards the mast, gets caught in the mast steps, and a huge 4-m-long tear appears in the leech area. I know the sail wasn't in prime condition, but this should not have happened, considering I had the leech area reinforced by the sailmaker on Lanzarote. I am shocked, for a brief moment. However, there is no time for that. Instead, I roll up the sail and go down to the forward cabin, where I have to remove both mattresses and all the slats, in order to fetch the second genoa.

 In the meantime, the sea has also been building up, growing ever steeper, as the old swell from the southwest comes up against the new waves from the northeast. *Jambo* is sailing under engine against the wind and the waves. The foredeck sways and moves up and down. But no other course would make it any easier for me to change the genoa. I quickly take down the old genoa and simply stuff it into the dinghy under the ropes, which happens to be stowed right side up so that I can put the empty reserve canisters there later. It happens to be very useful in this situation too.

I hoist the other genoa - it's newer and better anyway. When I'm done, after three quarters of an hour, it's already blowing 19 knots, and the first 3 m breakers are rolling towards *Jambo*. Working on a swaying foredeck is definitely no fun. Fortunately, in this emergency, I benefit from the experience gained on the outward voyage, when I hoisted the second genoa several times.

 Towards evening, the wind is blowing at 24 to 28 knots, still from the northeast. The waves reach a height of 3 to 5 m. I choose an upwind course of 60 degrees to the apparent wind. That should still be doable. I set both sails to quarter their size. The angry sea washes over *Jambo* again and again.

As night falls, the wind goes up to 32 knots. I have to reef again and make the sails so small that *Jambo* can still sail straight through the water. The genoa is at an estimated 4 m², and the mainsail maybe 3 m². I can reduce the mainsail continuously, thanks to the furling system in the mast, and it holds well at any size. I can't get the small reefed foresail trimmed perfectly, because the genoa sheet lead is too far back, even though it is already at the front end of the track, so it flaps a bit. I don't bother trying to add another pulley, because the waves are now coming over the boat more violently than anything I have ever experienced on all my trips so far.

I set the parameters of the electric autopilot to the toughest conditions, so that it turns the rudder fast and hard. The violent impact of the breaking waves repeatedly throws *Jambo* 20 to 30 degrees off course, and tough steering is necessary to get back on course.

It works: the angle to the apparent wind is 60 degrees, and 90 degrees to the true wind. So we have a strong drift, which is okay in these conditions. *Jambo* is coping very well, but clearly, we have reached the limit for an upwind course. Up to wind Force 6, I can usually sail all courses on *Jambo*. At Force 7, it depends on the swell, which is fierce so far out on the ocean, but I much prefer it to offshore, where shallower water or currents often mean sea conditions are even worse. At Force 8, I would sail actively downwind, keeping ahead of the wave, and at Force 10, I'd start praying. I would not like to try to master a severe storm. I have no idea if *Jambo* could cope. But good forecasts mean it is possible to avoid the storm fronts, as I have done here, so that I "only" have to deal with the tail end.

I also hadn't realised how inadequate my Garmin inReach Mini weather forecast really is, for conditions like this. Luckily, I can make up for that, thanks to the information I get from Anke in the back office, and from many other people I don't even know personally, who keep me up-to-date on the weather via their text messages. Without them, there would be no way to do this trip safely.

I can also rely on my autopilot, which steers *Jambo* very reliably in these heavy seas, so that I can even get a bit of sleep now and then, even though *Jambo* is completely swamped by waves several times. I don't actually see that happening, but I hear the blows and the water masses pouring over the deck.

I still have to recharge the batteries during the night of course. Since I can't use the generator in these conditions, I switch on the engine for an hour at midnight, and again early in the morning.

Friday, 22 May, 12th day's run 132 NM, total distance 1474 NM, position approx. 31.5 °N 55.5 °W, 6 Bft northeast, course north northwest

Soon after midnight, the wind starts decreasing. By morning, it is down to Force 6 again. The sea has also calmed down a bit. The waves are still up to 4 m high, but they are much longer and less steep, which means *Jambo* is no longer washed over, and is sailing merrily over the wave crests and down into the troughs.

All is well, and I seem to have survived the worst of it. My strategy of heading east paid off. The low-pressure area caught up with me in the end, but it had lost so much strength by that time that I could cope. I could also have headed southeast, which might have been even safer, but then I would have been far off course.

Another option would have been to head west, allowing the storm to pass to the north, and put it behind me sooner. But I didn't have a detailed enough forecast to be able to assess this. There is always the risk of a storm failing to progress as planned. If it unexpectedly and suddenly changes direction, moving further south in this case, you end up caught in the middle of the storm zone.

I add a satellite phone and a wind forecast package to my list. I will look into this next winter to find the best solution. It could well be Iridium Go and PredictWind.

But for now, everything is fine. I can relax a bit, and ease the sails to pick up speed.

Then I suddenly see something ahead, and slow down. It turns out it is a white buoy. *It must have broken free somewhere and found its way out into the open Atlantic.* Then I notice that the waves are bypassing it as if it were anchored. At 4000 m water depth? I don't think so. Maybe it is drifting very slowly because its mooring chain is still attached?

The wind continues to drop during the day to 20 knots. I tack to the southeast until the afternoon and then come about. We sail on into the next night, beating the wind at Force 5.

Saturday, 23 May, 13th day's run 104 NM, total distance 1578 NM, position approx. 32 °N 54.5 °W, calm

I stay up all night as the wind falls asleep. It is almost calm with changing winds from the north. Mostly I use the engine, but can sail again from time to time. The two extremes are that close.

Sunday, May 24, 14th day's run 105 NM, total distance 1683 NM, position approx. 33 °N 54 °W, doldrums

Calms are worse than storms, they say. I agree. Either weak winds with constant wind shifts keep you on your toes, or you have to sail under engine and use up your fuel, which is the scarcest resource for me. In previous centuries, it would have been water, and if it got too scarce, the sailors threw the horses overboard to reduce water consumption. That is why this area is still called horse latitudes to this day.

There is a pronounced and extensive area of high-pressure ahead to the north. Due to my escape course to avoid Storm Arthur, I have come a long way east, and can no longer cross the narrower band of high-pressure near Bermuda, as I'd planned. Instead, I have to face the high-pressure area here in the east, where it is really big.

I've turned the engine on. I think I'll have to motor sail for another 36 hours or so, or perhaps slightly less, if I'm lucky.

It is a beautiful sunrise with calm seas - an incredible sight. I fly the drone and get some fantastic aerial shots of *Jambo* cruising with the rising sun as a backdrop. Later, I decide these are my favorite shots of the entire trip. Of course, I enjoy this unforgettable moment with a cup of freshly ground, brewed coffee.

Then I make the most of the gentle ride to transfer some diesel from the canisters into the tank. I haven't used much fuel yet, and only refill 70 litres. I continue under engine, heading northnortheast, and only sail occasionally until the winds start blowing over 6 knots consistently. *Jambo* sails 60 degrees on the apparent wind. The course is about right, and our speed is a good 4 knots.

Monday, 25 May, 15th day's run 107 NM, total distance 1790 NM, position approx. 34.5 °N 53 °W, 4 Bft west-northwest, course east-northeast

The night is great! Although I do have to turn on the engine for an hour around midnight due to lack of wind. But after that, it increases continuously, and in the morning, I have wind Force 4 from west-northwest. In retrospect, 30 hours under engine isn't too bad, and means I have done all right coming through the high. I was able to sail into it, and set sail again quite soon on the way out. So it must have been about 350 NM wide. What I don't want to happen is for the high to move in a similar direction and at a similar speed to us.

During the night, I cross the Hamilton (Bermudas) - Ponta Delgada (Azores) line heading north. This is the first important milestone on this trip, and I should now have left the high-pressure zone between the two places behind me. However, there seem to be more lulls and more easterly winds to the east.

Today I change the boat's time for the first time, as I have now come a long way east. I change it from UTC -4 to UTC -3. Sunrise

245

is now at 5:22 and sunset at 19:39. As on the outward journey to Guadeloupe, I do not strictly adhere to the time zone division, but try to make sure the sun's highest point is between 12:00 and 13:00.

Tuesday, 26 May, 16th day's run 137 NM, total distance 1927 NM, position approx. 36.5 °N 54 °W, 4 Bft east, course north

I am cold, because it is now only 20 °C below deck in the morning now. I have been used to temperatures of 30 °C and more for months, and find it difficult to adapt to lower temperatures in such a short time. I swap my thin quilt for the thicker duvet because I am starting to freeze during the night.

I continue sailing north in the current wind. No passage is possible to the east just now due to lulls and the extended east wind situation. I hope I will find westerly winds at around 40 degrees latitude north.

Anke's flight to the Azores, scheduled for 11 June, is cancelled today by the airline TAP. We were expecting this, and have decided that we will not be able to visit the islands this year. We are already planning to make up for it when things get a bit more relaxed in the future. I would like to avoid a supply stop in the Azores, but at this point, I can't to rule it out completely.

If I don't visit the Azores and decide to sail non-stop to Germany, the question is: do I go north or south past the UK? The north might be a bit tiring because conditions can be rough, and heading south through the English Channel will mean it is difficult to rest properly, because my sleep intervals will have to be kept short due to heavy shipping traffic. I still do not know what I will decide to do in the end. I will wait and see how things develop, and what the wind is up to.

During the night, I reach another light wind area. The wind blows at around 7 knots and is decreasing. I manage to keep our speed up by sailing a broad reach. It is also colder and today, I am wearing long trousers for the first time in about four months. It feels very uncomfortable. But I guess I will have to get used to it.

Everything is blue!

What a beautiful morning! Blue sky, blue water and a light breeze. I sit on deck in the warm morning sun and enjoy the view into the distance with a nice cup of coffee. The ocean is mesmerising today in all its simple blue beauty. I feel deeply content and quite overwhelmed by this sight. The Atlantic Ocean captivates me. It's a truly special moment. Sometimes that is all you need when you are at sea.

Things are ticking along nicely just now, I am happy and I am feeling great. I have had a lot of fun on this trip so far. After seventeen days, I am also in good shape now, and have overcome my initial limpness and the lack of fitness I had to start with. When there is no choice, your body recovers fast. I can crank, sail and tack as much as I have to.

I have also found a good sleeping rhythm, or rather: I'm coping with the one I've got. Of course, it always depends on how often I have to get up to do sailing work in between. I usually sleep up to three hours because there is very little ship traffic. At present, a ship shows up on the AIS about every two days. In addition, I have both warning alarms turned on, which have always worked perfectly so far. So from my point of view, it is not too big a risk to sleep for these longer intervals.

You need a good portion of optimism, motivation and fun on a trip like this. Then time goes by relatively quickly. I am glad about every day I can spend out here at sea, although of course some days are more difficult than others are. Moments like this morning make up for them.

The trip is going well, I'm having fun, and the next few weeks promise to be very exciting and challenging, with more high-pressure zones, light winds and lulls, and perhaps some strong winds as well. I will have to manoeuvre my way through them skillfully. Let's see! But so far, this trip has been an unforgettable adventure for me, quite literally: a crazy experience.

Thursday, 28 May, 18th day's run 100 NM, total distance 2132 NM, position approx. 39.5 °N 54 °W, 3-5 Bft southwest, course north-northeast.

The night goes well and is relatively calm. In the morning, a strong current of about 2 knots picks up to the south-southeast. Apparently, the Gulf Stream makes a detour here from Newfoundland. But I am also very far to the northwest. Nova Scotia is only about 500 NM to starboard, and this could be the Labrador Current making itself felt here.

After two coffees, I go back to my warm bed, and we head further north for now, since the wind is supposed to be stronger there than in the south. There are some high-pressure areas lurking east of Newfoundland and northeast of Bermuda. The counter current is making my life a bit difficult now.

The whole afternoon I have wind Force 5 from the southwest, and it stays that way well into the night. But I gradually free myself from the counter current when it veers off to the left, heading southeast at a leisurely pace of 1 knot. I hope that tomorrow in the course of the day, I will be able to run with the Gulf Stream. *Jambo* moves leisurely to the north, sailing downwind.

<u>Friday, 29 May, 19th day's run 109 NM, total distance 2241 NM, position approx. 40.5 °N 53 °W, 4 Bft west, course north-north-east</u>

I am awakened by the sound of banging sails, with the wind actually threatening to fall asleep. I lower the sails, start the engine and sail north at 6.5 knots, because that is where there should still be some wind. In the east there is calm. After a few hours, wind really does start coming from the west at 13 knots. I probably managed to escape another calm by the skin of my teeth. That was lucky!

During the night, I cross the 40th parallel north, which is a second milestone. I never thought I would ever be just 400 NM south of Newfoundland.

In the morning, it is foggy for the first time, which gradually dissipates in the morning sun. Apparently, this is due to the effect of the cold water Labrador Current. In former times, you could expect to face icebergs here this time of year, starting from the 40th degree of latitude, which the Labrador Current carries far to the south. In times of global warming this phenomenon has probably shifted further north. Unfortunately, I will have to head further north than I would like, and further west too, in order to find winds that are more favourable.

The day pans out very well. Despite all the signs, it is lovely and warm again, so I can do without my long trousers today. I am pleased about that. And I also manage to find the wind, which goes up to 21 knots, and even have to reef the sails for the first time in ages, after so many days of light wind. This is the perfect wind to sail all the way home. It should stay like this.

But the next high-pressure area is already astern, and seems to be following us. It is moving north from Bermuda, and could catch up with me in two days' time. That would mean another day or two of calm. Of course, I could do without that. I'm still trying to decide how to deal with this high. It depends on the storm's further course and speed. At the moment, it is approaching at about 200 NM per day. If it sticks to that speed, I could let it pass to the east. Therefore, I will stay on a northerly course for now. I find it thrilling to deal with the weather systems here, and develop the right strategy.

I have a great sailing afternoon, slightly downwind, at wind Force 5. In the evening, unfortunately, the wind dies down again, and the current runs at 1 knot in a south-southeast direction, so we don't make much way.

I look at the pilot charts for June for the North Atlantic, and am now actually in the zone where icebergs are to be expected. Fortunately, so far I have not seen any. Then the wind goes down to 3 Bft. I have to stay on my north-northeast course, and try to find the wind. There is still a calm in the east.

Saturday, 30 May, 20th day's run 126 NM, total distance 2367 NM, position approx. 42 °N 51 °W, 4-5 Bft southwest, course north-northeast

The iceberg furthest southeast is located northwest of 44 °N 46 °W according to the US Navigation Center (https://www.navcen.uscg.gov/). Jörg, from the *Aurelia,* passed this information on to me. Many thanks for that at this point! It is approximately on my course, and I make a mark in the sea chart. I will try to keep southeast of this position if I can. I wasn't expecting to have to deal with icebergs before I set off on this trip. But of course, I take the topic very seriously.

I am starting to feel a bit boxed in as far as my course options are concerned. In the east, there are high-pressure areas with calms expected, in the north there are the icebergs, and further west is not an option, since in my view I have already come close enough to the American coast. Naturally I don't want to head back south either. It is maddening, and certainly dampens my spirits a bit. So I sail between icebergs and calm areas on a northeast course, trying to stay clear of the icebergs as far as possible, and hoping that the calm won't affect me too badly.

The wreck of the Titanic lies at: 41° 43' 55'' N, 49° 56' 45'' W. In the afternoon, my bearings show I am 145 degrees and 43 NM away! Many thanks to André in Marienfeld (German town) for sending me that piece of information via the Garmin.

In the evening, about one and a half hours before sunset, fog forms over the water, becoming more and more dense. The wind is still blowing at Force 4 from the southwest, but is slowly dying down and recedes as we approach the high-pressure area. Quietly, *Jambo* glides through the thick fog into the night. *When will I be able to set course east at last?*

Sunday, 31 May, 21st day's run 103 NM, total distance 2470 NM, position approx. 43 °N 49 °W, 3 Bft south, course east

It is still foggy as the sun comes up with an estimated visibility of 200 m. Meanwhile, I am now at the foot of the Grand Banks, close to the 1000 m  depth line, and only about 280 NM southeast of Newfoundland. I really can't go any further north now, the threat of icebergs is simply too great, and I don't want to travel further up the continental shelf. I have always had a lot of respect for continental shelves because the waves can pile up oddly there. Of course, I have never sailed here before. I don't know the character of the sea, or how the current conditions, caused by the Labrador Current and the Gulf Stream, affect things. But the high-pressure area that has been on my heels for the last two days is moving along as expected, and is now already roughly starboard astern.

In the cold Labrador Current, and in dense fog, shivering with cold, I change the sail position. After what feels like endless days heading north, with icebergs ahead, I can finally select an easterly course and confront the high in the east! This is the perhaps the most moving moment of the whole voyage, unforgettable! Even now, when I look back while writing this, I am gripped by emotion. I guess feelings run deep after weeks of solitude, struggling with the weather systems and almost despairing, before the tide finally turns. After so many days, so far off course that I'm almost in Newfoundland, this is the turning point.

The centre of the high-pressure area will pass me to the north today, moving in an easterly direction. As it does so, the wind will shift from south to south-southeast, and later to southeast. The only thing I have to do today is wait until the wind has shifted and increased enough for me to be able to gain space, sailing east close to the wind.

The fog is finally dispersing, the sun is shining and a gentle current flows towards the east-northeast. Things are looking up!

I get a great update on icebergs from Greg, in Vienna. He writes to the U.S. National Ice Center directly, inquiring about ice at my position, and receives the following reply from the Command Duty Officer: "The area he is in now has no sea ice, but may have icebergs."

Thanks for that! The so-called Mean Maximum Iceberg Limit line extends to 40 °W. Within this line, icebergs are to be expected. East of it, there are no icebergs until almost Greenland. Even though the risk is low, I keep my radar on all the time now. I have marked two warning areas, where the alarm goes off if any objects appear. Smaller icebergs probably won't be detected, but they also pose less of a risk. Anything as large as a medium-sized buoy can be detected at short range, and the larger icebergs of course, at longer range.

Further east, there is still a calm and no way through. So once I get past this high-pressure area, I will probably continue on a northeasterly course between the calm in the east, and icebergs in the northwest. Sailing here in this sea area is hugely challenging, but it is a thrilling adventure at the same time.

Monday, 1 June, 22nd day's run 142 NM, total distance 2612 NM, position approx. 43.5 °N 46.5 °W, 3 Bft southeast, course northeast

We are making good progress! My strategy of passing through the high-pressure is working. The high-pressure area is moving exactly as predicted. At this point, a big thank you to Chris from *Quick*, who sent me the times and positions of its centre. Now I am already sailing on the far side of the high-pressure area, I have 8 knots of wind from the southeast, and an additional Gulf Stream of 2 knots. Another big thank you goes to Arno from *Elas*, for sending me information and coordinates of the Gulf Stream. Thanks also go out to Anke, and Christoph, in Siegen, who provide me with daily updates, and of course to all the people for the information, tips and good wishes that reach me via their text messages.

All the kindness is fantastic. I may be traveling solo, but I don't feel all alone. My trip has become a small community project, including lots of people I don't know personally, who don't know each other either. It is astounding.

The most challenging part of my journey home comes next: crossing the northern North Atlantic. However, I feel very confident that I will manage it with all this fantastic support.

Jambo has had a good cleaning over the last three nights. Due to the fog and almost 100% humidity, there has been a lot of dew, especially at night, which trickles down every surface in small streams, dripping everywhere - from the boom, from the bimini, from the rigging and from the railings. The result is that all the salt and dirt have been rinsed off, almost like in a car wash.

The 22nd day's run is 142 NM, which is a good distance, and confirms that the tactics of following the high have been worth it. This time it was easier, because the front moved through faster than the previous ones did, which were more stationary. The key was all the accurate information, along with the Gulf Stream, which fortunately happened to be just where I needed it most.

In the meantime, I sail on the so-called Great Circle route. This is a classic sailing route from the ports on the east coast of the USA to Great Britain and Scandinavia. It has several arms. The northernmost route leads to Scotland and Scandinavia, another branch to Oban in Scotland, and three southern ones take you to Southern Ireland, the English Channel and the Mediterranean.

I have to choose one of two variants. I can either sail through the English Channel to Germany, or else sail north past Scotland into the North Sea, and then set course southeast towards Heligoland. Always assuming, of course, that nothing serious happens on board, and that I am still fit. These considerations are always part of a long voyage. The Azores would be a good place for an emergency stop. But I am confident that everything is going to be all right! Both routes are about the same distance now, so I don't have to make up my mind just yet.

<u>Tuesday, 2 June, 23rd day's run 141 NM, total distance 2753 NM, position approx. 44 °N 44 °W, 4 Bft east-southeast, course northeast</u>

During the night, I reach the third milestone of my journey, the same longitude and latitude: 44° 28'. The wind shifted to east-northeast during the night, and I have come a bit further north than I actually wanted. The current is moving southeast at about 1 knot, and it is cold and very foggy again. I seem to be back under the influence of the Labrador Current again, instead of the Gulf Stream. The wind is supposed to shift back to the southeast later, and then I will try to get on a course east-northeast as best I can.

There is a lot of shipping traffic for a change, at least by my standards. Two freighters pass me a short distance apart, the *Shandong Hong TU,* 2 NM away, and immediately after that, the *Regius,* just 1 NM away. This is a welcome test for my two AIS alarms, which both go off as intended.

Then I decide to tack after all, as the wind is gradually dropping, and set course to the south-southeast. Cruising upwind, I hit the same longitude and latitude again for a second time, at 43° 57'.

Unfortunately, the wind also decreases to the south. Apparently there is another calm approaching, so I head northeast again, where there is supposed to be more wind. Also in the medium term, this seems to be a more promising way to go east than in the more southern latitudes. The weather systems are very dynamic here, so I expect a few light wind days, and some calm ones either way.

In the afternoon, the wind fortunately picks up again, and with a good wind Force 5. I actually need to reef for once. *Jambo* is reaching. A light current sets off to the northwest and makes the waves a little longer, which means the ride is very calm and pleasant. From time to time, the direction of the current changes. This suggests large eddies. I am still in the area where the Labrador Current and the Gulf Stream meet.

In the evenings, it is foggy and cold, and I have started wearing a sweater below deck, since the temperatures barely reach 20 °C now. In the morning, when it is coldest, it is only 17 °C, and my diesel heater is broken. I couldn't get it repaired in the Caribbean, of course. They know more about air conditioning than heating there. When the generator is running, I switch on the small electric marine heater now and then.

<u>Wednesday, 3 June, 24th day's run 151 NM, total distance 2904 NM, position approx. 46 °N 42 °W, 4-5 Bft southeast, course north-northeast</u>

What a beautiful morning! I am greeted by blue skies and sunshine! It is warm, at least compared to the last few days. The wind is also playing along, and things are going very well. I enjoy my coffee on deck and warm up in the sunshine. I feel top fit in every way, and could climb a mountain (of course, there are not too many of those here).

Then suddenly I catch a glimpse of a blowing whale to starboard, and then I see it again! I don't know what kind it is, but it looks magnificent!

The whole morning goes well, but from noon, the wind starts to decrease, introducing the next phase of weaker wind ahead. Also a catamaran ahead seems to be on a similar course. Dieter, from *Damile* sends me an interesting update from the shipping news in my current area:

GRANIE 17:28 UTC, 46.71388 °N 39.623 °W, speed 7.3kn, course 84 °, wind 7 knots south.

ESPIRITU 12m sailor 47.03206 °N 22.1316 °W, speed 4.4kn, course 79 °, wind 12 knots east-northeast.

The *Granie* is a catamaran about 100 NM northeast of my position and probably sailing under engine. At least, that is what I assume, with 7.3 knots speed and 7 knots of wind. Many thanks for this information to Dieter.

I am now about 450 NM east of Newfoundland, and think this is about half way if it turns out to be a non-stop trip. With 2900 NM behind me, there must be fewer nautical miles ahead than I have covered so far. I am not so good at estimating the number of days though. If there are any more lulls, then in the worst case it could take longer than twenty-four days, although I don't think so. I still haven't decided yet how I am going to sail. Shall I go north or south past the UK?

The northern route appeals to me very much - up there in the Roaring Fifties, sailing in stronger winds. After all, I've been dealing with moderate and weak winds, which is not typical. I am in what is called the westerly wind zone, but instead of westerly winds, I keep encountering easterly winds, due to the pronounced high-pressure situation over the North Atlantic. The way the high-pressure areas are shifting now, is one reason in favour of the northerly route.

Another area of high-pressure is supposed to be moving south from the northeast. It is quite a crazy constellation: one high is stationary, the other is moving north, and now one is moving south straight ahead. Coping with the systems is still the greatest challenge for me. Understanding the weather, getting between the systems, and dodging the lulls as best I can is more demanding than the sailing itself.

Sunset! It gets chilly immediately, and fog slowly begins to form over the water. The sea is calm, with only a shallow swell from the previously stronger southeast wind, gently rocking *Jambo* up and down. The wind drops, only blowing around 10 knots from the southeast.

I remove the foresail pole, and let out the sails for Force 3, so that *Jambo* can sail along leisurely, at 60 degrees of apparent wind. The wind is supposed to turn south later, but at the moment, it is not making any moves in that direction. In the saloon below deck, it gets cold really quickly, and I climb into my cosy bunk in the forward cabin, and keep warm as best I can, wrapped up in two blankets.

Thursday, 4 June, 25th day's run 103 NM, total distance 3007 NM, position approx. 47 °N 40.5 °W, 3 Bft south, course northeast

This morning it is overcast and cold. The sea is glassy and there is only a light breeze. I sleep in, and can hardly persuade myself to leave my warm bunk. I stay in bed for an extra hour after sunrise.

At some point, I manage to get up after all, to have some breakfast. Unfortunately, I forgot to turn on the bread machine at 4 o'clock this morning, because today is actually bread baking day. So I turn on the Honda generator to charge the batteries, and at least make some fresh coffee. I can turn the Honda off again after an hour, because the batteries will be charged then. The baking machine needs about two and a half hours. I lie back in my warm bed and look forward to the bread. Again, it is the simple things that please me and keep my spirits up.

Today I change the ship's time for the second time. Board time is now UTC -2. Sunrise is at 4:47 am and sunset is at 8:34 pm.

I do an inventory of all supplies, water and fuel. After 25 days, the status is as follows:

Drinking water: 90 litres, enough for about 30 days
O-juice: 30 litres, enough for about 60 days +
Food: (way too much), enough for 60 days +
Yogurt: 1.5 kg to be eaten in the next few days as the expiration date has already passed.
Canned fruits enough for 25 d days +
Coffee beans: 6 kg, enough for 120 days + (there will be no shortage of them).

Bread:
Baking mixes for 20 loaves, enough for 60 days

Beer:
My trips are always non-alcoholic, but I have a few beers of course.

Fresh water:
I started with 300 litres in the inboard tank.
Plus 155 litres stowed in the forward cabin, in reserve canisters and 5 litre bottles.

Additionally, I have collected 20 litres of rainwater.
That makes a total of 475 litres.
Amount consumed so far 230 litres.
Amount left 245 litres, enough for about 25 days.
Petrol for the Honda generator:
I started with 110 litres.
Amount consumed 50 litres.
Amount left 60 litres. That is enough for about 30 days.

Diesel:
I started with 260 litres.
Amount consumed 80 litres.
Amount left 180 litres.

So that is all right then. I can carry on sailing without having to worry about supplies for another twenty-five to thirty days or so. I don't think that my journey is going to take that long though.

Friday, 5 June, 26th day's run 102 NM, total distance 3109 NM, position approx. 48.5 °N 39.5 °W, 3-4 Bft south, course east-northeast

During the night, I am stuck in a calm, and have to change course for a short time until the wind picks up again. In the early hours of the morning, a good wind Force 4 from the south settles in at last. The current runs with us and it is raining a bit. I feel I am closer to the centre of the high-pressure area to the east of me, so I bear away in a more northerly direction, until I find a good Force 4 again. That is the position in the high I would like to hold for as long as possible. But at some point, of course, our ways will part again, and the wind is expected to turn to southwest later. For now, I enjoy the ride, with *Jambo* making 6 to 6.5 knots of speed through the water on a beam reach. And the current helps too.

Today I cook a very tasty meal. As a lover of Indian cuisine, I have some Indian spice mixtures on board. I conjure up a garam masala dish based on a tomato-olive-cream sauce. My favorite Indian dishes are ones with lamb or chicken. Of course, I don't have any meat left, so I replace that with canned tuna. It is delicious. The way to a man's heart is through his stomach, even at sea!

In the evening, unfortunately, the wind dies down, and *Jambo* glides into the night in a weak wind. So once again all we can do is - wait for the wind.

Saturday, 6 June, 27th day's run 115 NM, total distance 3224 NM, position approx. 49 °N 37 °W, 2-3 Bft southwest, course east-northeast

The night is not so good. The wind is very changeable, so I have to gybe several times to make any progress. As so often, I find that light winds are more work than strong winds, and by morning, I am exhausted.

Also, the forecast is bad. No wind is predicted until the day after tomorrow. At least the weather is all right. Now and then, the sun comes out between the clouds. The sails bang, which makes me wince every time, and is so frustrating. I follow a slightly more northerly course, but the wind remains weak at around 9 knots from the southwest. *Jambo* makes little way ahead of the wind.

I spend the morning in bed and catch up on some sleep I missed during the night. In the afternoon, there is a bit more wind, and the day turns out better than I had expected in the morning. As before, the goal is to manoeuver through the high-pressure areas as well as possible, and to find more stable westerly winds.

<u>Sunday, 7 June, 28th day's run 134 NM, total distance 3358 NM, position approx. 49.5 °N 34.5 °W, 5 Bft south, course northeast</u>

I tend to go further north than east, which makes sense, because going north shortens the distance I have to travel east a bit, since each degree of latitude to the north reduces the distance between the degrees of longitude. The two-dimensional nautical chart is deceptive. It shows the northern latitudes clearly distorted by the Mercator projection.

That is why I prefer northerly courses to southeasterly ones. By tomorrow, there should be good southwesterly winds, and then I will have to decide in the next few days whether to sail north or south past the UK.

I think I am now on the last third of my journey, which means I have to stay attentive and concentrated, and make sure I am not careless. Mishaps and mistakes tend to happen towards the end of my trips, when my concentration starts declining. I can't allow that to happen, because I still have a very long way to go. A sailor's greatest enemy is his own carelessness! This is definitely true for me.

My Garmin forecast predicts wind Force 7, and it looks as if a strong wind field coming from the west is catching up with me. I brace myself for choppy seas and stronger winds, take the Honda generator below deck for safety, test the engine, brace the boom on both sides, and make sure nothing below deck will be tossed about.

Fortunately, this prediction is wrong. As we head into the night, the wind blows from the south at Force 5, gusting to 6.

Monday, 8 June, 29th day's run 137 NM, total distance 3496 NM, position approx. 50 °N 31 °W, 4-5 Bft west, course northeast

During the night, I reach 50°N latitude, the fourth milestone of this cruise. The sea is chaotic and choppy due to a swell at right angles to the sea state, and a slightly opposing current. *Jambo* is rolling strongly on a downwind course. Thick fog surrounds us, and below deck, it is bitterly cold.

At noon, the sea calms down, because current and wave are moving in the same direction again. But a weak wind field is approaching aft, and the wind is already starting to drop.

I am now almost in the middle of the northern North Atlantic, and check to find the best port of call in case of emergency (as the crow flies):

733 NM to Horta in the Azores
990 NM to La Coruña in Spain
957 NM to Falmouth in England
823 NM to Cork in Ireland
941 NM to Oban in Scotland
846 NM to Reykjavik in Iceland
851 NM to Ikerasagssuaq in Greenland
929 NM to St. John's in Newfoundland

Of course, how fast I can get to one of these places depends on the wind. But I think I could make it to the Azores in six days. However, the further east I get each day, the easier it will be to reach Cork in the south of Ireland. I am keeping my fingers crossed that all goes well, and I won't have to make an emergency stop.

The night is really good. A mini-high passes through quickly, which I survive without needing the engine. The wind has returned with Force 5 from the southwest. I am very pleased with the last day's run of 136 NM. I set the mainsail only, on a downwind course.

Normally I would only set the genoa, but I want to go easy on it, as one of the three tapes holding the ring on the clew is slightly torn. It's nothing serious yet, but I need to keep an eye on it. The furling mainsail looks completely unaffected by what it been through so far. It last saw the sailmaker over 10,000 NM ago. I have one mainsail in reserve. Although I am not worried, I am being cautious.

Today I finally decide to sail the northern route around Scotland. I have left the decision open as long as possible, and on the course so far, both routes through the English Channel and past Scotland, have been similar in length. Now I have to decide on a route. I had been thinking about it for several days and it is my first choice.

I set the next waypoint to Rockall Trough accordingly. I will sail on from there to the northern tip of the Hebrides. The Rockall Trough lies between Ireland, in the southeast, and Bryony Bank in the northwest. This is where the continental shelf begins, and as always, I plan to adopt a conservative strategy when moving from deep to shallower water. If there are more strong winds, and the sea is very choppy, I want to sail into the trough from the southwest. That way I will be protected somewhat from the Atlantic swell by Bryony Bank. I could also sail between the Hebrides and Scotland if necessary, if things are too unpleasant west of the Hebrides. This part of the sea is famous for being unpredictable. It is still quite a long way away though. About 700 NM. First, I need to find the right wind and the best passage.

Today I change the time for the third time. Board time is now UTC -1. Sunrise is at 4:38 and sunset at 21:16.

I reach a fifth milestone when I pass the same northern latitude as my home port, Enkhuizen, in the Netherlands, (52° 42' N). It is almost at the intersection with the western longitude of Horta (28 °37' W).

Wednesday, 10 June, 31st day's run 143 NM, total distance 3775 NM, position about 53.5 °N 27 °W, 4-5 Bft west, course northeast

Another morning, and a familiar picture outside: light fog. It is overcast and cold, maybe 10 °C. It is not surprising, seeing as I am now already north of the 53rd parallel. Without a diesel heater, the cold is an additional challenge on this trip, which I severely underestimated.

When I started out from the Canary Islands towards the Caribbean in December, there was no Corona pandemic. At that time, Anke and I were planning to meet up again in the Azores. So I gave her all my sweaters (except one), when she flew home from Lanzarote in early January, to reduce bulk, and she was going to bring my warmer clothes to the Azores. In the saloon, the thermometer on the wall doesn't climb above 18 °C during the day; early in the morning it is 14 °C, and it is much colder in the footwell area.

Fortunately, I do have one sweater with me, which will just have to do for the next three weeks. I have to make sure my clothes don't get wet, because there is little chance of drying them. The good news is that my petrol supply is still very high. This means

 I can allow myself the luxury of turning on the Honda generator to run the small electric heater for an hour this morning. I warm up my feet, which I can barely keep warm. During the day, I spend a lot of time in my bunk, keeping warm under the covers. Temperatures will drop some more over the next few days, but should go up again after we round Scotland, and then head southeast on the North Sea.

This trip is also a trip through different climate zones. Less than four weeks ago, I was pouring Atlantic water over my head several times a day to freshen up. Today I have stowed away all my swimming trunks, and need a thick anorak on deck.

At midday, the sun actually comes out! It's lovely.

The day's run of 143 NM is also great. The last twenty-four hours have gone really well with mostly Force 5 wind from southwest. The Gulf Stream helps us along with another half a knot or so. This morning I set the next waypoint at 59.5 °N 3 °W. This is north of the Orkney Islands, and from there I want to head north past the Orkney Islands on an easterly course.

I looked at the strait between Scotland and the Orkney Islands on the map. There are the two passages: Pentland Firth and Liddel Eddy. The nautical chart warns of large currents and eddies. Since I don't know the sea area, and don't know what to expect, I want to avoid it if possible.

First, I have to find the best passage for the next few days in light winds. The sun is shining, it's 20 °C in the saloon and for once, the solar panels are able to charge the batteries again today! All is well!

Then I see a seagull that sitting on the solar panels. I don't like that at all. For one thing, they affect the power output, and they leave their excrement everywhere. I chase it away by clapping, and think that I am rid it. But a short time later, it's back again. This time it ignores my clapping and refuses to budge. I have to wave a piece of wood in front of its beak before it finally flies off.

I watch it fly away, and land behind *Jambo* in the water, only to take off again shortly afterwards, fly an arc around the bow, and then head for the solar panels from port, where it lands safely again, and settles down to rest. I have no choice but to chase it away again with my piece of wood. We repeat this scenario several times, and I wonder who is going to give up first. Somehow, I don't think it is going to be the seagull, so I change tactics and try to prevent it from landing in the first place. I am able to confuse it enough to stop it landing the next time by waving my stick and shouting loudly.

Unfortunately, this success is short-lived, and bird actually manages to land again the next time. I chase it away again, but of course only briefly. On the next approach, the seagull misjudges the landing, and falls on board next to the equipment rack, where it lies on its back on the port side, screeching and flapping its wings. I am able to nudge it overboard. That must have given it a fright, because I don't see it again after that. Fortunately, because I was about to give up at any moment.

Thursday, 11 June, 32nd day's run 111 NM, total distance 3886 NM, position about 54.5 °N 24 °W, 1-2 Bft southeast, course east-northeast

Everything is grey!

A white-grey wall of fog stretches around *Jambo* at a distance of about 200 m, seamlessly merging into the grey of the sky, and virtually forming a grey dome around us. Dark grey waves appear out of nowhere from the wall to port, roll under *Jambo*, and disappear again into the grey wall to star-

board. In light winds, *Jambo* sails through this surreal scenery!

I've reached the high, and the wind dies down gradually to wind Force 1 to 2, which is no longer sufficient for sailing. So I put on the engine, because I have so much more diesel than I need for the remaining distance, because I have been so economical. After a short time, a stable Force 2 wind from the east means I could hoist the sails again if I wanted to. But I decide not to, because the batteries need loading, and I also want hot water for rinsing and showering.

When the engine is running, I can also run the heater via the inverter, since the alternator (115 A) with Sterling charge controller provides sufficiently high current, about 70 to 80 A. When the heater runs via the inverter, very high currents already flow in the 12 V electrical system, about 80 A for the 1000 W and half that for 500 W. In such applications, I check the cables to the voltage converter more often for temperature. So far, however, everything has been fine. Fortunately, the heater means it is a bit warmer in the shower.

After that, the day turns into a cold but sunny and beautiful sailing day, with mostly Force 3 winds from the southeast. I leave the cabin lights on all day. I don't have economy bulbs, and they provide a bit of warmth as well as light! 21 °C is today's peak below deck, together with the sunshine. I am satisfied.

<u>Friday, 12 June, 33rd day's run 112 NM, total distance 3998 NM, position about 55.5 °N 21.5 °W, 2-3 Bft southeast, course east-northeast</u>

The night is very pleasant. The wind blows with a light Force 3 from southeast. The current oscillates in the same direction between north and southeast with about half a knot, and helps or pushes our course in a better direction, for the most part.

In the morning, the wind seems to stay consistent around 9 knots, at least since sunrise. Gradually it starts to back off as well, turning *Jambo* on the wind to a more northerly course. The sky is overcast, but it is not foggy for a change. The temperature is about 10 °C outside and 15 °C below deck. I stay in my bunk a bit longer, and keep warm for another hour before getting up. I turn on the generator together with my heater for two hours. I have been using less fuel lately because the days are much longer now, over 17 hours, than they were at the beginning of the Caribbean trip at 12 hours, so the solar panels can provide power for longer. They usually cover all the power I need throughout the day, even when it is cloudy.

My fridge also needs much less power in these temperatures than at over 30 °C in the subtropical latitudes. During the day, I cool it down vigorously, and at night, I can even switch it off. I also don't have too much food left that needs to be cooled. I ate the last yoghurt yesterday, and the last bit of salami I have on the bread for tomorrow. Only a few eggs, margarine and jam still need cooling. I filled the fridge mainly with drinks, which store the cold during the day when the electricity is flowing from the solar panels, and keep the temperature down at night when the fridge is off. This works well. Next winter, I intend to refit some things on board so that in the future, I will only depend on such measures to save electricity, in an emergency.

I'm on target course east-northeast, to waypoint 59.5°N 3°W, and turn on the engine. Of course, I let the heater run on 500 W until there is more wind. There should be more wind in the east, and more wind is predicted for tonight for my current position.

Saturday, 13 June, 34th day's run 111 NM, total distance 4109 NM, position about 56 °N 19 °W, 4 Bft north-northeast, course east

During the night, I can switch off the engine and sail again with a weak Force 3 wind from northeast. The wind increases to Force 4 from north-northeast. *Jambo* is on a close-haul and makes good speed. The bread is baking, and the generator and heater are running. Lying in my warm bunk, I am looking forward to breakfast.

The wind increases continuously up to 15 knots, so that I decide to reef. Even though I am slowly getting closer to the coast, I'm still very conservative in order to protect the rig.

A light, southeasterly current pushes *Jambo* to starboard, and I stay hard on the wind to gain further northerly latitude and keep on course for the Orkney Islands.

I change my bunk and move from my forward cabin to the leeward bench in the saloon for the night, as it is far too bumpy with an upwind course ahead. *Jambo* slams into the trough of a wave violently several times. It has been a long time since I had to sleep in the saloon on this trip.

Today I change the time for the fourth time. Board time is now UTC. Sunrise is at 4:21 and sunset is at 22:03.

Until midnight, things go really well: course 65 degrees and about 6 knots speed. I lie down around 22:30 and set my alarm for midnight.

When I wake up, the first gusts of wind are already up to 15 knots. Shortly before half past one, they reach 17 knots. So I quickly get dressed, turn on the deck lights and reef the genoa. After that, the gusts die down again, and with 12 knots wind, of course, the sail is too small. Suddenly we slow right down. Our course is pretty awful. I check the drift: 2 knots to the south, which means more than 1.5 knots of current. The speed is almost gone with only Force 3 from northeast. So I have to furl out again. After that, I can only get courses of 90 to 115 degrees, with good speed, but in the wrong direction - I lose northern latitude! But there is nothing I can do. Almost spellbound, I just stare at all the displays with a feeling of despair until 2:30, when the wind turns a bit in my favour, to the north again. Then I lie down. At about 4 o'clock I gradually wake up as it starts to get light. Again, it is very gusty and rough, with winds around 16 knots. I grab a coat and reef the sails. The current is still running at over 1.5 knots.

Bryony Bank is now about 50 NM to the east. I am on the continental shelf, and crossed the 1000 m depth contour earlier without realising. It is only 290 NM to the Hebrides. Wind and current favour the more direct course west of the Hebrides, and I leave Rockall Trough to starboard.

I think that the current conditions should start to improve at Bryony Bank at the latest, with less than 200 m water depth or west of there. Of course, I didn't get much sleep during night. But that doesn't matter, because as usual I can catch up on sleep during the day.

First, I need a coffee. So I switch on the generator and then the coffee machine. But something is wrong, and instead of rinsing, a warning orange triangle with an exclamation mark lights up. *Not the coffee machine!* I think. Agreed, yesterday it got splashed with some salt water through the open window. But it should be able to cope with that. It always has done so far. So I look in the instruction manual, to see what the lamp means, and it says insert brewing pump. *Thank goodness!* It is just that the flap on the side was open. It must have come loose during the pitching and rocking.

Shortly afterwards, I'm sitting in the saloon with my coffee and the heater blowing on my feet, hoping that the current will subside soon, and *Jambo* can resume a better course.

I also decide on my final destination today: Heligoland, with no scheduled stopover. If everything goes well, I could be in the Orkneys on Thursday, and on Heligoland the following Monday or Tuesday. Let's see - of course anything can happen.

It has been five weeks now. What a long time! I was interested to see what it is like to be alone at sea for such a long time. So far, I am doing well. Physically, I feel in top shape and I am not finding the sailing work too difficult. I'll probably have to get used to going for walks again after my arrival, because that exercise is missing, of course. I'm almost always in a good mood, only the lulls get to me every time. Mentally, I think, I'm all right. I can still calculate the day's run, change the time on board, determine the course and set it.

In the evening, I leave Bryony Bank. For the first time in a long time, the depth gauge has registered the seabed again. The display shows 200 m depth. The small island of Rockall lies 50 NM off the port side. There is still a light current off to the southeast. Towards evening, the wind turns a bit to the right, and takes *Jambo* on an easterly course once again. That is not okay, because I want to go northeast.

<u>Monday, 15 June, 36th day's run- 141 NM, total distance 4385</u>
<u>NM, position approx. 57 °N 12 °W, 4 Bft N, course northeast</u>

The wind gradually shifts back during the night, and this morning it is already coming from the north with the prospect of north-northwest. Wind speed is down, but I am still on course for the Orkneys! It is 340 NM direct distance to the waypoint 59.5 °N 3 °W. The plan for today is to gain as much northern latitude as possible at adequate speed, and then pass the Hebrides with a wide berth. I wonder if the wind will keep up.

The sea is very calm. With just the occasional wave to slow her progress, *Jambo* settles into her stride. I update my local weather data. Things are looking good, although there is a period of weak wind on its way. The currents are intriguing. At times *Jambo* sails through streams that suddenly accelerate her speed over ground from 6 knots to 8 knots, pulling her eastwards. I would love to stay in them for longer but it's impossible, as they seem to be flowing diagonally. Three times, we manage to run with them briefly. Overall, the current is moving more or less in the right direction.

The archipelago of St. Kilda off the Hebrides, is roughly 100 NM dead ahead, high tide there is at 14:23 hours ship's time. The influence of the tides is becoming more substantial now, and I expect that to continue until we reach Heligoland. As always, it is both a curse and a blessing.

Nonetheless, this morning's sailing is beautiful and exhilarating, and I can't wait to see how the afternoon will play out. The wind gradually subsides, dropping to 10 or 11 knots.

The afternoon is as good as the morning. In fact, I even manage to find the North Atlantic Drift, the extension of the Gulf Stream, which flows past the Hebrides. Now things really speed up – out of the norm for me. The current increases my speed by about

¾ of a knot. The wind from north-northwest picks up again, blowing at around 12 to 13 knots. The current has a double positive effect on sailing speed over ground, adding additional propulsion as well as increasing the relative speed to the wind. Sailing close-hauled, the increased apparent wind speeds *Jambo* along so she travels at 7 knots or even 7.5 knots. We make excellent progress, and I am delighted.

Tuesday, 16 June, 37th day's run 149 NM, total distance 4534 NM, position approx. 58 °N 8 °W, 3 Bft N, course east-northeast

Today my Garmin inReach Mini seems to have poor reception, meaning that not all messages get through properly. Some cannot be received, and others are incorrect. As communication with text messages is very time delayed at the best of times, it is even more difficult to get any weather forecasts today.

St. Kilda is directly abeam of me during the night, and in the morning, the Flannan Isles are about 7 NM to starboard ahead. Visibility is poor as it is hazy and overcast, with light drizzle. The temperature is about 10 °C. Because of the poor visibility, I cannot actually make out the islands, but I am approaching the coast.

Finally, my VHF radio springs back to life and I get information from the info channel. I still don't have any FM radio or mobile phone reception yet.

Then at last there are only 3.5 NM to the Isle of Eilean A' Ghobha. I can see three islands clearly on the radar. Then, suddenly, I see them shrouded in mist to port.

Land Ho!

Abeam to port, 2.5 NM, 9:55 UTC, finally after five weeks! I am returning to civilisation. I have FM radio reception now, and can listen to Scottish music playing, although there is still no mobile phone reception yet. Then I hear a ping, and the first WhatsApp message comes through. Suddenly there is a torrent of short acoustic signals, ping, ping, ping, as I receive all the messages from the past five weeks. It feels like having a party!

Mobile Data!

Seeing land is great, but the real surge of joy comes when I get mobile phone coverage. Mobile data! I feel like a changed man - as if I have woken from a dream, all my energy comes racing back. I can see the bar for cell-phone reception and even have LTE!

I send Anke a photo of me right away and a short while later we can actually talk on the phone! We are so happy to hear each other's voices after all this time. We can hardly stop talking, as there is so much to say. What a moment - I am back!

Next, I do a weather check on Windfinder. It isn't great. There is a substantial calm for the next couple of days, but nothing can dampen my spirits. I post a quick update on Facebook. It is just a few more nautical miles to the north tip of the Hebrides - through the mist I can just about make out the shore.

Incredible! I have left the North Atlantic behind!

The new wind forecast, with a calm in the north of Scotland, means I abandon my original plan to head past the Orkney Islands to the north. I now have the option of sailing through one of the following seaways: Pentland Firth or Liddel Eddy. I find further information on the Internet. The Pentland Firth is notorious for currents of 10 knots or more, as well as turbulence and breaking tidal waves. The Liddel Eddy looks a bit more friendly on the map. I set the next waypoint 219 Dover M, south of Hoy, which I hope to reach in eighteen or nineteen hours. The distance is roughly 95 NM. That should be doable. The wind will decrease during the night so I will be motor sailing until I get there, before heading on through one of the straits. That is the plan.

Today I change the clocks for the fifth time. The boat's time is now UTC +1, the same time as in the UK. Sunrise is at 4:22 am and sunset at 10:38 pm.

Wednesday, 17 June, 38th day's run 120 NM, total distance 4654 NM, position about 58.5 °N 4 °W, calm, course east

During the night, I reach my sixth milestone, the shortest night with 5 hours and 35 minutes of darkness. In fact, it doesn't really get dark at all, because twilight in the high latitudes lasts almost the whole night.

In the morning, I am north of Scotland, in dense fog, under engine. There is hardly anything to see, not even the Scottish coast, which lies to starboard. It is bitterly cold. This is probably an unrecorded milestone: the coldest morning of the trip.

I switch on my heater and run it through the inverter, exceptionally on 1500 W. After a short time, something starts crackling behind the backrest of the bench on the portside. Luckily, I look immediately. And see that a flame is already coming out of the battery main switch installed there, which I use to disconnect the voltage converter from the mains when I don't need it.

I always have my fire blanket at the ready. It is stored aft, next to the galley, in case there is a fire on the stove. Thank goodness! I grab it and quickly smother the source of the fire. By now, it is smoking considerably, and it's getting worse. I rush on deck to catch my breath. Below, I can see the smoke is spreading and getting denser.

I take a deep breath, hold it, go down to the saloon and open the first windows. Then I hurry back on deck to take a second deep breath and head back to the saloon to open the other windows. The smoke gives me a headache, but it goes away quickly later.

It doesn't stop smoking at all. I take another gulp of air up on deck and go back to the source of the fire, holding my breath. I lift the fire blanket, and see there is still a flame.

Why?

Then a thought pops into my head: The cable insulation melted, it must be a short circuit. Of course, that kind of fire doesn't need any oxygen and can't be smothered with a fire blanket. I tear out the cable feed, make sure the wires aren't touching, put the fire blanket back, and rush back on deck, into the fresh air. Shortly afterwards, the smoke subsides. I let it drift off, then look under the fire blanket, to make sure the small fire is out.

I have just realised how easy it is to lose your boat in a fire, if you can't extinguish it fast enough. I was very lucky to be sailing under engine power when it happened, with no heeling, so I could open the windows quickly and see what I was doing. I got off lightly once again.

After the fire, the first thing I have to do is get 220 V again, because I need a coffee, and want to bake some bread immediately. Unfortunately, I don't have any reserve wires on board. But when I had added three batteries on Martinique, and the third one did not fit in with the others, I had connected it with longer pieces of wire. So I now disconnect that battery, and use the wires to connect my reserve inverter. I need two cups of coffee to calm my nerves. I turn on the bread maker.

Next I have to clean up the remains of the fire. I get rid of all the grime and wash the area thoroughly with vinegar cleaner. Still, it smells like burnt plastic in the saloon.

What caused the fire?

Of course, high currents were flowing at the time, as I had the heater running on 1500 W, about 125 A. The cables are designed for that, and the switch can stand 250 A. In fact, everything should have been fine. I will have to investigate the cause properly later. For now, I am heading on towards the North Sea. I have to concentrate on that first, and push the topic aside for the moment.

Then I reach my seventh milestone, the most northern point of my trip at 58° 42.8' N 3° 13.5' W.

It is in the afternoon, and the sun has been out again at last for a very long time. Immediately it is much warmer. I pass the Island of Stroma. It is an unforgettable sight: this island with the white lighthouse and the white spray splashing against the brown cliffs. Further up, I see green fields and a few houses. Perhaps the view seems so magnificent because I haven't seen anything like it for weeks. For a brief moment, I consider dropping anchor in the bay, and imagine crossing over to shore, walking in the green meadows, and lying down in the grass to be warmed by the sun.

Then I stop daydreaming. There is no chance of going ashore, because of the strict entry regulations for Great Britain. A 14-day quarantine in a so-called port of entry is compulsory. Landing here would be illegal.

So back to reality and into the Pentland Firth. With high concentration we continue. The water is almost as smooth as glass, but I can see the first eddies appearing. From one moment to the next, the fog comes up, and I can't see the Island of Stroma anymore, although I am still very close. The fog is getting denser by the minute, and I have only 30 m visibility ahead, but above me, the sky is still blue. It is dripping everywhere, because the rig picks up water from the fog and releases it in thick drops.

I am in Pentland Firth, one of the world's most current-rich straits, which I have decided is preferable to Liddel Eddy. But my timing seems to fit, and at the moment the current is running along at only 2 knots. Muckle Skerry is already on port side. Not long afterwards, with precise conservative timing, I have almost made it through this notorious strait. At the same time, I have reached the North Sea, and set course south-southeast. From now on, it should get warmer every day. I can do with that, and of course with a little more wind.

That was my eighth milestone: sailing through Pentland Firth! My milestones are tumbling away. But this passage is well worth a milestone, as far as I'm concerned.

The North Sea!

I am now in the North Sea, in home waters – or as good as! I feel so happy, but I am also terribly tired all of a sudden, since I'm lacking in sleep. Sailing near the coast, single-handed, is a different story to being out on the open sea. I didn't get any sleep all day because of all the commotion caused by the fire, and then of course because of the trip through Pentland Firth.

I am only beginning to realise how exhausted I actually am. Nevertheless, this was a great day. *Ah yes, I almost forgot about the fire...* but there is another positive lesson to be learned. I see it as a kind of emergency fire drill. And from my point of view, I couldn't have handled the situation much better, I don't think. In addition, I take it upon myself to improve the cable layout. As a cause, I suspect a loose connection in the battery main switch. This caused a lot of heat to build up, which led to melting of the cable insulation, and ultimately to the short circuit, which was then probably to blame for the open fire. Well, that's my theory.

I melted down some tea lights when I had a moment today, and completely sealed the burned area with a layer of wax to contain the smell. I almost can't smell it anymore. During the next few days, I will air the saloon well.

On Monday, I should arrive on Heligoland, plus/minus one day, depending on how things go. But I have quite a few litres of diesel left, and can use some of it on the last leg if there isn't enough wind. In the evening, I am already under sail again. With the wind at 6 knots, gusts of 7 knots, and a current of one knot, we can go places - at least for the next few hours, until the current drops again.

Now I am sitting in the saloon, freshly showered, eating another snack and listening to the FM radio, as long as I am still close to the coast and have reception. From outside the sun shines into the saloon. It feels so good after the cold and often foggy weeks I have just experienced. I am satisfied and dead tired, looking forward to my interval sleep. I am exhausted, and immediately fall fast asleep. Around 9:30 pm, my alarm clock goes off, and I do my checks. Everything is okay and *Jambo* is on target. I miss the next alarm, and don't hear the next one until after midnight. Startled, I look at the time. Damn, I didn't hear the alarm clock go off! My first glance goes to the electronic nautical chart. Damn again: *Jambo* has been sailing the wrong course for hours and is in a wind farm area. I stumble on deck, and see the first wind turbines ahead. I had the autopilot set to wind angle. While I was sleeping, the wind shifted, sending me on a south-westerly course, directly to this wind farm. I can't believe I actually woke up in time!

<u>Thursday, 18 June, 39th day's run 114 NM, total distance 4768 NM, position approx. 58 °N 1.5 °W, 3 Bft northeast, course south-southeast</u>

The experience during the night gives me plenty to think about. It is the second mishap within twenty-four hours. As always, things start to go wrong for me towards the end of my trips. It is the same again this time, although I remembered this from last time, and tried to concentrate as best possible. But the trip has left its mark, and after more than five weeks at sea, I can't do everything the way I would like to.

I now have to adapt my rhythm to the conditions as best I can. Here on the North Sea the shipping traffic is huge, compared to the Atlantic. The list of AIS signals is pages long, while on the Atlantic, or north of Scotland, I never had more than five messages. I make sure I zoom right into the electronic sea chart so that I don't miss anything there either, because in addition to the wind farms, there are also oil and gas platforms. I have reduced my intervals of sleep after this experience back to 30 minutes. Further out, away from the Scottish coast, an hour may be possible again, but not here and now.

The course target is unchanged: Heligoland, bearings South Harbour: 123 degrees, 350 NM.

Friday, 19 June, 40th day's run 130 NM, total distance 4898 NM, position approx. 56.5 °N 0 °W, 3 Bft southeast, course south-southeast

During the night, I reach my ninth milestone: crossing the zero meridian. The night itself goes well enough, and for a long time I can sail on an almost direct course to Heligoland, until in the second half of the night the wind begins to turn right, first to east and then to east-southeast. *Jambo* turns, sailing close-hauled on a southern course.

Towards morning, I start the engine and go back to a direct course to Heligoland: bearing 120 degrees, 275 NM. There is still enough diesel to run the engine for another twenty-four hours at medium speed. The weather is cloudy, overcast and foggy. But it should clear up later. The bread is baking, and I am looking forward to breakfast!

My estimated time of arrival is now Sunday evening, if the wind comes as predicted. I take the opportunity to clean the bathroom, clean and restock the refrigerator. The free space after almost six weeks, is now filled with a few beers. I am looking forward to Heligoland!

<u>Saturday, 20 June, 41st day's run 148 NM, total distance 5046 NM, position approx. 55.5 °N 4 °E, 4 Bft southwest, course south-southeast</u>

At night, I switch off the engine, and under sail, I continue close-hauled on a direct course to Heligoland. The current runs to the east with about 1 knot, and helps us along. Heligoland is still on bearing 120 degrees, 141 NM ahead. The weather is very good, clear to cloudy, and it is getting warmer by the day!

Today I change the time for the last time. Board time is now UTC +2 and thus on the current time in Germany. Sunrise is at 4:59 and sunset at 22:25.

On the same longitude as my home port of Enkhuizen (5° 16' E), I reach my tenth and final milestone.

Direction and speed are super today. *Jambo* is still running well after 5000 NM, and has often demonstrated her strengths in weaker winds during this trip. We are approaching Heligoland much faster than expected, bearing south 122 degrees, 82 NM. I think that I will arrive tomorrow around noon.

Then it's off into the last night. There is so much going on here, now, as I am crossing one of the main shipping routes on the North Sea. The engine is running, and I have hauled in the sails as the wind has turned and become too weak. It might be possible to sail again later on. I pull myself together and make sure I concentrate. I have also put the radar on guard zone alarm, because safe is safe. I must avoid another mistake during the final nautical miles of my journey at all costs. That would be so typical. Things often go wrong at the last minute.

The sunrise is as beautiful as the sunset was last night. Heligoland is now about 30 NM ahead. I survived the night okay, and can't wait to get there.

In glorious sunshine, I can see Heligoland ahead, and take one last opportunity to fly my drone for some beautiful pictures of *Jambo* with Heligoland in the distance.

After that, I haul in the sails, and continue under engine. Heligoland is getting closer all the time. Now it is time to hang the fenders on the railing. It has been ages since the last time I had to get the fenders out. It takes me a moment to remember when that was. It was in March, over three months ago at Simpson Bay Marina on Sint Maarten. After that, I just anchored and sailed.

It is a really weird feeling. I had thought I would be immune to the moment, but that's not the case. Now, after six weeks, it seems odd for me to just sail into the southern harbour and tie up. After all, what comes next feels like a new phase of life lying ahead of me: life on land!

What's more, I'm returning to Germany after almost six months of life aboard and far from home, and *Jambo* has even been away for a whole year. *Jambo* has been a very good home to me during all this time. Of course, she is not so big, and sometimes I longed for a bigger boat with a lot of space. But as always in life, everything has its advantages and disadvantages.

Then I have to dodge a supply ship. It is my right of way, but I don't mind, and let it pass, of course. Shortly afterwards I reach the Sellebrunn W buoy, a cardinal mark. Although I have already visited Heligoland a few times, this is the first time I am approaching the island coming from the north. The sun is shining, and I have hoisted the yellow quarantine flag to port. Heligoland is now already very close, and on starboard ahead, I see Lange

Anna standing there. Of course, I have never seen her from this perspective before. How fantastic!

In the beautiful sunlight, the warm colours shine on me, contrasting with the deep blue of the sky, the brown of the rocky coast, and the green fields above, similar to what I saw off the Island of Stroma. Lange Anna stands majestically as we glide by, and greets me like a red stick of rock speckled in white icing, at least that's what she reminds me of. Of course, it is the droppings of the seabirds breeding there that shine so white.

A large federal police boat passes *Jambo* on its course north, but takes no notice of us. Then I am hailed on channel 16, and asked to switch to channel 68. Sailors moored in the northeast harbour get in touch with some information. How kind. Heligoland glides past so colourfully. Then Marlene and Bert from Trans-Ocean call me over the radio, as we had agreed beforehand, via the Garmin.

They want to welcome me and take a few photos for Yacht magazine. They are coming over now in their dinghy. Alex Worms, from Yacht, also wants to contact me in the next few days, to write an article for the Rolling Home Initiative.

Then I pass the entrance to the northeast harbour, and a beautiful view of the small village with its colourful houses comes into view. Already I can see a dinghy with the Trans-Ocean pennant approaching, and the two sailors from the sailing yacht *Heimkehr* greet me very warmly, in the name of Trans-Ocean. I am delighted about this, and we exchange a few words. They accompany me until I enter the southern harbour. Many times, I have entered here, often in bad weather. I sail through the outer harbour, and Marlene and Bert overtake me with the dinghy. I hang out the fenders on both sides, the lines of course, are already prepared.

Jambo and I enter the southern harbour, and I look around to see where there might be room. There are only a few boats at the middle jetty, and I head for a sailing yacht to berth beside it. The couple of sailors there have spotted me already, and are standing on their port side to take my lines. Everything works really well.

We made it!

After 42 days and 5130 NM, I moor at 11.30 am in the south harbour of Heligoland. I am extremely satisfied, and very happy. The German couple next door has no idea that an ocean passage of several weeks lies behind me. Bert and Marlene come to *Jambo* in the dinghy, and say how great she looks. You would never know she had been on such a long trip.

We drink a glass of champagne and enjoy the warm sun. They take a few more photos, and invite me to breakfast, which I gratefully accept. Their delicious salami tastes amazing this morning. The two sailors who radioed me from the northeast harbour come by for a chat. Marlene and Bert give me a mouth and nose mask, which is mandatory when shopping and in restaurants. I have to get used to the new rules here first.

Then I am back aboard *Jambo,* and start tidying. Ten bags of rubbish have accumulated, but I can dispose of them here. Then I go to the harbour office. I register, and pay harbour dues for three days. Water is next on my list of to-dos, because my tanks are empty. Fortunately, I meet the caretaker at the sailing club, who turns on the water at the middle jetty for me, so I don't have to walk too far with my 20 litre canisters, which I lug back and forth twelve times, until I have 240 litres in the tank. That should be enough to get along for the next few days. Below deck, I also clean up a little. Some visitors pop in, who have travelled to Heligoland especially to see me. How nice is that? I am chuffed to bits. Many thanks for it!

In the afternoon, after I have tidied up and unwound a bit, I finally grant myself a well-deserved jetty beer, which tastes simply excellent after forty-two days at sea. A Carib at the central jetty on Heligoland.

I have arrived safely at last.

Link to video

Epilogue: Review and Outlook

The next few days are quiet and relaxing; I walk a lot, sleep a lot, go shopping and enjoy two wonderful evenings with Marlene and Bert at dinner, in nearby restaurants. I have a lovely time. During the first two nights I wake up suddenly, and since *Jambo* is lying so still, my first thought is, *we are not moving! Another calm!* It takes me a moment to remember that I have already arrived, and am firmly moored in the harbour on Heligoland.

After three days, I say goodbye to the beautiful island on a lovely day, and cast off. Anke and I have chosen Zeeland in the Netherlands to make up for the sailing holiday we couldn't take together in the Azores. It turns out this is a good decision, as we are able to move around almost normally, despite the pandemic. We protect ourselves as well as we can with our masks. We meet more lovely people, including Alex Worms, from the sailing magazine Yacht, who interviewed me a while back. It's nice to meet up with so many people I met on the social networks. When you see each other in the flesh for the first time, it is almost like meeting old friends.

I'm gradually settling down in Zeeland, and getting used to the new rhythm of things. I don't feel like going home yet, because *Jambo* is still home to me.

But what a trip! Everything worked really well. I made three big mistakes: the torn genoa, the fire and sailing into a wind farm. I was lucky, and got off lightly. And I am more aware of these issues now, having learned from my mistakes.

This was my longest trip to date. For a long time now, I have wanted to carry on sailing until I eventually want to stop, and find out where my limit is. I don't think I have found that limit yet. Until I reached the Hebrides, I had found a rhythm where I felt I could have continued sailing like that for weeks, although I would have preferred to be sailing in a warmer climate. I found the cold very hard to deal with for two weeks, in the high latitudes - I didn't expect it to be so bad. I spent a lot of time in my bunk under two blankets, trying to keep warm. It would have been easier with working diesel heating, of course, but that would have meant using a lot of fuel. And I can't say if it would have been enough to keep warm.

I learned so much on my Atlantic circuit, and the list of things I want to retrofit on board kept getting longer. I'm not sure if I will manage to do everything, but here's what I have planned:

- Electric windlass
- New battery bank (lithium 600 Ah)
- Watermaker
- New voltage converter 3000 W
- New life raft
- New fire extinguisher and two fire blankets
- Saildrive seal change
- Have engine leakage repaired
- Change engine switch panel
- Mount several small holding rails in the saloon at different places
- Stainless steel anchor protection at bow
- Seal deck cable holes
- New bilge pump
- 100 A battery charger
- Plus many other small things

Jambo is coming out of the water in Sneek in the Netherlands at the end of September. That is earlier than ever before, due to the pandemic. So the saildrive seal can be changed, and the engine leak fixed then.

Where do I want to sail to next?

On my first Atlantic crossing from Lanzarote to Guadeloupe, I had thought about it already. I have friends in Australia, and I have promised to sail over in *Jambo* to see them. That is not the only reason why Australia really is our next dream destination. I hope nothing comes up to stop us, and the pandemic doesn't slow things down for too long. Onwards and upwards, or as I like to say:

To the horizon and beyond...

See you again soon! I can't wait!

Acknowledgements

I would like to thank so many people for helping me to make this journey possible:

Anke, for her tremendous support, always looking out for me, even from far away, holding the fort back home and sending me all the important information from the back office.

Tobias Lepper, from Lepper Marine, who was my technical backup, and sent me everything I needed in case of emergency.

Trans-Ocean and Intermar for the Rolling Home Initiative, especially Astrid Ewe (TO), Johannes Frost (TO) and Hans-Uwe Reckefuss (Intermar).

Christoph Feld, in Siegen, who sent me vital information about weather and routes on the way.

Christian Buschfort, from *Quick*, who turned out to be a high-pressure draft expert, and also provided me with excellent weather data.

Arno, from 'the sailing yacht Elas' blog, an expert on currents, who also copied all the Garmin MapShare messages to me, and summarised them in a file.

Greg, in Vienna, who provided me with important information about icebergs, and always cheered me up in his inimitable way.

Dieter, from the *Damile*, who sent me information about on-going shipping traffic.

Tim, who provided me with information about Heligoland, before I arrived there.

Marlene and Bert Frisch, from the *Heimkehr,* for an extraordinary reception off Heligoland, and the two beautiful evenings we enjoyed there together.

And everyone who kept their fingers crossed for me on my trip, followed my journey, and sent me such lovely messages when I completed my Atlantic crossing.

Boat Type

BAVARIA 34 Holiday

Year of construction: 12/2008

First launch: spring 2009

Length: 10.71 m

Width: 3.60 m

Draft: 1.55 m

Waterline: approx. 9.7 m

Total weight: approx. 7 tonnes

Furling main approx. 25 m²

Genoa approx. 30 m²

Delta anchor, galvanized, 16 kg

50 m hot dip galvanized chain 8 mm

Anchor line lead 40 m

Volvo Penta D1-30 with 27Hp

Alternator 115 A

Starter battery 68Ah AGM

Sterling charge controller

Saildrive

3 blade folding propeller

Dinghy Marinepool 2 1/2 person

Outboard motor 6hp

Raymarine 240e radiotelephone

Two handheld radios (Standard Horizon)

Chart plotter below deck B&G Zeus3 12"

Chart plotter in cockpit B&G Zeus3 7"

Wind sensor WS310

Rudder feedback sensor RF25

Precision-9 Compass

Triducer DST800

BT1 Bluetooth Base Station

B&G Triton^2 Speed/Depth/Wind

B&G Triton^2 Autopilot Controller

NAVICO NAC-2 Autopilot Computer

NAVICO WR10 Autopilot Remote Controller

SIMRAD ForwardScan™ XDCR

B&G 4G Radar

AIS easyTRX3S-IS-N2K-WiFi

Webasto air heater EVO 3900 with 3.3 kW (still defective)

Hot water boiler 40 litres

Battery charger 45 A (220V)

Supply batteries 2*170 Ah (defective) 3*108 Ah

Voltage converter 12 V to 220 V, 1500 W, constant 220 V for whole on-board circuit and switchable to shore power

Fresh water tank 300 litres

Holding tank 75 litres

Diesel 150 litres plus 5*20 litres reserve

Petrol 10 litres external tank for outboard engine

Solar system:

4 semi-flexible modules of 120 Wp each, 2 modules are connected in series at a time

2 solar charge controllers Victron 100/20

MMSI: 211638460

Call sign: DJ6493

The Limfjord Anecdote (2018)

What a day! Running aground and getting stuck!

We are in the middle of a great sailing cruise from Copenhagen across the Limfjord to List on Sylt, when we get into a real mess. Who we are? My wonderful boat *Jambo*, of course, a BAVARIA 34 Holiday, Wilm, the helmsman, aged sixty-eight at the time, and me, Martin, the skipper, fifty-four years old, but still feeling like I'm in my mid-thirties.

This year, like every year, I planned a nice summer cruise for us. After sailing to northern Spain last year, this time we headed to southern Norway and western Sweden. I had sailed *Jambo* from the Netherlands to Oslo in two legs, and then cruised from there to Copenhagen, with my partner, Anke. It was as good as a dream. But that is another story.

Jambo stayed in Copenhagen for three weeks while I had to work. Then my helmsman, Wilm, and I arrived in the last week of August to start the return journey to the Netherlands.

I haven't been to the Limfjord yet, and am looking forward to sailing there. We make good way to the small town of Hals, on the east coast of Denmark, and the entrance to the Limfjord, with everything going as expected.

With the Limfjord ahead, we have chosen the island of Livø as our next stop. It is about 50 NM away. We will also come past Aalborg, the largest city in the area.

In the morning, I notice our batteries have not charged under engine overnight. I rarely switch to shore power at night, as we are usually fine for a night or two with the 115A alternator, a small battery bank of 360Ah, and a 1500 watt voltage converter. But I need to check out what's wrong later when I get a chance.

The day starts with strong winds up to 33 knots from southeast. We are still having breakfast when suddenly a woman knocks on our boat. It is the harbour master, and she needs our help, because a sailing yacht has broken loose. Two men are already there, but they can't get it moored again without more assistance. Wilm and I throw on a coat, and hurry to help. We soon see the 43-foot yacht that has broken loose, banging its bow against the side of a smaller yacht. It's a sight that probably hurts every sailor to the bone. The four of us are able to secure the larger yacht.

After we are all safely back on board, we cast off and head out of the harbour at nearly full throttle on the way out, so that we do not drift too much in the narrow exit. We make good time out of the marina on a broad reach course, and are pleased about the good wind to start with. Before Aalborg, it decreases significantly, so that we have to switch on the engine. This gives me the opportunity to go check the electrics, while Wilm takes the helm. We pass through the bridges in Aalborg with some waiting time, and on we go. I remind my helmsman that the buoyage changes behind Aalborg, as we are sailing to the other side of the sea. Green is now on port and red on starboard.

I am busy below deck trying to find out what is wrong, and have my head deep in the small engine compartment measuring the electrical voltage at various points when the alternator is running. Fortunately, I always have a voltage tester on board. The voltage at the starter battery is 15.5 V. It should definitely not be that high. The consumer battery is not charged at all now. I measure the voltage at the isolating diode, and find the fault: The alternator is supplying 20.8 volts, and the isolating diode is burned out on the supply side.

I'm busy thinking that it's probably the charge controller, when suddenly my helmsman shouts, "We've run out of depth!" I get out of the engine compartment, almost hitting my head, and yell, "Reverse the throttle!" The next moment, I hear the engine howling, and revving even higher. I charge on deck, yank the throttle into neutral, and then reverse at full throttle almost in the same instant.

But we're at a standstill, no longer making any way, in any direction at all. We've grounded at full throttle, and *Jambo's* bow is pointing slightly upwards. I ask Wilm: "Why didn't you kill the engine?" and he replies: "You shouted full throttle!"

I'm stunned and can't believe it.

But I pull myself together and look around. There's a green buoy 300 m behind us and one 300 m ahead. We must be on the line to the left in the fairway. But wait a minute? There is an easterly cardinal marker about 100 m to starboard ahead, and we're well southwest of it. I plunge below deck and check this on the electronic chart. Sure enough, it confirms that we are off the fairway.

The water depth is only 0.6 m any further west here. Our shallow keeler with a draft of 1.55 m is no longer sufficient. So this was clearly a steering error, and I am pretty upset.

Up I go again and reverse the engine until white smoke comes out of the exhaust. We only move what feels like a few inches. I stop. Ruining the engine isn't going to get us out of here now. The wind is still coming from the southwest, and *Jambo's* bow is facing north-northwest. It is not perfect, though, because on one side the wind pushes us to starboard, where there should be more depth, and on the other side a little forward, where it is shallower.

We set the mainsail anyway, hoping to heel a bit to reduce the draft. *Jambo* does indeed heel a little, and I reverse full throttle back again, unfortunately without any noticeable effect. We have been stuck for almost three quarters of an hour now.

I look around. There are no other watercraft to be seen, no humans, not even on shore. It is just an ordinary Monday with rainy weather. The sailing season is probably over here, at the end of August. We have seen only three motorboats so far all day, near the bridges in Aalborg. There also seems to be no professional shipping west of Aalborg either. Those ships probably all approach Aalborg from the Baltic Sea, since it is shorter, and the fairway is wider and deeper than coming from the North Sea, where we are going.

I make up my mind to drop anchor, and crank it tight with the winch, helping to move *Jambo* astern.

This is easier said than done. First, we have to get the dinghy ready, which is tied up amidships on the upper deck. Then we have to lower it into the water, attach the outboard motor, take out the fuel canister and put it in the dinghy, and get the paddles out of the locker. Where did I put the red emergency stop cable last time? In case we need it to start the boat. Fortunately, I find it after a quick search.

Of course, the outboard motor doesn't start. I pull the starting chord several times, like a madman, but I can only pull it out halfway. It must be jammed somehow. I'm not just frustrated now, I am starting to despair. I thought I had already reached my low point earlier on. But it can be even worse it seems.

Of course, that doesn't help either. So I open the hood of the outboard motor, and find a plastic hook that seems to be blocking the starter. I hold the hook up with one hand, and pull the chord with the other. Immediately the outboard starts up happily. Now all I need is to take a breath and gather some strength.

I am already soaking wet with sweat under my weatherproof jacket. It keeps on raining lightly.

I go over to *Jambo's* bow, pick up our 15 kg plough anchor along with 6 m of chain, and the start of the anchor line, and carefully pull the anchor line out astern behind me, trying to make sure it doesn't get caught up in the small outboard propeller. Of course, that is exactly what happens. Why oh why? It is as if nothing can go right today. But we soon get the line freed. Meanwhile, Wilm takes the other end of the anchor line, feeds it through the railing onto the starboard foresheet winch, and fastens it there. I run the line and chain as tight as possible, and drop the anchor about 40 yards from *Jambo*, hoping it will hold fast.

Wilm starts cranking the line tight while I get back on board. The anchor doesn't seem to be holding well, and can be cranked quite easily. Just in case, we try reversing at full throttle ... again to no avail.

So here we go again!

We crank the anchor all the way in, and I pull in the last bit by hand with the chain leader: "Boy, it is heavy! What did it catch down there?" I mutter as I struggle to raise it to the surface, until finally, a clump of silt and water plants appears. I pull it up far enough to be able to free the anchor of its additional ballast.

By now, we must have been stuck here for two hours. We have completely lost track of time, and I have to reconstruct the chronological sequence later. Somehow, in moments like these, you lose touch with the rest of the world and what is happening outside. We haven't eaten since breakfast, and it's already afternoon. But no one is hungry in this situation. We haven't had anything to drink for hours either, but we don't even notice we are starting to get dehydrated because the work is so tiring and sweaty. We just stay focused, and keep fighting to somehow reach our goal.

I sit in the dinghy and start the second attempt. I raise the anchor, and go aft. This time without wrapping the anchor line around the propeller. Aha, the learning curve effect! I tighten the line, drop the anchor, and head back to *Jambo*. This time the anchor holds better, not completely, but fairly well, so we get good tension on the line. I give full throttle backwards, and ... Nothing, absolutely nothing happens!

Jambo seems to be digging her heels in, as it were, after all our attempts, as the bow now seems to be sticking out a little higher.

In the meantime, the wind has shifted in our favour, and is now coming off the port side with Force 4. So we also set the genoa, and *Jambo* leans a little more to the side. Maybe it will be enough. We start the next attempt to free her. Under full sail, with the anchor line taut, aft, I give full throttle astern, and ... Nothing happens!

It is not as frustrating as it was at the beginning. Somehow, we are getting used to all the failures. Now I decide to connect the anchor line with the spi halyard to heel *Jambo* over even further. At least we still being creative.

Once again, it takes a lot of effort to attach everything accordingly, so that the spi halyard is linked to the anchor line. Again, Wilm tightens the anchor line. *His shoulders will probably hurt a lot later.* But I don't feel too sorry for him. I am still fuming after his error at the helm.

A driving error? It was a bit more than that: overlooking the cardinal marker, not keeping an eye on the depth gauge, not immediately taking his foot off the pedal and shifting to reverse, waiting for instructions, and then understanding and doing exactly the opposite. Now is not the right moment to even think about it.

The anchor line is slowly tightening. Unfortunately, the anchor doesn't hold as well as before because the angle of pull is steeper now. But we can heel *Jambo* a little more; I estimate about 20 degrees by now.

We try again. By the way, we keep the engine running the whole afternoon to make sure it can cool down between the freeing attempts, and so as not to risk the starter battery running down because of too many restarts. Under mainsail, with the anchor line halfway tight on the spi halyard, I give full throttle astern and *Jambo* ... doesn't budge an inch.

Now we are slowly running out of ideas. I am still considering tying all the lines on board together in order to fasten a long line to the buoy aft, and pulling from there as well. With all the mooring lines and the foresheet lines, it might be long enough. That is when I see a small boat in the distance, to the west. It seems to be heading east, in our direction. Hopefully, it won't turn off somewhere soon, and will pass us instead. It slowly approaches, and turns out to be a very small fishing boat of about 6 to 7 m, under Danish flag with a two man crew. They drive over to us and ask what is going on.

We share our predicament, and they immediately offer to try to pull us out. I want to give one of the men my line, but he thinks his might be better. I offer him a couple of beers in return. He agrees. That's fine, but he's not getting half my boat. *I am being too suspicious*. According to maritime law, half the ship's value is due after a successful salvage, if you take the other boat's line without reaching a price agreement first. So now, we have a verbal agreement to buy them both a couple of beers if they can help.

He pulls with what feels like 10 Hp, we crank the spi halyard at the same time, and reverse full throttle. But we still don't move. We try different angles for about half an hour. Then we break off, and the two men recommend we call 112 and ask for help. They say goodbye in a friendly manner, and we watch, as their boat slowly grows smaller in the distance. We are alone again, all alone.

The feeling that we have done everything possible spreads. I reject the idea of trying to reach the buoy with a long line, because effort and chance balance is no good. We need professional help! Of course, that won't be cheap. "I guess you'll have to reckon with at least 1,000 euros," I say to Wilm. But it doesn't matter at the moment, because somehow we have to keep going. The tides here are only about 10 cm. So a high tide is no use to us either.

So I call 112 and am connected to the Danish rescue centre by a friendly person who speaks good English. Again, the employee on the other end of the line is very friendly, and after exchanging some information, when he finds out that we are Germans, we switch to German. I am always surprised how many people I have met on my cruises in Norway, Sweden and Denmark can all speak our language, as well as English. Unfortunately, I don't speak a single Scandinavian language.

The rescue centre wants to try to organise a towing service, but that is not so easy. At the same time, the surrounding shipping traffic is informed, via channel 16, that the sailing yacht, *Jambo*, has run aground at our position. *Great, then it will probably be all over the papers tomorrow, with Jambo's name everywhere. It's embarrassing enough as it is.* I don't think that anyone listening will be rushing to help. I imagine that everyone is probably sitting comfortably, warm and dry on their boats, perhaps even having an early dinner, with a glass of wine or beer, listening to the radio messages and thinking: *Poor things. We'll keep our fingers crossed for them!*

We give up, resigned to waiting, when suddenly another sailing yacht passes by. I only notice them late, when they are already almost starboard abeam. They radio us to offer help. The yacht is about 13 m long, with an older couple on board. "They probably have a bigger engine than the small fishing boat that was here before," I say to Wilm. We fetch the 40 m line out of the forecastle, and I head over in the dinghy with the line in tow. But I don't quite get there, because my line is too short. The yacht can't get closer either because it is too shallow. Somehow, we manage to get close enough for the sailor to throw me a line, which I connect with ours. I return to *Jambo*.

So, here's to a new attempt! The towline is attached to the starboard stern cleat. The sailing yacht pulls, we crank and give full throttle backwards ... but unfortunately, we still don't move.

After a few attempts, we give up. Then the man radios me to suggest that we take the anchor line off the spi halyard, and he will try to pull from there, once. Sounds like a good idea. At this stage, any plan is fine by us. We rearrange everything, putting the anchor line back on the winch, and attaching the towline to the spi halyard.

Full throttle reverse again, as we crank the anchor line in. The yacht pulls hard on the mast, which has a real effect. *Jambo* heels to, about 50 degrees, and suddenly she starts, yes, she really starts, to move slowly, very slowly, and then faster and faster, and then we are finally free. Free, free, free! Hooray!!!

We thank them profusely, feeling incredibly relieved, untie the towline, and wave goodbye. Then they are gone. However, there is no time to catch our breath, because we are still at anchor, which has not held that badly. With the wind up to Force 5, it takes quite some time to lift the anchor. We almost run aground again on the other side of the fairway. That would have been all we needed.

We reach the next marina in Gjøl at 7 pm, and moor there, totally exhausted.

What a day! Once again, we have learned something new: The engine power of a medium-sized sailing yacht is enough to heel *Jambo* so strongly that she can get free again, if she is really stuck.

By the way, I did manage to charge the batteries with the alternator during the trip, by connecting the supplier circuit to the starter battery circuit at the isolating diode. If the batteries weren't charged completely, the voltage drop was so big that around 14 V were applied to the batteries. Which was enough to get by.

And did I forgive my helmsman Wilm? Yes, of course! *Jambo* was fine and no harm done. We are still great friends, and often laugh about the story now.

That's life! All's well that ends well!

Abbreviations and Explanations

Bft - Beaufort (measure of wind speed).

Heave-to - how to stop your boat under sail. The foresail is backed, i.e. on the wrong side of the wind. The boat does not move, but drifts downwind in an upright position.

Windward side - facing the wind

Leeward side - away from the wind

Genoa - main headsail

Sheet - line for the sails

Port - left tack

Starboard - right tack

NM - nautical miles

Knots - cruising speed in knots, 1 knot = 1.852 km/h

Fenders - air-filled plastic bumpers to protect the hull when docking

Tack - change of direction into the wind

Gybe - change of direction before the wind

Day's run - daily distance travelled

Windex – weather vane on the masthead

Mariniero - naval staff

Atlantic Circuit

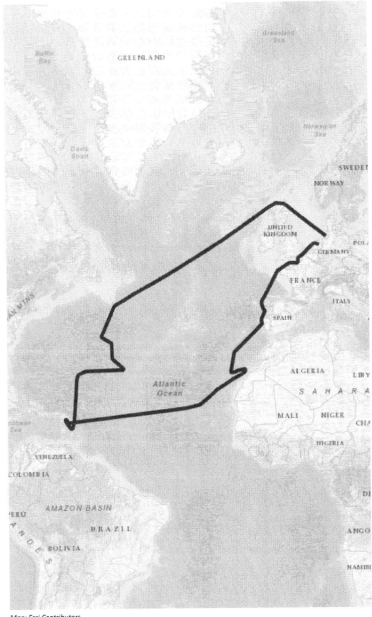

Map: Esri Contributors

Made in the USA
Las Vegas, NV
21 December 2022

63706776R00171